W9-DAF-434

MICHAEL SARRACINI   SCOTT MCGILLIVRAY

CASH FLOW
FOR LIFE

*Create Lifelong Passive
Income through Real Estate*

VISIONARY
STRATEGIES

Cash Flow For Life
Published by: Visionary Strategies
Copyright © 2011

All rights reserved. No part of this publication may be reproduced, stored in
a retrieval system, or transmitted, in any form or by any means, electronic,
mechanical, photocopying, recording, or otherwise, without prior written
permission of the publisher.

Printed in the United States of America
First Printing: June 2011

Neither the author nor Visionary Strategies, Inc., in any way make any warranty,
guaranty or representation, expressed or implied, as to the potential volume, profits,
or success of any activity or undertaking described herein.

All information related to the potential to earn money or realize a profit from any
activity described herein was received from third parties and was not created or
verified by the author or Visionary Strategies, Inc., or any agent of either of them.

Neither the author nor Visionary Strategies, Inc., in any way warrant or confirm the
accuracy of any information provided herein.

The reader should conduct an independent investigation into the information
contained herein before taking any action.

The success or failure of any undertaking described herein or based on information
provided herein may involve financial risks solely dependent upon the reader's own
ability and efforts, changes in technology or shifts in market realities.

Finally, nothing contained herein should be construed as legal advice.

Regulations vary from state to state, and change from time to time.

Consult your own independent legal counsel as to the legality of any
undertaking before taking action based on information contained herein.

Cover Design: Freddy Solis
Interior Design: Tressa Foster
Production Management: Dean Enterprises LLC

Table of Contents

Introduction

Before you start flipping through and looking at chapter titles for hints as to what you're going to read in this book, ask yourself the question, *"Why am I here?"*

Whether you ordered this book or you're checking it out in the bookstore, why ARE you here? When we ask this question of people who attend our meetings, seminars, or real estate investing courses, we hear some of the same reasons over and over.

"I hate my job".
"My job's OK, but I want more than a paycheck".
"I'm keeping up, but I'm not getting ahead financially".
"I need to secure my retirement future".
"I want to be wealthy and not worry anymore".
"My stock and bond investments aren't growing".
"I need to diversify my investments".
"Sorry, wrong room. Can you direct me to the Chiropractor's Convention?"

Actually, we only heard that last one once. And other than that last one, those are all good reasons for people to attend a seminar or for you to read this introduction.

The good news is that no matter which of those reasons apply to you (third door on the right for the last one), the help and knowledge you need to begin changing your life are in the pages of this book. How can we promise this? Well, we didn't have this book as college students when we were waiting tables, sharing rent, and sitting on recycled furniture. We had no cash, no savings, and no real estate knowledge. The extent of our real estate financial knowledge was figuring out how to divvy up the rent among roommates and how to deliver the rent check to our landlord every month.

We didn't write this book just to motivate you--we wrote it to give you a jump-start on a path to lifetime cash flow through rental real estate investment. We definitely will add to your motivation and build your enthusiasm; however, it won't be with "you can do this" mantras. We'll say it only once here: "You can do this". You'll be able to succeed in real estate investing not because we'll hype you up, but because we'll tool you up with education and resources.

From the first chapter and our "aha moment," we're going to share our successes and our mistakes as we went from broke students to owners of properties generating hundreds of thousands of dollars of cash flow and wealth we never even dreamed of when we were poor college students working at a restaurant.

We did it and it worked and made us money, so we're going to tell you what to do and how to succeed. If we made a mistake and took a financial hit, we'll tell you about that, too. Ask a room full of millionaires how many have never failed in a business and you won't see many hands raised. Ask how many of them learned something valuable from a failure and you'll get a room full of hands.

The good news is that we're going to give you valuable knowledge gained from experience. We've already made the mistakes so you don't have to. You get the benefits without the financial pain of the mistakes.

Not Just "Do This" and "Don't Do That"

There's a lot of value in learning what to do and what not to do before you buy your first rental property. However, if that is all you find in this book, we've failed in our goals for writing it. This is really a book full of HOW to do it information, tools, and resources.

From the basic mathematics of cash flow, we take you through the more advanced concepts and calculations you'll need to understand your market and market trends. You'll learn to evaluate properties, set rents, acquire and deal with tenants, as well as how to manage your properties and grow your business. Our advice includes how to grow your business into multiple companies with enormous cash flow and leveraged tax and liability strategies.

There are 27 chapters in this book, and this is our promise to you: There is not a single chapter that doesn't contain concrete, detailed, money-making tools and resources, as well as the education necessary to build your real estate investment business.

On top of all this great information, we want you to take advantage of the resources available on our website

www.scottsinvestorsedge.com

These resources are free for you to use anytime! If you're nearby a computer, take a few moments to visit the site right now and have fun with it.

If you opened this book looking for the Chiropractor's Convention, put it back. If you want to secure your financial future with "lifetime cash flow," keep reading.

CHAPTER 1
Walk the Talk for Lifetime Cash Flow

∞∞

When we first met in college back in 2000, the phrase "lifetime cash flow" had not entered our minds. Cash flow definitely was a prominent consideration for two students of limited means working their way through school. But our cash flow considerations were week-to-week, with no cash flow thoughts beyond making the next month's rent.

At that time, any relationship past a casual recognition of each other's existence wasn't one of mutual consent. Two "type A" personalities, we found ourselves clashing in debates and classroom discussions. We had no plan to build on our testy relationship. It seems that our professor had other ideas, teaming us up on a supply-and-demand economics project.

Working together to develop a business model that addressed supply and demand issues seemed to be the perfect middle ground for our personalities and interests. We plowed into the task with a productive synergy that soon began to produce results and created not only a productive partnership but a close friendship as well.

We got jobs as waiters at the same restaurant and we could usually be found on breaks and after our shifts on the restaurant patio sharing ideas to flesh out the project. Over a couple of beers, we would write notes and ideas on cocktail napkins. We would share tables and help each other in the restaurant and then spend late night hours studying and developing the project.

We continued to pick up as many shifts at the restaurant as possible, and decided to move into a house together with three other college friends to split the rent. Money for rent, tuition, and books pretty much exhausted our disposable income. The great thing about the restaurant job was that we could bring home leftover potatoes for dinner and lunch the next day.

One of our monthly tasks was to take turns collecting the rent from the other three tenants and depositing it in the landlord's bank account. We were sitting there on an old couch left in the house by the previous tenants, dining on leftover potatoes. Nobody else was there, but if they had been, we're sure

∞∞

they would have enjoyed seeing that light bulb come on over our heads when the conversation turned to making the rent.

> *"Hey Michael, there's another hole in this couch. Maybe we should buy a cover for it".*
>
> *"Unless you're hiding a bank account somewhere, I think you can forget about buying anything this month, Scott. I just collected and deposited the rent for the landlord and we're broke again. And I'm getting very tired of potatoes".*
>
> *"Yeah, a menu change at the restaurant would add some variety to our lives. I never really paid attention before, but isn't this monthly rent deposit about $500 more than our landlord is paying each month for this place?"*
>
> *"Scott, we've been working on this in class. He has the supply and we provide the demand, so I guess that's his reward for getting it right ... hmmm?"*
>
> *"Michael, are you thinking what I'm thinking? While we're eating leftover potatoes on a ratty couch, our landlord is sitting in another city putting $500 into his pocket every month".*
>
> *"Yeah, and while he's sitting there checking his bank balance, we're studying and working 14 hours a day and don't have a dime left to spend after we send him that rent!"*
>
> *"Man, it just got brighter in this room. We need to buy a house and fill it with student tenants!"*

It all came together in that conversation: the rent receipt, our long hours of work and study, empty pockets, and that class business model. That evening we went from "not a clue" to a blinding flash of the obvious. We needed to go out and buy a rental house.

Why should we be putting that $500 into our landlord's pocket every month when we could be putting it into ours? All we'd have to do was to buy a house nearby and rent it out to students. Of course, then we would need to buy another and keep doing it, multiplying that $500/month into a real business cash stream.

We Took the Hard Way – Now You Reap the Benefits

Who are Scott McGillivray and Michael Sarracini, and why are we able to claim that we'll move you through a process to lifetime cash flow? First of all, we're record-keepers. We've made a ton of mistakes building our real estate investment business. What is most important to you is that, from the first day, we documented every lesson learned and every tweak of our systems.

Our journals of activities, mistakes, and successes became the plan as well as our encyclopedia of investing. If we came across a problem or situation a second time, we simply referred back to our journal to see how we handled it successfully the last time. Then we applied the process to the new situation. What is just as important is that we could look back and see how NOT to handle a new situation, since we had also documented our failed or money-losing situations.

Jumping right into business without experience wasn't an easy process. What we found when our feet hit the street was that we were hyped up but we didn't have the tools or knowledge to implement a foolproof plan. We had a handshake introduction to real estate investment when we really needed a mentor relationship to guide us.

We needed someone who could and would "walk the talk" with us. We're not suggesting that we wanted someone to be with us to offer on-the-spot advice. Instead, our need was for an executable plan. We needed a plan developed around a set of well-defined goals, and we needed the knowledge and tools to implement the plan successfully. Half of that plan would need to include what to do to ensure real estate investment success. The other half of that plan was just as important: We needed to know what not to do. We needed the experience of "trial and error," with someone else making the errors.

A great deal of our life experience comes through trial and error. We make mistakes and hopefully we learn from them. We also hope that the mistakes aren't too painful and too costly in relation to the value we receive. One thing we can tell you for sure: mistakes when you're learning real estate investment through trial and error cost money--sometimes a whole lot of money.

Although we didn't find that mentor, we forged ahead, had successes, and made mistakes. Through it all, we kept records of both. Because of our obsession with documenting every success and mistake, we feel comfortable with setting a goal for how we will help you succeed.

Our goal is to eliminate for you the expensive process of trial and error.

Let's talk about goals for a moment, since we will be setting out investment goals throughout this book. We just gave you the first one, which is the need to eliminate trial and error in your real estate investment process. This is our goal, and three words explain our attitude about goals:

Goals are mandatory.

It's an attitude that will work for you if you develop goals realistically. Setting goals shouldn't be a haphazard process. They should be carefully thought through. Setting realistically attainable goals allows you to consider them *mandatory*. If your goals are realistic based on your financial abilities and the time you have to invest in this business, then you'll attain them. We didn't set that first goal of eliminating trial and error for you without thinking it through very carefully and making sure that the resources were available to make it happen.

The Pareto Rule

The Pareto Rule is named after the Italian economist Vilifredo Pareto. In 1906, he noted that roughly 80% of the land in Italy was owned by 20% of the population. He noted that there must be some correlation to other earthly things, since 20% of the pea pods in his garden contained 80% of the peas. Some people have come to call this the 80/20 Rule.

Sales trainers like to cite this rule, telling wannabe sales people that 20% of them will end up making 80% of the money. Whether in real estate, used cars sales, or retail, many people believe there is validation for this rule. We're not here to tell you that 20% of real estate investors make 80% of the money, though the rule may apply. Instead, we have our own rule.

The 10/30/60 Rule of Real Estate Investment Success

In our discussions with attendees at our seminars and with students in our courses, it's clear that very few of them are there because they have a love for real estate. They're there because they have a definite idea of the lifestyle they want, and they want to learn how to create that lifestyle. Real estate investment is the vehicle that will carry them to their destination.

You are probably reading this with many of the same lifestyle goals and questions. You want to know how real estate can be used to provide a comfortable, or even wealthy, lifestyle.

From our early seminar and learning experiences, followed up by trial and error, we have come up with our own rule that will assure your success in attaining that lifestyle. Our rule is the **10/30/60 Rule for Real Estate Investment Success.**

> **10% is Motivation.**
> **30% is Education.**
> **60% is Implementation & Mentorship**

Motivation

First, we believe that you're motivated or you wouldn't be reading this. However, motivation doesn't come from just being told that "you can do this". Motivation builds on that belief, but the bricks and mortar of that building are knowledge and tools that reinforce your belief that you can successfully create lifetime cash flow from real estate.

You want to learn whether real estate investment can improve your life, and if you believe that it can, you want to go out and get started. We want to feed that motivation and make it stronger. We'll accomplish our goal for you through a plan and realistic goal-setting process that will soon make it clear to you that this will happen.

The 10% motivation part of our rule is easy, because you come to this book motivated. It's also easy for us because we don't have to try to figure out what to write or teach that will motivate you. We know what motivated us: getting successfully past our mistakes and repeating our successes.

Education

While education isn't the major requirement in our rule, that doesn't mean we don't value it. It's imperative that you learn about your market area, real estate investing principles, and how to actually use your knowledge and not just amass it for the sake of bragging rights.

In this book, you're going to be thoroughly schooled in everything from market research to valuation and property purchases, and even on how to be a successful landlord. Education is a super-critical component of our program and of your success. The only reason you're less than halfway to success with just motivation and education is that the proper focus of your motivation and the right implementation of your education is absolutely critical.

Implementation & Mentorship

Logically you might argue that if you're motivated and if we provide you with a thorough real estate investment education, you will end up successfully managing properties for lifetime cash flow. If that were true for all people, then most of the real estate investing courses out there would be turning out the majority of their students as highly successful investors … but they aren't.

It's Like Losing Weight

How many people start a new year with a resolution to lose weight and shape up? It's a very large number. Many buy some diet and exercise books, and many more join a gym with a plan to work out regularly and drop those pounds. They're motivated, they have some education, and the gym provides equipment for weight loss. Yet how many successfully lose a significant amount of weight?

That number is much smaller. However, when we look at a TV show like "The Biggest Loser," we find a high percentage of the participants losing a lot of weight. Even those who don't make it all the way to their weight loss goals generally have lost a lot of weight, though not as much as the winners.

What's the difference? The diet books and eating advice is the same. The gym equipment is the same. The motivation is the same. The huge difference is in group participation and the mentorship of the trainers. Success comes from the support and experienced help of others. That's what we're going to bring to you in your real estate investment activities.

The 60% piece of the success plan is the mentorship, planning, and goal setting. We're here to provide this piece for you, both through this book and follow-up mentorship. Avoiding mistakes by capitalizing on our experience and record-keeping will get you started right and make your real estate investment for cash flow much more profitable from the very first property purchase.

You need a great deal of experiential information. Knowing what is likely to happen if a certain course of action is taken can be learned by doing it through trial and error. Or, for a much less expensive lesson, you can learn from others and benefit from their mistakes and successes.

First, it's a lot less painful financially and emotionally to learn from others' experiences. Second, it's a lot faster.

*"If I have been able to see further
than others, it is because I have stood
on the shoulders of giants".*
—Sir Isaac Newton

Sir Isaac Newton's statement shows that he clearly understood why he was able to make such rapid scientific advancements. He learned what others did and then advanced their actions. He didn't start from scratch or reinvent the wheel. You're going to learn what we have done, how to implement it, and how to advance from your experiences.

Now you know why Implementation & Mentorship are 60% of our success rule. It's taking the motivation and education to the next level. It's providing the help in implementing the plans, setting achievable goals, and making those goals a reality.

Motivation and education get you so far-- 40% of the way. Implementation & Mentorship take you all the way. You'll get all three in this book and from our mentorship, but in the proportions that will assure your success.

LEARNING FROM OUR MISTAKES

Sitting on that ratty couch and hatching the idea, as we did, is an example of a "dream," not a plan. However, we weren't daunted, and began to talk to real estate agents who happened to lunch at the restaurant where we worked. It seems that real estate agents go out for lunch a lot! So we ran our plan past someone almost every day. While they were nice people, most of them seemed to be a bit careful about providing encouragement to two college students with no money who wanted to buy a $200,000 home as a rental property. We understood, but we kept explaining the plan to anyone who would listen.

Negativity Kills Success

While the real estate agents were not interested due to our apparent lack of experience and cash for financing, there were others we encountered who were downright negative about our goals. Whether family, friends, or college acquaintances, there were plenty of people around who believed that there was little or no chance for us to succeed. They had horror stories about failed ventures, negative press about real estate market activity, and plenty of negative sentiment about our lack of experience and money.

You know the type. When you hatch an idea and verbalize it, the first thing out of their mouths is a statement as to why it can't work. It's just their nature, and maybe they have firsthand experience. Maybe they are extremely risk-averse, and the thought of investing in rental property is scary for them. However, that's their nature and their experience. You must put all of this negativity into its proper place – the trash!

We had our big picture plan, but we knew we needed more information and some help to get it going. We went to seminars, workshops, and even the Renovation University at Home Depot on Sunday mornings. We wanted to learn everything we could as fast as we could, and nobody's negativity was going to slow us down.

Finally – A Helping Hand

When we finally found a real estate agent who was either really hungry or took pity on us, the hunt for that first home was on. Our journaling nature came in handy as we looked at house after house. We learned something new in each of them, and we kept those notes.

Of course, being the very renter types who would end up as our target tenants, we knew the features of a house that would make it rentable to college students. We quickly learned the values of properties and had a very clear idea of just what the perfect house would be for our purposes.

Using our project business model, we plugged in the numbers for the property we wanted. The profitability and return on investment numbers looked great. Though family and friends were less than enthusiastic about our purchase, we managed to pull together the financing to buy our perfect house.

By the time the house was ours, we already had multiple rental ads in print and on the Web. Our business model made it clear that vacant time is a drag on profits, so we wanted to get that house rented quickly. This brings us to Lesson #1, duly recorded in our journals.

LESSON:
Don't set up multiple showings at the same time!

We ran an ad and stated a time for potential tenants to meet us at the house. While it seemed efficient to us at the time, when we arrived for our first showing, there were four groups of five people each waiting to get in. While that was bad enough, over the next fifteen minutes, seven more groups showed up. It seems that running a specific day and time in the ad wasn't the best of plans.

While it was a trying experience, the result was awesome. Eight of the groups wanted the house. This meant that we got it rented that same day. Now, that's reason for celebration, but we were actually disappointed. This experience clearly showed that there was demand far exceeding our single house supply. We had really needed seven more houses that day, and they would all have been rented!

LESSON:
When there's demand exceeding supply – do something.

We went right out and looked for another property. We had a business model that was validated by our first purchase, and we had the numbers to prove it. While buying two homes that first year was ambitious, we had ready renters and didn't want to waste the opportunity.

When we found a suitable house, we called the seven groups who lost out on the first one and offered it before we'd even bought it. We had committed renters before we had even signed the purchase contract.

LESSON:
When something works, keep doing it. When it doesn't, make a note.

From these first two houses, we leveraged our knowledge and kept building on our cookie-cutter approach. Cookies are a good example, because a recipe doesn't always work, whether for ingredient reasons or preparation errors. We definitely made errors. Some of those errors were really costly. They weren't all errors in the valuation or purchase process. There were also mistakes made as landlords, in property management, and even in rent collection and eviction when things didn't go well.

During the following years, we would religiously document failures and successes in detail in our journals. These journals became an encyclopedic reference and the origination of this book and our "Successful Landlord" training courses.

Motivation: Let's get back to our 10/30/60 Rule. You're motivated, maybe even more so now because you've seen that two broke college students can build a major cash flow real estate rental business from being renters. You're 10% of the way to lifetime cash flow.

Education: Now you know that we have books of notes on our processes, failures, and successes. We have the education you'll need to replicate our success, and we're going to share a huge body of educational rental property investment information with you here. You've just increased your progress toward success to 40%.

Implementation & Mentorship: Remember our goal in serving your needs: *"Our goal is to eliminate for you the expensive process of trial and error"*. And, don't forget that we consider our goals to be mandatory. We are committed to providing you with the motivation, education, tools, and resources to go all the way in achieving 100% success in real estate investment.

EVOLUTION OF A SUCCESSFUL BUSINESS MODEL

In this first chapter we shared our college living and financial experience with you to set a baseline for your future success. You simply can't get any more broke than we were, and you can't have less knowledge about rental property investing than we did when we had that conversation on the ratty couch.

Since 2000, we've bought and sold a great many rental properties, interviewed countless tenants, and made a whole lot of trips to the bank with rent checks. We've produced training courses, workbooks, and a full educational institute. Through the wide reach of television and the quality concepts of our Success Academy, we've been able to help tens of thousands of people in more than 15 countries realize the potential of real estate and use it to change their lives.

More than that, we've helped them realize the potential in themselves, see their amazing capacity to take what we have taught them, and become wealthy real estate investors. Now it's your turn.

ACTION STEPS

Take a pen or pencil and write down your idea of what success in real estate investment means to you right now.

Then make a bullet list of your assets that will help you achieve that success. No great detail needed now, but do list things like:

- "I have $xx,000" to invest".
- "I am willing to move cash from other investments like stocks and bonds".
- "It's time for me to set serious goals and build a plan".

That's all you need to do right now. It's an exercise in clarifying why you want to become a cash flow real estate investor and why you believe you can be successful.

WHAT'S NEXT?

If you aren't totally convinced that real estate rental property is where you should be placing your money and investing your efforts, the next chapter will make it crystal clear for you.

CHAPTER 2

Real Estate is a Most ABLE Investment

Too few people realize the amazing advantages realized by holding real estate as an investment. Investors complain about their stocks and bonds as they watch values fluctuate and inflation erode the value of their investments.

Our goal in this chapter is not just to illustrate the advantages of real estate investment but to compare it to stocks and bonds. While those investment types are fine for certain financial goals, there are certain disadvantages that come with investing in stocks and bonds. Real estate investment avoids these disadvantages and even capitalizes on the situations that create them.

Here are the very "able" characteristics of real estate investment.

SCALABLE – A HUGE PIE WITH A SLICE FOR YOU

The real estate pie is so unimaginably huge that you only need the tiniest slice to become wealthy. It's scalable, so you can increase the size of your slice whenever you want. There are more than 150 million homes just in the U.S. and Canada, so finding the right investment properties for your financial plan will not be a problem.

Most investors begin with a single home, buying it for rental income and the other financial advantages of real estate investment. Once they're enjoying these many advantages, it's a logical next step for them to buy another, then another. Some will move into multi-family and apartment investment to take advantage of the economy of scale enjoyed by owning multiple units in one place.

What type of rental properties you end up owning isn't important, as long as they help you meet your investment and lifestyle goals. How quickly you expand your holdings is also entirely up to you. Remember our first landlord experience during college.

> *"Scott, there are seven groups all waiting to see our only rental!*
> *Get over here and give me some help showing it".*
> *"I'll help, Michael, but let's rush them through because we need to*
> *go out right afterward and buy another one!"*

AVAILABLE – ANYONE CAN BUY IT

Anyone over the legal age to enter into a contract can purchase and own real estate. Whatever your gender, race, social status, religion, or income, real estate is there for you, without bias in its return on your investment.

In many areas, even a minor can own real estate if purchased with the signature of a legal adult guardian. Corporations, non-profits, and institutions all own massive amounts of real estate. It's an investment asset that is available to just about anyone.

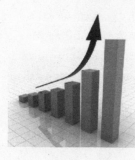

APPRECIABLE – IT INCREASES IN VALUE OVER TIME

Historically, real estate has consistently appreciated in value over time. The asset is worth more each year it is held. Don't expect that with a vehicle or other hard asset, since they depreciate the day they leave the showroom.

Stocks

Volatility is a term often used when talking about the stock market. How a public company is run and mistakes in service delivery or production can cause shares of stock to lose value. "Buy low and sell high" is a well-known goal of stock market investors. However, it is uncertain whether this strategy will work or if just the opposite will happen.

Bonds

Bonds are purchased by many investors late in life because they're less risky than stocks. They are purchased because they provide regular, though low yield, interest payments without the risk of stocks. They do not appreciate in value, paying out only the initially agreed-upon return.

The consistent appreciation of real estate has a lot to do with the fact that there's a limited amount of land, and the cost to build on it has usually increased each year due to inflation in labor and material costs. More bonds and stock shares can always be issued, diluting the value of previous shares in some cases. Land, on the other hand, is a finite commodity.

RENT*ABLE* – CASH FLOW FROM PEOPLE WHO PAY TO USE IT.

Remember when the light bulb went on over our heads in that college rental? A whole new world opened up to us when we realized that our landlord was clearing $500/month over his costs every month when we scraped together our rent.

Buy a stock and hold it, and you won't see them paying you regularly unless it's a dividend paying stock. If it is, then the price performance is a trade-off, since it will not be a stock that gains significant value during your holding period. Stocks gain when companies plow profits back into growth. When they give profits to shareholders as dividends, growth suffers and share value doesn't increase appreciably over time.

Bonds will definitely provide you with cash flow, but you lose any appreciation potential. For the security of a promised interest rate payout, the investor forgoes any increase in value over time.

Real estate is the only asset class that will pay you cash every month even as it is appreciating in value. Add this cash flow advantage to the others in our ABLE list, and you'll readily see why real estate investment is a reliable path to your future financial independence and the lifestyle you desire.

HEDGE*ABLE* – HEDGING OTHER ASSET CLASSES

All financial investment advisors tell their clients to

"diversify". However, most of this advice is in the context of buying different classes of stocks or bonds, or buying stocks in different industries as a hedge against losses. The idea is that by holding stocks in technology and in durable goods, for example, you may have some protection against losses if one industry class is losing value.

They'll also advise that holding some bonds will hedge against stock market fluctuations. You will continue to draw the interest promised by the bonds and can wait out the stock market to see if you can recoup your stock losses in the next uptrend.

Those are great strategies if you're trapped in those two asset classes, stocks and bonds. However, when inflation is in the picture, and it always is, neither class benefits. While some industry stocks can benefit from inflation in their product prices, just as often their production costs rise as well, so profits are stagnant, and stock values are too. If it's a dividend-paying stock, or a bond with a fixed interest rate, inflation takes a heavy toll on your returns.

Real estate can be your hedge against those perils. What happens when labor costs go up? How about when the price of lumber and building materials are rising? It becomes more expensive to build, and home prices normally move up as well. Your rental property's value goes up with inflationary pressures, making it a perfect investment hedge in a market with rising prices.

But there's another advantage and it's about rents: your cash flow can increase as well. If inflation is driving up home prices, then it's likely there is some upward pressure on rents, as well. Fewer people will be buying, which means more renters. More renters mean greater demand. We're back to that college project again. Increased demand brings opportunity for rental property owners.

LEVERAGE*ABLE* – A LITTLE MONEY CONTROLS A LOT OF ASSET

OPM, Other Peoples' Money, is the way to leverage your available capital and control a lot more asset with less money out of your pocket. Next to cash, real estate is considered the most stable asset to own. This means that banks and other lenders will give you money to purchase real estate because they see it as a secure investment.

All of the advantages we've talked about in this chapter so far are valued by lenders. They see a stable asset that isn't going to be moved and can't be easily destroyed. Insurance offsets risk of structure damage or destruction, as well. Lenders also know that real estate has historically always grown in value. They also have extra security in that they can take the property if you do not make the required payments.

For all of these reasons, you can use less of your cash as a down payment, and use the lender's money for the remainder of the purchase price. You can control 100% of the asset value with only 5% to 20% of your cash invested. And you're getting that other 80% to 95% of the rental cash flow, not the lender.

Visit our website for a great example of two different leveraging scenarios:

http://scottsinvestorsedge.com/book-resources/leverage-sisters

IMPROV*ABLE* – ADD VALUE EASILY

While many rental property real estate investors buy, hold, rent, and then sell properties without making improvements, there is the potential to do more. Making improvements to a property in the right way will add value to the property in excess of the cost of the improvements.

Remodeling or adding square footage to a home will increase its value. Owning a $100,000 home and doing an addition or remodel costing $15,000 will usually add more than that cost to the value of the home immediately. That's just the beginning, though, since now the basis for future appreciation is higher, as well, so your ultimate return on improvement investment will be compounded.

Then there's that great kicker that we could readily see in our college rental property investments: immediate rent increases and better cash flow. If adding a bedroom would accommodate another tenant and increase the rent, we would recoup our costs very quickly and realize added ROI into the future.

TAX ADVANTAGEABLE – GREAT TAX BENEFITS

One thing that always erodes your investment returns on bank accounts, stocks, bonds, and other equities is taxes. In areas with progressive tax rates, the better you do the more you're taxed as a percentage of profits, so you are penalized for success. There aren't many ways to minimize taxes on these types of investments, since there aren't really any deductible costs for holding them.

Real estate, on the other hand, enjoys many tax advantaged strategies. Depending on your country and state of residence, there are many deductions and tax reduction strategies available:

- Capital gains deductions on principal residence
- Deductions of state and local taxes on rental properties
- Closing cost expense deductions on rental properties
- Rental and management expense deductions
- Insurance for rental property is deductible
- Marketing and advertising expense deductions
- 1031 tax deferred exchanges in the U.S.

It's easy to see that there are a number of excellent and legal ways in which to maximize your return on investment in real estate by lowering your tax liability.

STABLE – SLOW TO RISE AND SLOW TO FALL

Now if you really want "stable," bonds will provide stability in value. Unfortunately, the trade-off is a paltry return on your investment, sometimes not even enough profit to outpace inflation. This isn't the path to riches or a better lifestyle. It is more of an attempt to maintain the status quo, and much of the time it doesn't even achieve that goal.

Real estate has proven to be one of the most stable investments in existence. There are market cycles in real estate as in any investment, but over time the predictability of real estate investment values and returns has been a great draw for investors.

LIVABLE – EVERYBODY NEEDS A HOME

In early 2011, National Geographic Magazine stated that the world's population was approaching 7 billion people and that it would be around 9 billion by the year 2045. All those people have to eat, so food is a major necessity. They all need a place to live, so housing will always be a requirement with increasing demand.

We're back to that college project yet again. Supply and demand are the basics of commerce and prosperity. People will always need a place to live. More people bring greater demand for housing, and rising prices are the economically logical result.

Once you are out there building your real estate rental property inventory, you'll experience a comfort level from the reality of statistics like these. Owning an asset that is destined to experience increasing demand far into the future is better than holding any stocks or bonds.

LEARNABLE – ANYONE CAN LEARN HOW TO DO IT

The higher mathematics required for rocket science make it a calling beyond the abilities of much of the population. However, real estate isn't rocket science, and the things that need to be learned to be a successful real estate investor are easily learned by anyone who wants to invest successfully.

First, real estate is all around us. You need only walk around to see real estate in every direction and of every type. Learning about real estate is much easier when examples are virtually everywhere we look. We can walk into buildings, learn about construction, and see what people need and want in places where they work and live.

Whether we're sleeping, walking the dog, working, or shopping, we're doing it in real estate. Everything we need to help us learn about real estate is right in front of us every day, in all of our activities.

If we want to know what current tenants are demanding in the way of rental home amenities, we can invite ourselves in to take a look. We can call up a rental management company and ask them to show us the properties they manage that command the highest rents, and they'll take us right in for a look and some education.

The math required for real estate investment success is far from rocket science stuff, and there are many software programs and specialty handheld calculators that can do it for us. If you can read and listen, we can help you to become a successful real estate investor living the lifestyle you've dreamed about.

PEACEABLE – SLEEP WELL WITH REAL ESTATE

Take a moment and skim back over the previous 11 "able" characteristics of real estate investments. How do they make you feel about real estate investment from a risk perspective? When we ask our seminar and course attendees this question, they don't have to think about it. They always say that it makes them feel comfortable with real estate as their path to financial independence in a low-risk but high-reward business.

You'll experience peaceful sleep, unlike millions of people who go to bed wondering where the stock market will open in the morning because there was bad news the day after the close. Your investments are where you can see them and monitor their condition.

ACTION STEPS

Take a piece of paper and write down each of the 12 "able" characteristics in this chapter. Leave some room between each for a couple of notes.

On a scale of one to ten, with ten being very important to you and a major factor in your decision to invest in real estate, rate each factor's importance to you, your investment and lifestyle goals. Also, if something comes to mind about why a particular item appeals to you, write that down. Sometimes our past experiences, particularly with other investment types, will cause us to highly value some of these characteristics.

Perhaps you've been in the stock market during one of the periodic crashes and lost a major portion of your net worth. Or maybe you've tried bonds and found that inflation took most of your profits, leaving you with less than bank passbook interest as a return on your investment. It doesn't matter, since you're just comparing the many benefits and strengths of real estate investment with other investment activities.

WHAT'S NEXT?

We've done a general assessment of your investment knowledge and financial capabilities. However, now that you have a better picture of the advantages of real estate investment, we'll go through a more detailed assessment of your abilities and the resources you are willing to commit to your real estate investment business.

CHAPTER 3
Determining Your Investing Resources

In the previous chapter you learned how very ABLE real estate investment is for securing a financially independent future. Now it's time to show your how *able* you are to accomplish your goals and become a successful real estate investor.

This isn't a pass/fail exercise based on how much money or knowledge you have available right now.

> "Hey Michael, there's another hole in this couch. Maybe we should buy a cover for it".
>
> "Unless you're hiding a bank account somewhere, I think you can forget about buying anything this month, Scott. I just collected and deposited the rent for the landlord, and we're broke again. And I'm getting very tired of potatoes".

We went right out not long after that conversation and purchased our first rental house. And then we did it again in the same year. So it's not about whether you have money now or not. However, knowing what you do have, or how you can free up some cash, is part of setting up a realistic time frame for reaching your objectives.

Notice that we're talking about timelines rather than an exercise to determine whether you have the resources to start your real estate investment activities right now or not. We'll show you that you are ready now. Whether it's cash in the bank or the will to succeed, you have the basic necessities to begin your real estate investing business. This chapter is about assessing your abilities, temperament, risk tolerance, and financial condition so that you can use the information to set your goals and develop a timeline for reaching them.

As we move through these self-assessment steps, remember that you belong here no matter where you fit financially. You're in a very mixed financial group when we consider everyone reading this book. Some of you will be broke college students like the two of us were back then, some of you will be people with some wealth, and others will fall somewhere in between.

Those with businesses or greater financial resources are likely to have some of the financial evaluation pieces we discuss already in place. They can move through the exercise faster, even skipping areas. Those with little or no cash will find a great deal of valuable information here for getting on track with a plan and creating attainable goals. It doesn't matter where you fit into the activities in this chapter. It just matters that you know you DO fit.

This chapter isn't all about financial resources. You will be evaluating personal knowledge and attributes, as well. Some of this evaluation will influence early investment activities, and some will come into play farther down the road. This is the time to learn more about yourself and how this self-knowledge will fit into your investment activities and strategies now and in the future.

TOLERANCE FOR RISK

Starting out with a discussion of risk isn't meant to intimidate anyone, since risk is part of any investment activity. If it wasn't, everyone would be rich, buying any stock on the exchange and watching it grow steadily in value.

In the previous chapter we gave you several reasons why real estate investment can be a hedge against risk. Real estate balances out an investment portfolio, substantially reducing overall risk. Owning real estate has historically been a stable and profitable enterprise.

Now is a good time to take a look at your personal attitudes about risk, decide how you will plan for real estate investment, and determine the timeline for growing your investment business. None of these actions are based on your financial situation. Whether you're sitting on a pile of cash or you're a financially-strapped student, knowing how you handle risk will help you set your goals and create a workable plan for the future.

Very Low Risk Tolerance
Whether you're rich or totally broke, if you fit into this group, you check

your pockets every morning for holes, since you don't want even a penny dropping out on the ground during the day. You take an umbrella to work even when the sun is shining and there's no prediction of rain.

Betting in the office football pool is out of the question. You end up with double and triple items in the kitchen cabinets because you buy them on the way home, thinking you may not have what you need to prepare dinner. You don't want to risk having to go out again.

If you see yourself in this description, it doesn't mean that you shouldn't start your real estate investing business. Actually, you're probably the person who will benefit most from this book and our mentorship. There is little chance of you building future wealth in any other way, such as investing in the stock markets. You couldn't sleep at night wondering what your stocks will be worth tomorrow, especially if there was bad news today.

Using leverage is something most of us do, whether it's a loan for a car or a home mortgage. So you likely have used other people's money to finance the things you need. Your low tolerance for risk doesn't mean you won't use leverage to purchase properties, just that you'll be much more careful in your valuation and selection of appropriate rental homes.

Rejoice, as you would probably never amass wealth in any other way, so this book, and ultimately real estate, will provide the tools and confidence for you to become a successful real estate investor with lifetime cash flow. Spend as much time as necessary to learn the math and evaluation tools for selection of properties. Develop a confidence in your ability to understand your local rental market dynamics, figure out what renters want, and learn what they'll pay to get it.

If you're in this risk tolerance group, you're in precisely the right place at the right time. Everything that successful real estate investment promises in the way of returns and financial security is available to you and at a risk level that will allow you to sleep soundly.

Normal Risk Tolerance

Most of us fall into this group. We leave the umbrella at home even if it's cloudy. The weather person didn't predict rain, so we take a chance. The office football pool is fun and it's just a buck, so why not?

We constantly arrive home from work and find we need to go out and get ingredients or basics to pull a meal together. If we don't have much money, we think we should put enough together to get into the stock market or at least buy some mutual funds to save for retirement. Those with some money are in the markets, watching the Dow Jones and trying to predict which industries and stocks to move into and when.

Stock market investment accounts, bonds, and mutual funds are common investment vehicles for the normal risk group. It doesn't mean that those in this category aren't cautious, and they certainly aren't happy when the market takes a dive and their investment account balances dive with it. However, they are optimistic that they will see growth over the long term.

Leverage is a tool this group doesn't mind using. Many will try to get the lowest down payment possible with a home mortgage, since they want to use their cash in other ways. Besides, the home will increase in value anyway, so why tie up cash unnecessarily? Some in this group will also trade stocks on "margin," using a leveraged account to control more stock than the cash they have available in the account to purchase it.

If you're in this group, it's easy to get excited about your financial future and lifetime cash flow. Maintaining a balance and only taking on realistic risk should not be a problem for you. Perhaps running through that last batch of numbers one more time before signing a purchase contract is a good idea, since your excitement can bring about hasty decisions at times.

High Risk Tolerance

Those in this group don't even own an umbrella. They are the ones who set up the office football pool, and they're constantly trying to up the stakes.

Using leverage is second nature to this group. They trade stocks on margin and end up with "margin calls" to put more cash into their trading accounts when the market is down and they exceed the margin lending percentage they're allowed.

If you're in this group, you're not worried about what's in the cabinet or fridge for dinner because you have a bet with a co-worker with dinner as a payoff. Whether you win or lose, you're going to a restaurant.

You're already seeing yourself sipping cocktails on a beach in front of one of your retirement homes. This real estate investment thing is just what you needed to offset the lousy performance you've been experiencing in your other investment accounts. Our goal for you is to try to keep you from skipping whole chapters and jumping into highly leveraged property purchases without the due diligence to cover your ass . . . etc.

Visit our website and take our interactive risk assessment test to find out which risk category you are in, you may be surprised with the answer!

http://scottsinvestorsedge.com/book-resources/risk-assessment

Every Risk Group Wins

Wherever you fall in the risk tolerance spectrum, you'll find what you need to succeed in this book and with our mentorship programs. We'll keep you on track for lifetime cash flow through rental property ownership.

YOUR CURRENT KNOWLEDGE LEVEL

How much do you know about buying, selling, and renting real estate? Whether you've never owned a home, or you've bought and sold several for personal residences, real estate investment in rental properties involves a whole new knowledge set.

- Attention to zoning issues
- Property condition evaluation and repair/renovation estimation
- Local, regional, and national real estate market trends and what they mean to the rental property investor
- Property valuation to assure the right purchase price to achieve investment goals
- Rental market demographics and trends
- Purchase, holding, and liquidation costs for the investor
- Property management from legal and financial perspectives
- Tax considerations in real estate investing

There's more, but that should give you an introduction to the components of a successful real estate investing business.

Our goal is to eliminate for you the expensive process of trial and error.

Remember that quote from Chapter 1? Here's where it begins to take on real importance. The first thing you should do is to realistically assess your current knowledge. From "my parents own a home and I live there" to "I've actually rented out a home before," it's important for you to recognize your knowledge, strengths, and weaknesses early in this process.

Even if you've done some rental property investing, you're reading this because you believe there's more to learn. We told you in the first chapter that we were one thing above all--record keepers. We kept journals of every success, mistake, and detail of our rental property investing, and we still do the same. You're here to take advantage of these journals and to use this book and our mentorship to take you to a new, exciting, and highly profitable real estate investing business threshold, no matter what you know at this point.

Regardless of your present knowledge, we'll get you where you need to be. What's important now is to take some time to stop and write down what you know, including what you don't know or think you should learn to become successful in creating lifetime cash flow.

CASH ON HAND

Try not to go to the elitist or the paranoid extremes here. Whether you're sitting on a pile of cash or sitting on a ratty couch with holes in it, there is information here for you. Your starting point is to determine what you have available for real estate investment cash, or how to begin to free up some cash so you can get started.

You're Sitting on a Ratty Couch

OK, so you've got zip for cash. Maybe you're like we were, in college and struggling to make rent, with a job after school and late night homework. Maybe you're one of the millions in this country who is just making it from paycheck to paycheck, never managing to save much money at all. The cash you have in your bank account isn't enough to carry you for a couple of months if your income stops.

Now is the time to sit down and determine where your cash is going every month. It's called a budget, and you'll need to develop one right away. How

much is coming in and where does it go out? We're here to help.
Use our living expense and home operating expense spreadsheets at our
website at http://www.scottsinvetorsedge.com/book-resources/livingexpense
and http://www.scottsinvestorsedge.com/book-resources/operatingexpense.

Don't miss a penny that you spend. Keep a small notebook or recorder
with you. Note every expenditure, no matter how small. One student was
absolutely amazed at his monthly coffee house expenses once he took the
time to keep up with them.

Once you've determined where your money is going, it's time to see
if you can re-route some of it to better uses. What about a straight coffee
instead of a latte? One student simply quit using the coffee house as a study
hall, and her expenses dropped by around $80/month!

Study where your cash goes and how you can cut your expenses. Instead
of thinking about a $3.00 specialty coffee, think of that $3.00 as a square
foot of flooring in your rental home. Now you have something to build on!
Each coffee you avoid is adding square footage to the first rental home you're
going to buy. Here's a screen shot from a randomly selected search result for
flooring prices:

Pergo Elegant Expressions Now Available For Less Than $3 Per Square Foot Through Best Laminate

Best Laminate is now offering Pergo Elegant Expressions laminate floors for a special price of just $2.87 per square foot, a significant price reduction. Best Laminate specializes in top quality laminates, including cheap Pergo floors. Remi Swinrzak

Now you have a whole new way to look at that cup of coffee.

Later in this book we'll give you some ideas for raising funds for
investment, as well as how to borrow intelligently. Right now, you should begin
to build on your own resources before you look to use Other Peoples' Money.

You're Sitting Pretty

OK, so you're not sitting on a ratty couch. "Sitting pretty" can cover
a wide range of financial situations. You're possibly sitting on some cash,
maybe a lot of it if you grew tired of stock market gyrations and put your
money into interest-bearing accounts.

Maybe you have bonds that could be liquidated to free up some cash for
real estate investing. What about retirement accounts? Or, you could still be
in the stock market but could sell some of your holdings to free up cash for
real estate investment. Is there cash in your home that could be used?

FINANCIAL STATEMENTS

If you have an accountant to do this for you, or they're already doing it for you, great! If not, you need to get an accurate picture of your financial position at this point in your real estate investment education. We provide some help on our website at http://scottsinvestorsedge.com/book-resources/income-statement, with a sample income statement and balance sheet.

If you have a business, you're already familiar with income statements and balance sheets. These financial evaluation tools should be applied to your personal financial situation as well.

Your *income statement* will document the sources of your income and the amounts. It will also list and calculate your expenses, ending up with a profit or loss at the bottom, just as if your personal life is a business. It's like an ongoing movie of how you make money, how much you make, and how you spend it.

While you may be sitting on a high dollar leather sofa instead of a ratty couch with holes in it, you still must account for your income and expenses to see where you can improve your financial position to free up funds for real estate investment. In fact, you'll probably find more areas in which to save than our financially-challenged readers.

For a downloadable Income Statement that you can use visit
http://scottsinvestorsedge.com/book-resources/income-statement

As for the *balance sheet*, it isn't a movie, it's a snapshot. It represents your financial position for one moment in time and for the numbers entered then. The calculations in the balance sheet result in your *net worth*, a snapshot of the net result of your assets and liabilities.

By revising your balance sheet twice each year, you'll be able to track your progress in reducing liabilities and increasing assets. And cash is an asset, so lifetime cash flow will result in a balance sheet that will put a smile on your face and money in your accounts.

For a downloadable Balance Sheet that you can use visit
http://scottsinvestorsedge.com/book-resources/income-statement

RESOURCES REVIEWED

In this chapter we want you to assess the current resources available to you at the beginning of your real estate investment activities. Through this book and our mentorship, you'll be constantly improving both your knowledge and your financial position. Tracking that improvement will be exciting and will clearly show your progress toward lifetime cash flow.

ACTION STEPS

1. Think about your tolerance for risk and where you fall in the examples. It doesn't matter where, but it will help you with what to focus on in your training.
2. Do the knowledge exercise. Sit down and write down what you know about real estate--buying, selling, renting, and the financial aspects of real estate investment. Write down where you need to add to your knowledge, as well.
3. Develop a budget or income statement that clearly sets out where every dollar comes from and where every dollar goes.
4. Determine where you can cut expenses and improve your cash flow. Every dollar you save can be returning cash flow later, through real estate investment.
5. Get an accurate picture of your current financial situation and what you have available for investment right now. Remember, if it's nothing, it's not a problem. It just means you need to work on other resources, and we'll help.

WHAT'S NEXT?

Financial leverage is part of real estate investing and an important one. In the next chapter, we will learn more about leverage and see some useful examples.

CHAPTER 4
Leverage and Using It Wisely

At this point you should have a really good idea of what you know, what you need to learn, and what your current financial resources are to get started with real estate investing. You've already begun a plan to work on your financial position in order to free up cash for real estate investing. And, even if you're cash poor and just getting started, you can expect more resource tools from us later in the book.

For the moment though, let's assume you have the down payment or more, in cash for the purchase of your first rental property. This will help us talk to you about leverage--the use of OPM (Other People's Money).

LEVERAGE IS A GOOD THING

The U.S. housing and mortgage markets took a huge hit in the period from 2007 through 2010. There were plenty of stories about careless lending practices and risky loan products. All of that bad news could lead one to believe that borrowing and leverage are not a good practice.

This couldn't be farther from the truth. Assume for a moment that you're filthy rich. We mean sitting on millions, or maybe even billions, of dollars. You want to put your money to work, but you don't want to do it in a risky way. You want to loan your money to people who will pay it back with interest that you can count on for years into the future.

Historically, home mortgages have been the most secure forms of investment. People will put off a lot of things and be late on other payments, but they will always try to make that house payment on time. Nobody wants to lose their home. So your money looks like it will work best for you at low risk by lending it to people buying homes.

Now add to your money the money of millions of other people with less wealth, who buy mutual funds or stocks that invest in mortgages. Suddenly there is a whole lot of money looking for borrowers. Add some government guarantees to lower lender risk, and you have a perfect storm of money looking for someone wanting to buy a home with leverage.

The mortgage industry is gigantic because it's good for all of the participants and the economy. And it's going to be great for your real estate investing business, as well. If real estate rental property investing required a full cash purchase of every rental home, there would be very few homes for rent out there.

Even if you have a large amount of cash, do you want to buy homes for cash and rent them out? Maybe, but you can do a lot more if you use leverage.

LEVERAGE EXAMPLES

Remember that this book is all about Lifetime Cash Flow. Plus, we want to remember all of the other great benefits of rental property ownership. It would seem that multiplying our properties would also multiply our benefits. This is true, as long as we do it well and with prudent investment principles and strategies.

Leverage Example 1 – No Leverage

You're a real estate investor sitting on $100,000 in cash. You want to purchase a rental home, and you want to pay cash for it. You know that you can get a renter into the home with a monthly rent payment of $650.

To keep things simple and only focus on leverage, we'll work these examples with only principal and interest payments, and we'll ignore taxes and insurance for now. Also, we won't consider closing costs. So, we have no mortgage, and rent payments of $650 coming in every month.

We also know that we'll see some appreciation in the value of the home over time, and that we'll get a tax break or two for expenses related to the ownership and management. However, since we don't have a mortgage, we won't have mortgage interest deductions.

Let's do the calculation for simple return on investment and cash flow.

Cash flow is $650/month x 12 = $7,800/year
$100,000 invested
$7,800 / $100,000 is 0.078 or 7.8% Return On Investment (ROI)

Remember that we're ignoring other expenses and taxes to simplify our comparison, so this return looks better than it would be in reality. However, we'll do the same for our other calculations in order to focus solely on the effect of leverage.

Leverage Example 2 – 50% Leverage for Two Homes

Now you've decided to buy two homes with mortgages instead of one home with cash. So, we'll put $50,000 down on each of two homes. We'll assume that they're similar $100,000 homes that will rent for $650/month each.

It's a good time for interest rates, and you find that you can get a mortgage on each of these homes at 5.25%. So, borrowing $50,000, each of the homes would be purchased with monthly mortgage payments of $276. Since our rents are the same $650 as in the previous example, we're realizing a cash inflow of $7,800 each, or $15,600/year for the two.

Payments total $6,624/year for the two homes.
$15,600 in less $6,624 out leaves $8,976/year cash flow
$8,976 / $100,000 = .0897, or 9.0% ROI

We've still invested our $100,000, but we now have more than a 1% better return on investment. That's $748/month, or $374 each per month in cash flow for each home. We've used OPM to add money to our monthly take. All of the other benefits of rental property ownership are in place, and we can now deduct the interest payments on the properties from income, as well.

Better than that, we have two homes that will enjoy value appreciation. That appreciation will not be diminished by the fact that we took out mortgages. We've increased our yield and doubled our anticipated appreciation gains, as we're gaining on $200,000 in assets. We're controlling $200,000 in assets with $100,000 of our money.

Leverage Example 3 – Three Homes with 67% Leverage

We're now going to borrow $67,000 on each of three homes. It's possible to get mortgages with 20% or more down, so it's possible to use your $100,000 to buy four homes with $25,000 down payment for each. However, rents don't justify that much leverage and may not justify three. But to show you one more leverage example, we'll move forward with buying three homes.

We'll stick to our mortgage interest rate and rents from the previous examples. So let's see how it breaks down.

Three loans at $370/month x 12 months = $13,320/year outflow
Three renters paying $650/month x 12 = $23,400/year inflow
$23,400 - $13,320 = $10,080/year or $840/month cash flow
$10,080 / $100,000 = 10% ROI

We've added to our ROI over the purchase of two homes and over the purchase of the single home with cash. We have all of the other tax and rental property ownership benefits still in place for all three properties. We went from a monthly cash flow of $650 to one of $840/month. While this isn't a big jump in cash flow, we're going to be anticipating appreciation on $300,000 in assets, which is three times what we would be getting based on a single purchase. Our $100,000 is now controlling $300,000 in assets.

Deeper Analysis of Our Examples

Our examples to illustrate leverage were just that--examples. However, would they have been good investments? It should be obvious now that leverage can be a really great thing for the rental property investor. However, it must be used intelligently, as too much leverage can backfire on the investor. Later we'll show you how to look at return on investment and monthly cash flow with a much more fine-tuned approach.

In fact, buying three homes with these numbers would not have been a good idea. Taxes, insurance, and expenses would have dramatically reduced your cash flow. The examples were to show the effects of leverage. Getting more in rents or paying lower mortgage interest may have made these viable investments, but that's why we want you "loving the numbers, not the homes". Our mandatory goal is......

Our goal is to eliminate for you the expensive process of trial and error.

Trial and error with leverage isn't something you want to do. We're going to make sure that you know how to get to the real numbers and use them to avoid leverage errors. Using leverage wisely can multiply your return and speed your progress toward your goal of lifetime cash flow.

LEVERAGE RISKS

Generally, when you hear about an investor running into trouble and losing properties to foreclosure, it's because they were over-leveraged. Obviously, no leverage would mean they owed nobody, and they'd have those homes. They may have been too aggressive in borrowing, or they failed to plan for possible vacancy losses or rent decreases. Let's look at some of the factors that make too much leverage a risk.

Rent Trends

What if there's a big apartment building spurt in your local area, and suddenly the inventory of nice rental units jumps up? There are plenty of places for renters to consider, so the landlords will have to become more competitive with rents. If your cash flow on a rental unit is too low, you could find yourself with negative cash flow very quickly.

Let's say you took on the three units in our third leverage example. We're still not talking about expenses, but your cash flow on those before costs and taxes is only $280/month each. Let's say that your expenses were $140/month each. Your net cash flow would only be $140/month each. That's why it was a good example of leverage, but probably not a good one for smart use of leverage.

Having to reduce rents even a small amount to compete could take away most if not all of your positive cash flow. And that's not taking into account vacancy periods when you're getting no rent at all and trying to compete to get a new tenant at the new reduced rent levels. In this situation, you could easily find yourself with negative cash flow.

Increased Costs

Taxes can, and do, go up. Repairs happen and utility bills increase. There are a number of expenses that can increase at any time. While a healthy market may allow you to pass those costs on to your tenants as increased rent, leases keep it from happening right away. A sick market would cause lower cash flow with increased expenses, since you usually can't ask for rent increases in a highly competitive rental market.

Vacancy and Credit Losses

Whenever a unit is vacant, cash flow is zero. People move, and you try to be on top of the situation and have a new tenant lined up to move in right after you clean and rehab the place. However, sometimes tenants don't stay through their leases, or they fall on hard times and do not make their rent payments on time. The more you're leveraged the more this can hurt you.

LOVE THE NUMBERS – NOT THE HOUSE

We'll keep bumping into this advice. You're buying the numbers, though they look very much like a house. Falling in love with a home may work for your personal residence, but it can be financial suicide when purchasing a rental home. We're going to give you a whole lot of instruction in the "numbers" of rental property investment. Using our material and mentorship, you will NOT end up in leverage trouble due to the normal ups and downs of rental property ownership.

While leverage is something you'll employ to grow your business, you'll use it only when the numbers work. Leverage is nothing to fear. You should embrace it as a tool to achieve your real estate investing goals. This book and our tutelage will provide you with the knowledge and ability to use leverage wisely and stay out of trouble due to the normal gyrations of your market.

ACTION STEPS

Get out some paper and a calculator and do some of your own leverage calculations. Try to get "real-world" with them. Look in the paper and find single family homes for rent. Use the rents they're asking for your calculations.

Take a stab at what the home may have cost the owner/landlord using comparable listed pricing in the area. Better yet, try to get sold prices if you can. Reduce those list prices by 10% to 20%, as you'll rarely approach asking price on homes you purchase for rental. We'll teach you about that. Then do the calculations as in our examples.

Do the first one with a cash purchase, then do another with 50% leverage, and another with 67% leverage. Or pick your own numbers. This is just practice to learn the effect of leverage. Don't get discouraged if your cash flow numbers are low, since you're not working with actual purchase prices. We're going to give you information and tools to make bargain deals, so you only spend the minimum you need to pay to get the numbers you want.

WHAT'S NEXT?

In the next chapter, we'll talk about the importance of credit, how credit scoring works, and how to improve your scores if they're less than stellar. Excellent credit over the long haul will allow you to borrow money at a much lower cost, raising your profits and cash flow.

CHAPTER 5

The Importance of Credit & Your Scores

Real estate rental investing is a business, and your profit margins will be determined by a number of important variables.

- The purchase price of the rental home
- Mortgage interest rates
- Taxes and insurance cost
- Repairs and maintenance
- How much rent you can charge
- Vacancy and credit losses

All of these factors are important. Incremental savings in any of them will contribute to your bottom line. If you can't get the numbers right for a deal, then it shouldn't happen.

"Love the numbers, not the house".

Of the six factors, four can change at any time. Only two are fixed: the purchase price of the rental home and the mortgage interest rate (most of the time). Adjustable Rate Mortgages (ARMs) offer fixed rates for a specified period; after that period, the rates can, and usually do, change. Lower rates are the enticing factor about ARMs, and we'll go into detail in the mortgage chapter. Using our "Strong ARM" approach, you'll get the best of both mortgage worlds. Learn more about this approach later in this book.

ARMs introduce some interest rate risk, which directly impacts cash flow. For investors with a lower risk threshold or a need to peg income more closely, we recommend sticking with fixed rate loans.

We'll go into detail later about these two types of mortgages, but for now we want to address the importance of your credit score and history and how they impact your mortgage interest rate and your bottom line.

Let's look first at the difference over time if you pay a 1% higher mortgage interest rate on a $175,000 loan.

5.75% rate on $175,000 loan = $1,021/month payment
6.75% rate on $175,000 loan = $1,135/month payment

Those are the principal and interest payment amounts. We have purposefully left out taxes and insurance in those numbers, since they are not necessary for our comparison. You can see that the higher rate is costing an extra $114/month.

No matter what we're charging for rent, we can easily see the effect of this increased cost on our ROI. We're paying an extra $114/month, which amounts to $1,368/year in extra cost. Let's say that we put $50,000 cash into the down payment and closing costs.

$$\$1,368 / \$50,000 = 0.027 \text{ or } 2.7\%$$

Our return on our cash investment in this rental is 2.7% lower because of this 1% increase in the mortgage interest rate. It's interesting to note that many supermarkets operate their entire business on net profit margins lower than 3%.

Of course, we can look at it in straight dollars, with $1,368/year amounting to $13,680 over ten years. Every day, new loans are issued to people at 1%, 2%, or higher premiums in mortgage interest because of their credit history and scores.

CREDIT SCORES & THEIR IMPACT

College students these days get credit card offers in the mail, often before they've even graduated from high school. Back when we were counting the holes in that couch, we didn't get offered credit cards. We didn't even think about going out and getting them. Who needed one more payment every month? Making the rent, eating, and buying books was our focus. It's a different world today.

In 2008, one resource placed the average U.S. credit score at 692. Two years later, many reports indicated that it had dropped significantly and that as many as 33% of the population had scores that would keep them from getting a conventional mortgage.

Credit is scored in a range from 300 to 850. The higher your score, the better your credit-worthiness for the purposes of borrowing money. But it doesn't stop there. Insurance companies are also now checking credit scores and basing insurability and rates on them, in some cases. So your credit score can help or hurt you in multiple ways.

Don't be discouraged if your credit history has some hiccups. Actually, we know of one very successful rental property investor who got into the business when his credit was "in the crapper". Those are his words and just show that you can make this happen even if your credit score isn't the greatest.

However, you'll want to work on it. One lender gave an example of four borrowers getting a $200,000 fixed rate 30-year mortgage.

Margaret with a credit score between 720 and 850 – Margaret has always maintained an excellent relationship with credit. She will definitely reap the rewards when locking up this mortgage, as she's getting a fixed rate of 5.5%. Her mortgage payment will be $1,136/month, and she will pay a total of $208,808 in interest over the 30 year life of the loan. Though that may sound like a lot, check out our other borrowers.

Carl's credit score between 675 and 699 – Carl's been pretty good with his credit, but he has a slightly lower score due to a number of loans and high limits, not because of any bad entries. He will have an interest rate of 6.25% and pay a monthly payment of $1,231. He will pay $243,316 in interest over the life of the loan, which is much more than Margaret's interest and could have paid for the really nice RV he's always wanted.

Beth is a little on the wild side with a credit score between 620 and 674 – Some late payments and a repossessed car a year ago are hurting Beth's ability to get a good mortgage. She will be required to pay an interest rate of 7.4%. Now the loan payment will be $1,385/month, and Beth is going to pay $298,513 in interest. She'll be buying furniture at the secondhand store due to this higher mortgage payment.

Dennis has a credit score between 560 and 619 – Dennis has always tried to have fun in life, buying what he wanted when he wanted it and using credit liberally and not in the wisest of ways. Dennis will be offered an interest rate of 8.2%. Actually, he barely made the cut. This will result in monthly payments of $1,496, and total interest paid over of $338,383.

Dennis, at the low end of the credit score spectrum, will end up paying $360 more per month than Margaret, and $129,575 more in total interest over the life of the loan. That's quite a difference.

Let's just agree that you want to have the highest credit score you can attain and hold on to it. You'll be using leverage frequently to put deals together, and your cash flow will be very dependent on your cost to borrow money.

Because your credit scores are so important, you'll want to check on them from time to time. While there are a great many online sites offering free credit reports, they are mostly geared toward signing you up for a monthly monitoring service. If you think you need this, then check them out by doing a Google search on "credit scores".

However, there is a free government site that will allow you to get your scores once every twelve months as required by the Fair Credit Reporting Act. You'll get your reports from all three major credit reporting agencies. Go to http://annualcreditreport.com and sign up.

How Your Score is Calculated

Each of the three major credit reporting agencies, Equifax, Experian, and TransUnion, calculates differently, so your three scores will never be exactly the same. However, all three maintain detailed records of all of your credit accounts and your payment histories. Factors used to calculate your score include:

- your payment history
- number of open accounts
- history of recently closed accounts
- the length of your available credit history

- the types of accounts you have
- how many inquiries are on your account
- how new your accounts are
- the percentage of available credit line that you are using

The type of account definitely influences your scores. Generally, fixed consumer loans help more than credit card and revolving charge accounts. Sometimes consolidating several credit card accounts into one fixed payment loan can increase scores.

The percentage of available credit that you use is important to your scores, as well. If you keep your cards charged up to near their limits, this will reduce your score. Keeping your balances under 50% of your available credit lines will improve your scores.

FREEING UP CREDIT FOR INVESTING

When you require leverage and OPM, Other Peoples' Money, to increase your holdings and build your business, your credit scores and history will determine in large part how much money you can borrow. How much money you can borrow will impact your business growth and your cash flow.

The amount of debt you carry as a percentage of your income and assets will influence how much money you can borrow. Reducing the types of debt not necessary to your real estate investing will free up borrowing ability for property purchases.

The first thought most people have when they want to decrease their debt is to try and pay off their larger accounts first. While putting available cash resources to work in paying off debt is a worthy goal, this isn't the most productive approach. There is a faster way to reduce debt.

Stair-stepping Debt Payoff

Human beings who start processes that aren't necessarily the most exciting or entertaining, like paying off debt, need some reinforcement along the way. There is a better way to structure your debt payoff plan that will provide reinforcement as you go and speed the process as well.

Let's look at a sample consumer's accounts and see how this stair-stepping plan will allow them to reach their goal sooner and will provide them with reinforcement along the way. Here are their current accounts:

Account	Balance Owed	Monthly Payment
Mastercard 1	$ 1,200	$ 75
Visa	$ 1,900	$120
Mastercard 2	$800	$50
Auto Loan	$12,500	$ 450
Consumer Loan	$ 3,000	$ 250

This consumer wants to begin to pay off these accounts and he's in a hurry. He also currently has an extra $150/month available to get the ball rolling. So, what should he do to get these paid off as quickly as possible and get a little positive reinforcement along the way? What is that reinforcement? It's paid off account statements. Let's take it in ordered steps:

1. Start with Mastercard 2, the lowest balance. The consumer is already paying $50/month, so he adds the extra $150 to that and pays $200/month on this account. In four months, more or less, it will be paid off. We'll ignore interest for the moment and just estimate months until payoff.
2. Now that Mastercard 2 is paid off, go to Mastercard 1. He now has the original $150/month plus the $50/month he was paying on the other Mastercard, so he adds that to the $75/month he's been paying on this card. Now the payments are $275/month on this card. This balance will be paid off in about five months.
3. Attack the Visa next. The consumer has $365/month now to apply toward this card. In about six months it will be a nice zero balance and he can move to the next loan.
4. Adding that $365 to the $250 he's been paying on the consumer loan, he can begin paying it off at $615/month. In about five months he can kill this balance and start working on that car loan.
5. In about 20 months this consumer has paid off all of his revolving debt except the car payment. He is now saving

enough in monthly payments to buy a rental home. Or, he can kill that car payment and have enough for a larger rental home, maybe even two of them!

Not only has he paid off his credit card debt, but he's greatly improved his credit scores and has a lower debt ratio. This will help him get mortgages at much better rates and add significant profits to his bottom line throughout his lifetime of cash flow.

WHEN YOU WANT TO CHARGE ON A CREDIT CARD

Earlier in this chapter, we said, "Reducing the types of debt not necessary to your real estate investing will free up borrowing ability for property purchases".

The key phrase in that sentence is *"not necessary to your real estate investing"*. Credit cards can serve many useful purposes in getting your real estate rental investing business off the ground. The use of credit cards can speed the growth of your holdings and cash flow. Any use of credit to increase your knowledge in the right areas or to add a level of mentorship and training is an excellent use of credit.

We offer a Mentorship Program that you can learn about at our website at http://www.scottsinvestorsedge.com/book-resources/successacademy. Get rid of as much unnecessary debt as possible, as we've discussed in this chapter. However, if you need to add some debt to jumpstart your business and take you to the next level in record time, you will see that it can be an excellent investment. The result will be more immediate cash flow.

ACTION STEPS

If you don't have a recent copy of your credit reports, go to annualcreditreport.com and get all three now. Go through them carefully, as errors are common and you'll want to have any incorrect derogatory information removed right away.

Assess your debt status for possible improvement. If you find that some revolving and credit card accounts should have their balances reduced or eliminated, begin the stair-step process to get rid of them. You want to free up every dollar possible for your investing and future lifetime cash flow.

WHAT'S NEXT?

Since leverage is going to be part of your future in real estate investing, the next chapter will take you through the most common types of mortgages, as well as the positives and negatives of each.

CHAPTER 6
Understanding Mortgages

∞∞∞

We have learned about leverage and why we need it. We know that using Other Peoples' Money will allow us to expand our property portfolios and increase our cash flow. We also know that we can enjoy more appreciation and control more assets than our cash alone could have purchased.

It's time to get into some of the mechanics of financing property purchases with a primer on mortgages. Unless you've been a mortgage broker in the past, don't skip this chapter simply because it's not exciting enough for you. Learning about mortgages will provide some of the most exciting moments in your rental property investing activities.

When you find the perfect property that will command top rents, your next step is to buy it. Finding out that you can't get the right mortgage to make the cash flow number work can be a major disappointment. However, using your knowledge of mortgages to get the right loan that creates cash flow above your minimum requirement can be really exciting. When we say "love the numbers, not the house," the mortgage rate and mortgage payment are two of the most important numbers.

In real estate, leverage is normally in the form of a mortgage on the property. The property becomes the security for the money loaned, and the borrower must repay per the terms of the loan or risk losing the property in foreclosure. As rental property real estate investors using leverage, we'll be applying for mortgages that fit the numbers we need to make our deals and rental income cash flow work.

While the most popular mortgage in the U.S. is the 30-year fixed rate mortgage, there are a number of mortgage structures available to borrowers. The type and duration of mortgage selected will depend on a number of factors including:

- how long the property is to be held
- the desired interest rate to make the numbers work

- the borrower's credit profile
- the type of property

In rental property investment, you should always think about the numbers.

"Love the numbers, not the house".

One of the most important numbers is the mortgage rate, since it is a major part of your costs and cash flow. The type of mortgage can influence the cash flow enough to stop a deal in its tracks. On the other hand, the right mortgage can make a deal happen by bringing cash flow in line with requirements.

When we purchased that first property back in college, a mortgage was necessary, but we didn't have a clue about the different choices that may have been available to us. In our financial condition just getting one was exciting, so we took what was offered. We've learned since then that the type of mortgage can make or break a deal, or it can make it a much better cash flow generator.

Let's look at the most common mortgage types.

30-YEAR FIXED RATE

Fixed rate: the mortgage interest rate is fixed for the entire duration of the loan. If it starts at 6%, 20 years later it's still 6%.

The 30-year fixed rate loan is particularly popular with residential owner-occupants because they want the security of knowing that their principal and interest payments will not change for the life of the loan.

However, this secure feeling, due to a never-changing interest rate, comes with a price. Loans of shorter duration can be had at lower interest rates. The shorter the time frame of the loan, the lower the interest rate.

This is logical, since lenders want the best return for their investment. They are willing to trade some of that return for the security of a shorter loan term. Fifteen years of risk is half of the risk they take on when loaning money for 30 years.

Remember from our leverage chapter that some investors are more focused on long term returns than on a lower rate, so they are happy to loan money for 30 years in order to be able to project their income stream for that longer period of time.

Multiple surveys done between 2006 and 2010 have come up with different estimates of how long the average homeowner keeps a home. However, most of them showed the range to be between five and eight years. That's far shorter than the 30-year mortgages most of the homeowners took out.

As a real estate investor, you should have a plan for how long you want to hold on to your properties, including rental properties. The quick answer is "for as long as the cash flow works". However, if appreciation is going well, at some point you may find it more advantageous to sell the home and roll your profits into another home or two.

Whatever your plan is at this moment, you may want to look at other loan types and durations than the staple 30-year fixed rate loan.

15-YEAR FIXED RATE MORTGAGE

The quick analysis of this loan is that it's for half the time of the 30-year mortgage. However, the major consideration for the real estate rental property investor is that while this loan will carry a lower interest rate, the shorter duration will make the payments higher.

A quick check at the time this was written showed that several national lenders were quoting rates that provided a 5/8 point discount for a 15-year fixed rate loan. In other words, you would save .875% if you borrowed for 15 years instead of 30 years. However, the monthly payments would still be higher than the higher rate 30-year loan.

For this reason, the 15-year loan is not favored by investors. While there may be a reason for using this loan type, the higher payments make it much harder to reach monthly cash flow goals.

ARMS – ADJUSTABLE RATE MORTGAGES

Advantages

As opposed to fixed rate mortgages, Adjustable Rate Mortgages, or ARMs, have temporary interest rates that will adjust at some point in the future. Be sure you understand how much they might change and how this adjustment will be determined. Investors with a very low risk tolerance may want to avoid ARMS, even though they will be foregoing some cash flow to do so. If you want a really detailed education about ARMs, you can get it at the Federal Reserve's website. However, you will find enough information here to make sound decisions and use ARMs wisely if you find them appropriate for your property funding needs.

As far as understanding the most important things to be concerned about when using ARMs, you should know that:

- monthly payments can change, even if interest rates do not
- payments can go up, sometimes a lot
- payments can go down (if rates drop) or not at all
- the borrower may end up owing more than they borrowed
- there could be early pay-off fees

Comparing different ARMs and comparing them to fixed rate loans can be challenging because of the array of factors that go into their makeup. You need to know about:

- indexes, the basis on which ARMs are adjusted
- margins
- discounts
- rate caps
- negative amortization
- payments
- recasting (recalculation) of the loan

Remember that ARMs are issued at lower rates than fixed rate loans, sometimes a lot lower. The most common ARMs are 7-year, 5-year and 3-year. While 1-year ARMs do exist, we'll focus on longer duration ARMS, which are more suitable for use by real estate investors.

At the time this was written, national lenders were quoting ARM rates at the following discounts to a 30-year fixed loan:

- **7-year ARM:** -1.25%
- **5-year ARM:** -2.0%
- **3-year ARM:** -2.5%

It's easy to see that there is a considerable contribution to cash flow with these discounts to a fixed rate loan. Of course, you should try to match your anticipated holding period to the ARM duration, or you could end up having to refinance at a rate that will negatively impact your cash flow.

What About Dennis?

Remember Dennis from our credit chapter? He had a very expensive mortgage due to his low credit score. Dennis may want to consider an ARM for his loan. Reducing his high interest rate by a couple of interest points would make a big difference in his payment. The risk he takes on related to rates three years later can be offset by working on his credit score for that period. Bringing up his score could make it possible for him to refinance in three years, keeping his interest rate manageable.

An ARM for You?

There may be valid reasons for taking out an ARM even when you plan to hold the home past the adjustment period. One reason could be that you anticipate the ability to raise rental rates enough to compensate for the adjustment.

Using the 5-year rate discount, let's see how this can help our cash flow on a home purchased for $150,000 with $50,000 down. The monthly payment savings is $115/month. Over the five year period, we would realize an extra $6,900 in cash flow.

Looking at it another way, if you want cash flow of $500 per house, as we did in our college purchase, you would be getting an extra 23% return if you used the 5-year ARM.

HOW ARMS WORK

Adjustment Period

Using our three ARM examples, let's talk about adjustment periods. At the end of the period, it is typical for the ARM to adjust. So our 5-year ARM will adjust at the end of five years.

The Index

The interest rate on an ARM is made up of two components, the index and the margin. Generally the index is a measure of interest rates, while the margin is an additional amount above the index which is added by the lender.

In most circumstances, if the index rate rises, so does the ARM interest rate and the loan payments. If the index rate goes down, some ARMs will take their rates down as well, while others will not.

Lenders base their ARM rates on a number of indexes, with the most common being:

- the 1- year Constant Maturity Treasury securities (CMT)
- the Cost of Funds Index (COFI)
- the London Interbank Offered Rate (LIBOR)

When you're considering an ARM, make sure that you know which index is being used. Take a look at the historical fluctuations of that index to see what could happen to your future rates.

The Margin

The margin refers to the points added to the index rate by the lender. While margins can differ by lender, margins are usually constant for the life of the loan. The *fully indexed rate* is equal to the margin plus the index.

Index	4%
+ Margin	3%
= Fully Indexed Rate	7%

If the index in this example were to rise to 5%, the fully indexed rate would then be 8%.

Returning to our discussion of credit scores and their importance, we find that some lenders base their margin on your credit record. The better your credit record, the lower the margin.

Interest Rate Caps

An interest rate cap is a limit on how much your rate can increase when the index increases. They come in two versions:

1. **Periodic adjustment cap** – After the first adjustment, this limits the amount the interest rate can adjust up or down from one adjustment period to the next.

2. **Lifetime cap** – A cap that limits the interest rate increase over the life of the loan. U.S. law requires that all ARMs have a lifetime cap.

Payment Caps

Many ARMs also have payment caps. These caps limit the amount the mortgage payment can go up even if interest rates rise. It's not a free ride, however. If the payment cap reduces the increase that the index dictates, the balance is added to the end of the loan.

TYPES OF ARMS

Hybrid ARMs

Hybrid ARMs are often advertised as 3/1, 5/1, or 7/1 ARMs. They are a combination of a fixed rate period and an adjustable rate period.

- The first number tells you how long the fixed interest rate period will be.
- The second number tells you how often the rate will adjust after the initial period.

So a 3/1 ARM will go for three years at the initial rate and adjust every year after that.

Interest Only ARMs

This type of loan allows you to pay interest only, not principal, for a specified number of years, typically three to ten years. Your payments will start out low; then they will increase at the end of your interest only period.

Payment Option ARMs

A Payment Option ARM is an ARM that allows you to choose among several payment options each month. These typically include:

- A traditional payment of principal and interest – reduces the amount you owe on your mortgage.
- An interest only payment – pays the interest but does not reduce the principal amount owed on the mortgage.

- A minimum or limited payment – allows you to pay a set amount each month, but it may not be enough to cover the interest. This will cause the loan balance to increase.

Payment Option ARMs are not normally of interest to real estate investors, but now you know something about them.

However, sometimes one of the ARM options can be just the right type of loan for a rental property investor's needs and cash flow requirements. Knowing how they work and what to look for will help you know when an ARM is appropriate to increase cash flow and improve your bottom line.

THE STRONG ARM APPROACH

We love ARMs because they increase our cash flow early in the ownership period. However, when we're running the numbers, we're evaluating the home based on the fixed rate that may result at the end of the ARM's initial fixed period.

In other words, if we decide to purchase a home with a 5-year ARM to get a great interest rate, we'll still run the numbers based on what the rate is likely to be after that initial five year period. This means that we'll always have profitable investment generating the cash flow we want, but we'll be getting bonus cash flow for the first five years.

HELOC – HOME EQUITY LINE OF CREDIT

If you own a home, you can set up a line of credit to access your equity. Many investors have used this type of loan to buy their first property using equity from their personal residence. This loan can also be used to access funds for improvements to rental properties.

Significant equity can be tapped with this predetermined line of credit simply by writing a check. You can use the credit line or not, as you need it. Paying back the loan builds back the line of credit to be used again, as needed.

COMBO OR PIGGYBACK LOANS

Piggybacking one loan on top of another is the concept with these loans. A second mortgage on top of a first can allow the borrower to get into a property with a smaller down payment and no Private Mortgage Insurance.

When a 20% equity is required to avoid paying PMI premiums, a combo loan can help. By taking out a second mortgage to cover the difference between the available down payment and the 20% requirement, the PMI is avoided.

LOVE THE NUMBERS

Understanding mortgages and how they work is quite important in building a successful real estate investment business and lifetime cash flow. Selecting the right mortgage for your purchases is critical to cash flow considerations, as well as to your exit strategies.

Our Approach

An old axiom of investing is that you should never enter into an investment unless you know how and when you're going to get out of it. While you may not know precisely how long you plan to own a rental home, some idea of the time period will allow you to select from numerous mortgage options.

We are always working with you to build lifetime cash flow and generational ownership. Buying property to keep and rent out for cash flow is our approach. Owning cash-generating properties provides a valuable estate to be passed on to your heirs and to their children. So your overall plan is to buy and hold property for an extended period of time.

Of course, situations change and economic or investment considerations could result in the desire or need to sell a property. Learning about selling properties and maximizing your ROI is a part of the process, though long term ownership is the primary goal. When the numbers are right, cash flows to you. Always make the selection of a mortgage a high priority in your rental property investing.

ACTION STEPS

If you have a mortgage on your personal residence, get it out and take a look at it. Read the terms and conditions, and be sure you understand the interest and how it's paid.

Spend some time going through mortgage broker advertisements and materials related to ARMs. Learn the differences and similarities between the different ARMs available. Contrast the various ARMs to a fixed rate loan using actual numbers for a sample property purchase.

WHAT'S NEXT?

In the next chapter, we take you an important step closer to actually getting started purchasing a property. We help you to begin the selection of your investing team members. It's a team activity, so you'll want to build an effective team to help create your lifetime cash flow

CHAPTER 7
Building Your Success Team, Stage 1

Successful real estate investing involves a diverse group of people and skill sets. Building a real estate investment team will be critical to your success. Each team member contributes certain skills and value to the process and each has an important role.

However, always remember that you're the captain of the team. The more you learn about each of the team members' functions, the more able you'll be to select excellent team members and manage them effectively. So don't just choose a team and turn over total responsibility to them. Continue to evaluate their performance and see how they're contributing to your goal of lifetime cash flow.

We're going to help you build your team in three stages. These stages will correlate with how you're progressing with your investing. For the first stage, you want to engage a:

- Mortgage broker
- Real estate agent/broker
- Real estate attorney
- Property & liability insurance agent
- Home inspector
- Title/Escrow company

There's no particular order for contacting these resources other than the first contact. Contacting a mortgage broker first is very important when searching for your first rental home. Your mortgage broker will take a lot of information from you, assess your ability to qualify for a mortgage, and tell you how much you should be able to borrow.

This is important, since it gives you a budget to use when you go out to find that first rental property. However, let's qualify that budget first. If your mortgage broker says you can afford a $200,000 home and can qualify for the mortgage to purchase it, don't run out with that amount as your target. We recommend taking a conservative approach by using around 90% of that amount as your budget.

We'll talk much more in the Mortgage Broker section of this chapter, but just know that they should be your first contact. The other resources can be contacted in any order. While you may not be ready to give them any business at this time, you are bringing them an opportunity to work with a future highly successful real estate investor. Act accordingly and let them know that you're putting together a team that will be working with you in all of your rental property investing deals.

MORTGAGE BROKER

The mortgage broker you end up working with will have one primary role: getting you the mortgages you need to purchase your properties. Later, a smaller role will be to help buyers finance properties that you're selling as an investment exit strategy.

"Hey Michael! Now that we've found this great house and know we can clear $500/month on it, how do we buy it?"

"Scott, your guess is as good as mine. When we get off shift, let's do some Web research and see how people who don't have any money buy houses".

As you can see, we didn't have a clue. We had low incomes and no experience in real estate, so we figured there wouldn't be anyone out there willing to give us the time of day. That was true until we did some legwork and started asking questions. It didn't take long for us to learn about a mortgage broker over at the local mall.

We had no idea what criteria to use when selecting a mortgage broker. At that stage, just finding a broker to talk to us was a big step. This broker turned out to be very helpful, answering all of our questions, and we had a lot of them. Actually, you should place response and helpfulness right at the top of your list for attributes of a good mortgage broker.

Another area in which you should question prospective brokers is in the type of loans they handle and the banks they work with. Mortgage brokers are independent business people. They do not work for any particular bank or lender. This is one of the main reasons you want to work with one.

Brokers work with many banks and lenders, giving them the ability to shop for the right loan for your circumstances and financial abilities. If you go to an individual bank, and that bank requires 25% or more as a down payment, you're dead in the water if you don't have that much or don't want to put that much into the deal.

Mortgage brokers can shop around for lenders willing to accept the down payment you're able to provide. Of course, that's dependent on the appraised value of the property. Your broker will also know which lenders have the most liberal terms, lowest costs, and competitive interest rates.

It's logical to ask why banks would want to work with mortgage brokers. The fact is that banks don't have the resources to field a sales team to bring in loan business. They work with brokers because brokers bring them business. And the broker serves a helpful role by prequalifying buyers so the lender knows that the potential buyers are eligible for a loan.

There is an "underwriter" at the bank who will review all of the details and loan documents to make the decision whether the loan will be granted, but mortgage brokers give that process a faster start by gathering those documents and getting the necessary information from the borrower.

The underwriter holds all of the cards and all of the money, so they're the one who must ultimately be pleased with the loan package. However, when a mortgage broker brings a lot of business to a lender, they frequently become well acquainted with underwriters and can smooth your loan process.

A sports figure has an agent who negotiates deals for them, as well as product endorsements. You have a mortgage broker who negotiates with lenders on your behalf. The lender pays the mortgage broker a commission on the loan, and you'll also have some fees charged directly to you by the broker.

Always question the fees you are charged. Depending on where you live, fees may or may not apply. In Canada, we've always worked with mortgage brokers who get paid completely by the lender. However, in the U.S. there are fees frequently charged by the mortgage broker. They aren't necessarily paid in full by the lender.

While you'll want to build a relationship with a broker based on trust, in the beginning you'll want to ask about each fee, why it's charged, and if it's negotiable. "Junk fees" can drive up the cost of a loan to the point that it kills the deal because you no longer *love the numbers*.

Fees versus Points

While fees are normally paying for some type of service related to getting the loan, you can also end up paying points to do what is called "buying down the loan". This isn't a mandatory fee but a way to provide more money up front to get a lower long term interest rate. If the mortgage broker tells you that you can get a ¼ point lower interest rate if you pay one point up front, then you'll need to run the numbers to see if that option will work for you. A $150,000 loan amount would mean that you would have to pay 1% (one point) up front to get that lower rate.

Building a Relationship with a Mortgage Broker

By the way, that mall mortgage broker made out well by taking a couple of college guys under his wing. Over the next five years we did 13 deals through this broker, making a lot of money for everyone involved.

> *Our goal is to eliminate for you the expensive process of trial and error.*

Remember our goal. Over those first five years and subsequent years, we have learned a lot about mortgages and mortgage brokers. While it was trial and error for us, it's going to be a smooth and rapid development process for you through our mentorship.

A mortgage broker will come to value your business as you work together. If they do charge fees, you'll eventually be able to negotiate those based on the business you're bringing them. They may be willing to reduce your fees and accept only what the lender is paying them to originate the loan.

Questions to Ask to Select the Team Member

Right now you're trying to begin a relationship with a mortgage broker that you assume will continue through many deals. Later you'll have questions directly related to the deal of the day. Here are some questions to ask to start a business relationship when you aren't there looking for an immediate loan.

- **What types of loans do you handle?** – While some government-backed loans may not be available to investors, others are and the rules change constantly. Try to find a mortgage broker who works with lenders in handling everything from VA and FHA loans to specialty loan types for investors and multi-family properties.
- **How many lenders do you work with?** – The more the merrier here. More lenders mean more opportunities to find one that will work with you on a particular deal.
- **What is the typical timeline for each type of loan?** – You're just getting an idea of how long these mortgage processes take from start to finish. You'll want to try to have tenants ready and waiting for houses you buy, so knowing the time frame to find them will help a lot.
- **What are your broker fees?** – Get them in dollars or percentages and you will be able to estimate your costs going into a purchase. Fees change, so have them gives you periodic updates.
- **Get some recommendations for other team members.** – The mortgage broker will be working with title companies, insurance agents, real estate agents, and others. You might as well have them give you some recommendations for people to talk to for other team positions.

It isn't a terrible thing to change mortgage brokers or even to use more than one. However, starting a mutually productive relationship with one broker early on will help you concentrate on the other components of your business.

REAL ESTATE AGENT OR BROKER

Let's get the "agent versus broker" discussion out of the way now. While laws and business structures vary in different areas, the majority of real estate brokerages are set up with both brokers and agents. Here are the differences in status for most companies:

Broker

A real estate broker's license normally requires more training, as much as two or more years of experience as an agent, and more stringent education and testing requirements. In many brokerages, there is a single broker who is the "managing" or "sponsoring" broker under whom the other licensed individuals work as "agents".

In many areas there can also be "Associate Brokers". These people have met the requirements to be a broker, but they don't want the hassle or expense of setting up their own brokerage and managing agents. They would rather "hang" their license with another broker who becomes their sponsoring broker.

Agent

While "agent" has become a generic sort of term, in many areas it's a designation indicating that the person is licensed but must work under the supervision of a broker. It doesn't mean that you will not have a well-qualified person with a great deal of experience. Many agents are in the same situation as the associate brokers just mentioned. They don't want the hassle and extra expense of being a broker, and they're happy to remain agents for their entire career.

Generally, agents do not have the authority to bind their broker to any discounts of their standard commission rates or charges. For this reason, you may want to seek out an associate broker or broker if they're available so that you can get a faster and more reliable response to requests to adjust commissions to fit special situations.

However, at this stage you're probably going to be just fine with either an agent or a broker. Also, there are some services you're about to ask for from your real estate professional before you have any deals for them. You may find that working with a hungry newer agent will be better for you, as they'll be more willing to bend over backward for your business. You can grow your businesses together.

Through the information and mentorship we will provide, you're going to end up more savvy about your local real estate market than many real estate agents are. Early on, their experience and ability to help you through the home search and transaction process will be more critical than later, after you've built upon your experiences.

Who Represents Buyer and Seller?

In earlier days, all agents worked for the seller in an arrangement called sub-agency. The seller would retain a brokerage to list their home for sale, and when an agent or broker from another agency brought in a buyer, that agent became a sub-agent of the seller. This meant that both agents were now working for the seller and in the best interests of the seller-- not a good situation for the buyer.

While you'll still read poorly-researched or old material stating that your buyer agent works for the seller, in almost all areas this is no longer the case. Sub-agency is mostly dead.

With that said, the seller is still paying the entire bill via the commission that's split between the seller's broker and the buyer agent/broker. However, the buyer's agent owes no duties to the seller and has no responsibility to look after anyone's interests other than those of their buyer. Multiple Listing Services are the organizations formed for brokers to cooperate with each other to get properties sold. When a listing broker places a home in the MLS, a commission share is offered to other participating brokers if they bring a buyer. There's no set commission amount or percentage, nor is there a set share. However, they generally split the commission paid by the seller 50/50. So if the seller is paying a total commission of 5% to get their home sold, the two brokers would each get 2.5%.

Is Your Agent an Agent Under Agency Law?

"Agency" is a legal concept that can confuse people because so many real estate professionals are called agents. In fact, in the vast majority of transactions, the real estate agent is not the "agent" of the buyer or seller in the full legal sense of the term.

> *"Hey Scott! One of these contract documents says that our real estate agent isn't our agent. What's up with that?"*

> *"Maybe we shouldn't sign anything until we figure out just what she IS!"*

While you can find a lot of legalese defining agency and the relationship of the agent to their principal (client), let's keep it as simple as possible. If, as a buyer or seller, your real estate professional is a true agent in the legal sense, they are like an extension of you. They have the authority to act on your behalf in ways that non-agents cannot, and they have a higher level of responsibilities and set of duties called "fiduciary" duties.

In many areas, the creation of a true "agency" relationship requires a signed document in which both you and your real estate professional agree that they are your legal agent. The document will also spell out the relationship and duties of both parties. In some areas, agency can be "implied," meaning that your real estate professional acted in a way that implies they are your legal agent.

Trying to give you all of the possible relationships here isn't necessary, since one of your first questions to ask a real estate professional you're considering for your team is how agency and representation work in your area or state. And it's quite alright for them not to be your legal agent. The vast majority of transactions are done by real estate professionals in a non-agent status, using terms like "transaction broker," "transaction facilitator," or something else.

The key thing to know is that your real estate professional needs to fully explain the different representation options offered in your area so you can choose how you want to be represented. Generally, any choice you make will still ensure that your real estate professional is working in your best interests as a buyer, unless ...

Buying Through the Listing Broker or Agent

Many uninformed buyers believe that they will get more accurate and faster information if they just call up the broker or agent who has the property listed and work through them to buy it. While you may get a question answered a little faster, the cost for that speed could be excessive.

The listing brokerage has signed an agreement with the seller to represent them and to try to get the best price for their home. They are definitely working for the seller, so you need to be concerned about whether or not they can serve your best interests when they have made this written promise to the seller.

Using a different agent in the same brokerage that listed the home can still present a problem if the brokerage is the agent of the seller. Without getting too complicated, let's just say that having a real estate professional not affiliated in any way with the listing brokerage is always going to be the best way to know your interests are being served.

True Buyer-Only Agency

One representation option that's becoming more and more popular is a brokerage that only works with buyers. Normally such brokerages advertise their company as a "Buyer Agency" or "Buyer-Only Agency". They do not take listings. This removes the problem for a buyer of beginning to search for property with a real estate professional that turns out to be the listing agent or affiliate of a brokerage that is listing a property he wants to buy.

Buyer-only agency representation is the cleanest way in which a real estate professional can represent buyers, with the broker working completely in their clients' best interests all of the time. Since your primary activities early on will involve buying, not selling, this could be the type of brokerage you'll want to select for your team. Later you can add a listing brokerage for selling properties.

Real Estate Consultants

These are real estate professionals who offer other structures for payment for their services. They offer "fee for service," hourly rates, or flat fees for transactions. There is an organization that certifies its members with the ACRE acronym. It stands for Accredited Consultant in Real Estate, and their website is MyREConsultants.com.

There are hundreds of ACRE professionals in the U.S. and Canada. They offer alternative ways in which to use and pay for their services for both buyers and sellers. With the laws constantly changing and consumerism a strong force, there are many areas where it is legal for a real estate brokerage to charge other than a flat commission.

There are also many areas where it's legal for a real estate brokerage to rebate a portion of their commission to buyers. ACRE members use these and other billing methods to tailor their services to the needs of the client and save them money. This could be of value to real estate investors because it gives them the ability to pay less and thus increase return on investment.

Your market and transaction knowledge will soon be greater than the normal consumer's knowledge, so you may find that working through one of these real estate professionals can save you money--sometimes a lot of money--in a transaction.

Recommendations

It's an important marketing tool of real estate professionals to ask their previous customers to refer them to others. They'll keep in touch via mail and email, signing off with something like, "I appreciate your referrals". So it's usually easy to get a number of recommendations from friends and family of real estate people they have used in the past.

Remember, however, that you will be buying and selling in a real estate investing business, and your needs are not the same as those of a regular consumer buying or selling a personal residence. Investigate prospective real estate professionals and ask a lot of questions.

Check out their websites first, as this can tell you a lot about how they operate, what specialties they may have, and where they focus their business activities. Too many real estate websites will just be billboards for the agent, with testimonials and statements about how many deals they have done.

Testimonials are fine, but what else do you see on their site? Do they have market commentary and statistics? In other words, are they giving you helpful market information instead of just marketing themselves? It's not a deal killer, but you could find a really knowledgeable person because they take the time and effort to talk about events in the market and give property sales statistics.

Getting Automated Market Information

This is something you'll find mentioned on some real estate websites. Usually when you're on a search page looking at listings, there will be an offer to either create your own custom search or have one created for you. Once it's in the system, you'll be alerted to new listings that meet your criteria, as well as price changes on current listings that are a match.

> *"Michael, I love working with our agents, Bill and Monty! This Private Client Service thing is great".*

> *"Show it to me Scott. What's great about it?"*

> *"We give them our exact property criteria--home size, price range, areas, bedrooms, baths, and more. They set us up for automatic email alerts. The minute a new listing is posted, we get it in an email. I'm even getting them on my cell phone!"*

> *"Scott, I can already see us beating the other investors to the next perfect rental house. Set me up!"*

Taking this one step further, ask the agent if they will also provide you with periodic property sold reports. This will allow you to build your database of sold statistics, allowing you to make quick estimates of property values based on previous neighborhood sales.

Finding an agent for your team who will provide you with all of this automated data will allow you to quickly build a detailed market database that will help you identify future opportunities.

Ask the agents questions about the market and the numbers. You'll be able to tell from their answers if they are on top of it. Ask them about experience and their buyer/seller mix of business. Get their opinion on market conditions now and how they see the market moving in the future. This isn't because you want to base decisions on what they say, but more to see how well they know their market and how much thought they have put into analyzing it.

Friends Don't Make Good Real Estate Agents

Like any statement, there are exceptions, but there aren't many exceptions to this rule. Almost everybody has one or more friends or family members in the real estate business. You are starting a real estate investing business, and you must treat it like one.

Using what you learn here and doing the research to locate viable real estate professional candidates for your team, you will end up with the right match. Do not start with a friend or relative, since it will probably result in a strain on your relationship. You may prefer to choose another agent later, anyway.

INSURANCE AGENT

You may leave this team member selection until you actually are contracting to purchase a home, but you can go ahead and get an insurance agent lined up. You can start with recommendations from other team members, since mortgage brokers and real estate professionals deal with insurance agents every day. They'll know the ones who get the job done quickly, do it with minimum hassle, and have competitive, premium rates.

However, you'll also want to approach insurance brokers. Like mortgage brokers, they represent more than one insurance company. Unlike going into a State Farm or Farmer's Insurance office and being offered only their insurance brand, a broker can shop multiple insurers to better meet your needs.

Later, when we get into specific things to do in your home purchase process, we'll talk about dealing with an insurance agent to purchase a policy for the home you're buying. Right now, if you want to look into selection of a team member, it's a more generic process. Mostly, you are searching for responsiveness and good recommendations.

If you want to postpone this team member selection until you're actually purchasing a home, we'll go into detail at that point to help you know how you'll be interacting with agents in the process of purchasing your policy. It's likely you'll end up using the same agent again if they perform well for you.

REAL ESTATE ATTORNEY

In some areas, attorneys are involved in many or all real estate transactions. In the majority of areas, however, the real estate agents, brokers, and title companies are the ones who shepherd you through the process. Then an attorney is only needed for things like the preparing the deed, preparing other documents, or dealing with a problem.

In the purchase and sale of homes, the area where you do your investing will determine if an attorney is involved in all transactions. If not, then you still need to look for an attorney specializing in real estate for your team.

You'll be dealing with tenants and landlord-tenant law, so you definitely want to know the law and understand the right procedures and required documents. While you may be able to pick up a generic lease form off the Web or at the office supply store, it's not what a real business person will do when their survival is at stake.

You'll want to have an attorney who can look over and "bless" your lease contracts, tenant questionnaires, and other documents. This is especially true if you end up having to evict for non-payment of rent. Your attorney can advise you of the timelines for notifications and actions, as well as the proper wording of letters and notices.

Finding a Real Estate Attorney

Where you live and invest will determine if there is a "real estate specialty" designation for attorneys. If there is, this means that they have met certification requirements and have strong abilities and knowledge related specifically to real estate transactions. This isn't necessary, but it can be helpful as the first place you look for an attorney.

If real estate law is a specialty in your area, there will be a pronounced area of the Yellow Pages for those attorneys. You can also look on the Web for your area with search terms for "real estate attorney". Of course, recommendations are still one of the preferred ways to find the right person.

Ask your real estate professional for a recommendation, since they do enough transactions that they will regularly bump into situations that require attorney assistance. They'll also know which attorneys do a lot of the deed preparation for their closings.

Most attorneys will be happy to talk to you without charge when you tell them that you're a real estate investor and you want to develop a relationship to get your deals done and to get advice and services in handling your rental property business in the future. Speak to several attorneys and select one you can call on when the time comes.

HOME INSPECTOR

No matter how great a handyperson you may be, remember the adage that a writer shouldn't edit their own work. You need an independent and unbiased trained eye to help you evaluate a home's condition before you sign that purchase contract.

Many home inspectors gravitated to their profession from construction backgrounds. Question them about their construction experience, type of buildings they've worked on, and overall general experience with spotting and correcting problems. You aren't going to be hiring them to correct issues, but experience in fixing a bad roof or foundation is critical to recognizing what is wrong and estimating the extent of repairs necessary.

You don't want an alarmist, but you don't want a blind eye either. You want a thorough person with clear procedures. Most inspectors use a detailed checklist as they walk through their inspection to make sure they don't overlook items. Many also use software and handheld computers to speed the process of recording the inspection and reporting the results afterwards.

Recommendations from real estate agents can be helpful here, but be careful. If you find a real estate buyer agent who is very aggressive in protecting their clients' interests, they can probably give you a great recommendation for a thorough inspector who will make sure you have a full picture of the home's condition.

Homes of any age will have problems, so you shouldn't be waiting for perfection before making a purchase. However, knowing what's wrong and having a good idea of what it's going to cost to correct it will give you an advantage in your negotiations and cover you for future cash flow when repairs are necessary.

TITLE/ESCROW COMPANY

In some areas, title and escrow companies aren't used because attorneys handle the transactions. However, in most areas there will be a title company providing services to cover the property with a title insurance policy and help close the deal.

Someone in the transaction will be choosing the title company. Sometimes it's a matter of seller's choice, sometimes buyer's, but it's usually negotiable. Services will be provided to search the title history, determine if there is a clear chain of title, and insure you against risk of a claim that could threaten your ownership.

Where title companies are the main managers of the flow of the transaction, they are quite important in ways other than just providing a title insurance policy. If their procedures aren't efficient or if they are understaffed, they can be responsible for delays or problems. They can be very helpful as well, since they are coordinating a number of people and companies, including the lender, two real estate agents, insurance coverage, surveyor, and others.

This is another selection you may put off until you're actually ready to make a purchase, but some research now would be a good idea anyway. You'll want to get recommendations from real estate agents and mortgage brokers, and you'll want to visit the title company offices, too.

Ask each company for any sample policies or forms they can provide to help you be ready for your first transaction. This is good for knowledge, but is also a test of their responsiveness and desire to be helpful.

Ask about their fees, and see if you can get a schedule of title insurance premiums, which are usually based on property value. If they can give you a sample closing statement with detailed fees, you can learn a lot about the process and see what each company charges.

ACTION STEPS

1. Go to http://scottsinvestorsedge.com/book-resources/team-stage-one and download your stage 1 team worksheet
2. Get out there and start circulating and meeting people in the real estate and mortgage industries. Maybe even join an investment club, as you'll meet affiliate members there from all of these professions, including attorneys, home inspectors and more.
3. Using what you've learned in this chapter, start building your team. Don't overpromise business volume, but don't be shy about letting them know that you're a serious real estate rental property investor who wants a serious team.
4. Find the right real estate professional and get some automated reporting set up. Begin to build a file or database of properties listed and sold.

WHAT'S NEXT?

Next you should begin to feel more excited, since we're going to do some goal planning. Remember that we consider goals to be mandatory, so we want to help you create realistic, attainable goals. It's especially important to reward yourself as you attain them.

CHAPTER 8

Goal Planning and Goals are Mandatory

Everyone has dreams. We tend to dream about how we would like things to be in a perfect world. We dream of riches, importance, power, and happiness. We discount the probability of these things happening, simply because they are dreams. Saying, "I hope they call me for that dream job," is an example of this. Having a dream of the perfect job is nice, but we often feel we have very little chance of getting it.

We might think, "I hope I'm lucky enough to get a visit from the Publishers Clearing House people". This is a dream of winning a huge prize, like winning the lottery. Of course, these games of chance depend on luck and are very much outside of our control. Dreams and luck are fun, but we seldom see the good results we desire.

Goals, on the other hand, are planned outcomes based on logic and work. While a goal may seem similar to a dream, the outcome is much more predictable and can actually be a sure thing if:

- The goal is realistically attainable.
- The timeline for attaining the goal is realistic.
- You consider it mandatory and follow the plan to achieve the desired result.

Comparing dreams to goals is like comparing a rock garden to a vegetable garden. Dreams are like a rock garden. While it can look pretty and require little work, it provides little in return. Goals are like a vegetable garden, requiring planning, care, and work, but providing the outcome you expect and desire.

Pretend for a moment that you're attending a high level corporate management meeting of a computer hardware company. Imagine that the management team is setting production and revenue goals for the coming year. If this company has a history of profitability and meeting or exceeding their goals, there will be some very important things happening at this meeting.

1. There will be serious discussion of current conditions that may influence the setting of the goals themselves. Carl from Sales will present data about changing sales patterns for different lines. If demand has softened for some lines, there will be scaling back production of those and possibly ramping up production of others.

2. The participants will evaluate the production facility's ability to turn out product in order to keep from setting unachievable. Beverly from the assembly line will be called into the meeting to comment on the ability to meet production goals.

3. Careful consideration of the market, including what they can sell their products for and what it will cost to produce them, will result in revenue predictions on which they can rely. This discussion will involve Carl from Sales, Angela from Purchasing, and Bill from Human Resources.

4. Major processes will be planned with specific timed goals to make sure everyone gets their part done on time.

5. Incentives and bonuses may be put into place for key managers and production employees to reward them for meeting their quotas or goals.

6. All of this will be carefully recorded in minutes of the meeting. Then marketing and production plans will be prepared for distribution so that everyone is on the same page to assure the goals will be achieved. Madeline, the CEO, will appoint a team to prepare the reports and master plan. Then they'll have another meeting to go over these items to make sure that all first meeting goals have been addressed.

That last item is critical to your process, though smaller in scope than this large corporation's business. You must write down your goals. Planning what you need to do, scheduling and devoting the necessary time to do it, and recording all of this is critical. We consider it our job to give you the knowledge and tools necessary for you to do this planning and goal setting. We'll help you set realistic goals that will be achieved, and we'll remind you to reward yourself when they are.

Goal Types by Time Frame

We'll be working with two types of goals, short term and long term. For our planning purposes, we consider short term goals as those that can be attained in one year or less. We'll break those down even more into daily, weekly, and monthly goals. Consider short term goals as components of your long term goals.

Create your short term goals, making them a sort of to-do list. The daily goals must be attained each day, and the weekly and monthly goals must be completed on schedule. They build on each other. Breaking long term goals down in this way provides a constant stream of achievements, keeping you motivated to continue and reach the next goal.

Long term goals for us are from one to 10 years out and are made up of short-term "interim" goals. It's very possible you won't completely attain one or more of your long term goals, if for no other reason that you may change plans and reorient for a different, more important goal. An example might be a 10 year goal to own 20 rental homes. You may get halfway there and decide that you want to move to apartment purchases. You will probably end up with more units, but it's just a different plan and goal.

FOUR ELEMENTS OF GOALS

For a goal to be attainable and valuable to your plans, it must be constructed of quality elements.

Realistic

Especially when setting your short term goals, be sure to be realistic in your ability to achieve them. Setting unrealistic goals will result in failure to attain them and discouragement in the process. This risks your long term goals.

While you may want to set a goal to play professional baseball, if you don't have the ability and time to practice hours every day, it's very likely that it's an impossible goal. In the same time frame, setting a goal to play on a citywide softball team would be much better because you know you can make that happen in the time frame you set.

Don't set goals that are too easy, though. Set them as high as reasonably possible, then get down to work and attain them. The sense of accomplishment as you check each one off your list will spur you on to the next until you ultimately accomplish all of your goals.

Complementary

Your goals should complement each other and work together to help you to achieve your planned results. Setting a goal to buy five properties your first year, and setting a goal for the same year to take three months off to travel could be a problem. Make sure that you aren't setting conflicting goals, since one or more of them will probably not be attainable.

Measurable

In order to know if goals have been achieved, they must be measurable. Setting a goal to be rich in five years is too subjective. Setting a goal to have a net worth of $1 million in five years is something that can be directly measured.

Flexible

Goals aren't set in stone. They can and will change over time. Goals will evolve as your real estate investment business evolves. Our previous example of switching from single family residential homes to an apartment project is a good example.

Perhaps you had a goal of purchasing three homes in a certain price range during your first year. You may scale back the number of homes but buy higher-priced homes because the areas and rental income numbers justify it. Never hesitate to change a goal for a better result, but be careful not to change one just because you're having trouble achieving it. Be honest with yourself about why you are changing goals.

SUCCESSFUL GOAL SETTING

"Hey Michael. That first deal went so well and the cash flow is great. Let's buy five more because the rent demand is out there!"

"I'm with you Scott, but let's sit down and look at our available time and resources to be sure we aren't trying to move too fast for our abilities".

It's not rocket science. In fact, four simple steps will assure your success at setting and attaining your goals:

1. Write down your goals.
2. Review goals often for progress.
3. Develop plans to be constantly moving toward attaining them.
4. Follow through and implement your plan.

At our website at http://www.scottsinvestorsedge.com/book-resources/personalgoals, we have a set of forms to plan your personal goals, both short term and long term. Those are for personal goals. Then there is another set of forms for your property investment goals. While personal and business goals will mesh at times, they
are different and should be separated to help you track and achieve them.

THREE-STAGE ACTION PLAN

Your schedule will be up to you. However, to get you started, we've prepared a three-stage action plan which can realistically be achieved in five years or less. Change numbers or items to fit your situation, but take the time to do this right, since it's your plan for a successful real estate investing business.

Stage 1

Study the market, study the market, and study the market some more. The next chapter will give you much more detail about ways to focus on your local real estate market starting from a big picture view and zeroing in to specific details of properties.

Go to seminars, attend classes, join an investment club, and watch real estate TV shows. Read real estate materials in print and online. Subscribe to local real estate sites and blogs to get regular market updates and commentary.

If you're not already, start learning to be handy around the house. Once you're a successful investor with many properties, you can hire people if you want. However, early on you'll probably want to save money and cut costs to increase your ROI and get you into properties that will provide the best cash flow. Take some classes at Lowe's and Home Depot.

If you've begun to build your team, then you're already meeting real estate, mortgage, insurance, and construction people. Keep doing that even if you have made some choices. Networking will bring you opportunities, so keep meeting people.

Sample Goals for Stage 1

- **Cash flow:** $100/month minimum.
- **Time to achieve:** 12 months
- **Reward upon achievement:** $100 of luxury. Buy a bottle of fine wine, take a boat trip, or have a nice dinner.

You can change the numbers if you want, but keep these goals realistic and measurable.

Stage 2

You're continuing your education process and learning all the time. Build on your experiences. Record your experiences so that you can reference them for future decisions and activities. Do new things like refinancing, renovating, or researching different homes in other areas.

"Love the numbers, not the house".

Though you're trying new things to learn more, make sure that everything you do is profitable.

"Scott, it was a great idea to renovate that kitchen between tenants, because the new renter is paying $50 more in rent and said they loved that kitchen".

"The best news, Michael, is that we did most of it ourselves and it

didn't cost much at all!"

Remember to record all of the good and bad moments and decisions, especially those "ah-ha" moments. Your journal will become one of your most valuable tools as you grow your business.

Sample Goals for Stage 2

- **Cash flow:** $1000/month minimum.
- **Time to achieve:** one to three years
- **Reward upon achievement:** $1000 of luxury. Take a trip. Buy a new gadget or some furniture.

You can see the building process and movement through time. These are sample goals, and you can tailor them to your plans and abilities. Just make sure they meet the four elements for good goal-setting.

Stage 3

Keep expanding your business. Buy more properties while always "loving the numbers". Keep building on what you've learned in the first two stages. Continue your educational pursuits by reading and attending seminars, classes, and workshops.

Always be current in your market knowledge. Increase your knowledge of real estate investment calculations and market valuation techniques. Take classes on rental property management and how to be a landlord. Learn about landlord-tenant laws in your area.

While this may come naturally to you, go ahead and write down that you plan to feel much more confident. You've been constantly upgrading your knowledge and experience, and you have multiple properties all producing great cash flow, so you can feel confident. If you're still investing part-time, as most people are at this stage, consider taking it all the way and becoming a full-time rental property investor.

At the end of this stage, at about five years, have a meeting with yourself. Go over all of your goals and planning and see if you've accomplished everything you set out to do. Many find that they have exceeded their expectations and have blown right by their goals. Use this review to plan into the future for more expansion.

Sample Goals for Stage 3

- **Cash flow:** $5000/month minimum.
- **Time to achieve:** three to five years
- **Reward upon achievement:** $5000 of luxury. Buy a new car or some jewelry. Take a fancy trip.

Rewarding yourself is important. It takes a lot of work to get through each of these stages, and you want to take the time and spend a little money on yourself and family at each stage. You've earned it.

At http://scottsinvestorsedge.com/book-resources/three-stage-goals, you'll find a form to record your three stage goals. Use it and get started on your path to lifetime cash flow.

CHAPTER 9

Market Research for a Sound Investing Foundation

One major difference between a mediocre real estate investor and an investing star is market knowledge. It can seem a bit overwhelming at first, since there is a lot to learn and the market is constantly changing. However, market research needn't be a daunting issue in today's world of computers and the Internet.

Knowledge has never been more accessible to the individual, nor has it been available so quickly and efficiently as it is today. Lack of information is not the problem; there is too much information and the sources on the Internet are not always reliable. We're going to help you develop a research process that will give you what you need from sources you can trust.

THE GOOGLE EARTH APPROACH

It's really impressive to use Google Earth mapping to zoom in on an address. This technology is shown in the movies and used by spy organizations, and it really gets you from the big picture view right down to the street view of a building. It's a great example of what you need to do to build a useful body of market research for your real estate investing success.

The big picture is important. While world events do influence real estate in our local areas, starting our research from a national perspective is most useful. Ultimately, we will spend most of our time gathering information and researching market conditions on a regional and local level. All of it is important information; however local research will dominate our time and efforts.

WORLD EVENTS & INFLUENCE

While the U.S. and Canada are obviously big players in the world economy, events around the world can influence real estate markets here. As our stock and bond markets are affected by world events, they also have a profound influence on interest rates, including mortgage interest rates.

So it's important to at least pay attention to worldwide events that create movement in stock and bond markets. Also, since many ARM interest rates are based on bond and other market benchmarks, having a big picture view of world events is part of your market research.

For this category of research, just keeping up with the news is usually enough. When you're watching an international news report, notice how many times the commentator mentions the effects of these world events on stock and bond markets and interest rates. Or you can watch reports on CNBC or other financially-oriented networks to get the financial side of world news.

This global view is one piece of the market research puzzle, but "real estate is local," so remember to keep the international news in perspective.

NATIONAL REAL ESTATE MARKET RESEARCH & NEWS

With a very long common border, it's interesting to contrast the U.S. and Canadian real estate markets. During the U.S. real estate and mortgage problems from 2006 into 2011 and beyond, Canada experienced strong demand and rising prices in many areas, while the U.S. was in crisis mode with falling home prices in most areas of the country. So even with the proximity of the two countries, you can readily see that, at any time, there can be very different trends emerging or entrenched. National real estate trends and events are quite important to local markets. While we all understand that "real estate is local", demand and supply issues aren't the only factors influencing real estate sales volumes and prices in local areas. Even in a market with strong demand, if financing is difficult due to national mortgage banking issues, then many would-be buyers won't end up buying.

Let's look at some resources for national real estate trending and sales statistics in the U.S. There are comparable organizations and resources in the Canadian markets, as well.

National Association of Realtors

At http://realtor.org, there are reports, statistics, and surveys released regularly by the National Association of Realtors®. There is value in this information, but be careful to place the proper emphasis on it since this is a trade organization promoting the interest of their professional real estate members.

In the next chapter, we'll talk about searching the Internet and other resources to find property information. However, this chapter is about keeping up with trends and learning about real estate news rather than finding a property in a certain area at a certain price. The NAR does some interesting surveys of what buyers look for in properties, and this can give you good information about what renters are looking for, as well.

Standard & Poor's Case-Shiller Home Price Index

Home price indexes are ongoing records of home prices to help us to understand what has happened, and perhaps even to help us make educated guesses as to what will happen in the future.

The Case-Shiller Index, found online at http://www.standardandpoors. com/indices/sp-case-shiller-home-price-indices/en/us/?indexId=spusa-cashpidff--p-us---- does a concise job of giving an overview by telling us:

"Metro Area Home Price Indices are based on observed changes in individual home prices. The main variable used for index calculation is the price change between two arms-length sales of the same single-family home. Home price data is gathered after that information becomes publicly available at local deed recording offices across the country. For each home sale transaction, a search is conducted to find information regarding any previous sale for the same house. If an earlier transaction is found, the two transactions are paired and are considered a "sale pair". Sale pairs are designed to yield the price change for the same house, while holding the quality and size of each house constant".

By using prices for subsequent sales of the same home, this method yields a reliable record of how homes are appreciating or depreciating in a market. There are some checks and balances to help ensure that these are arms-length transactions with willing buyers and sellers. Case-Shiller uses publicly recorded information from government offices and tax assessors.

This index tracks 20 metropolitan areas around the U.S. There is more than 20 years of history for this index, so it's a great resource for getting a feel for how home prices have moved over a long period of time. Here's what a chart looks like for this index:

	2010 Q4 Level	2010 Q4/2010 Q3 Change (%)	2010 Q3/2010 Q3 Change (%)	1-Year Change (%)
U.S. National Index	130.38	-3.9%	-1.9%	-4.1%
Metropolitan Area	December 2010 Level	December/November Change (%)	November/October Change (%)	1-Year Change (%)
Atlanta	99.92	-0.9%	-2.4%	-8.0%
Boston	152.54	-0.1%	-1.0%	-0.8%
Charlotte	112.59	-0.7%	-0.7%	-4.4%
Chicago	117.86	-1.4%	-2.2%	-7.4%
Cleveland	99.73	-0.4%	-2.0%	-4.0%
Dallas	114.61	-0.2%	-1.1%	-3.6%
Denver	124.10	-0.7%	-1.2%	-2.4%
Detroit	65.93	-2.3%	-2.5%	-9.1%
Las Vegas	99.48	-1.1%	-0.4%	-4.7%
Los Angeles	170.99	-1.3%	-0.4%	-0.2%
Miami	143.11	-0.5%	-0.2%	-3.7%
Minneapolis	117.09	-1.3%	-2.2%	-5.3%
New York	167.86	-0.9%	-1.2%	-2.3%
Phoenix	103.10	-1.7%	-1.1%	-8.3%
Portland	138.23	-1.2%	-1.6%	-7.8%
San Diego	158.97	-0.7%	0.1%	1.7%
San Francisco	135.85	-1.0%	-1.1%	-0.4%
Seattle	138.70	-2.0%	-1.1%	-6.0%
Tampa	130.23	-2.6%	-0.9%	-6.2%
Washington	186.18	0.3%	0.0%	4.1%
Composite-10	156.26	-0.9%	-0.8%	-1.2%
Composite-20	142.42	-1.0%	-1.0%	-2.4%

Source: Standard & Poor's and Fiserv
Data through December 2010

This very popular index is used by many government and consumer economists to track home price trends. Some consider it to be limited somewhat by the fact that it's only measuring 20 metropolitan areas. To get a more universal perspective that takes in more of the country and smaller areas, the Federal Housing Finance Administration (FHFA) Index is another one to follow.

FHFA, Federal Housing Finance Administration Index

This index uses government backed mortgage data, so it provides easier access to data for smaller areas, including cities and towns. At the highest level, the index tracks Census Divisions:

Pacific Census Division: Hawaii, Alaska, Washington, Oregon, California

Mountain Census Division: Montana, Idaho, Wyoming, Nevada, Utah, Colorado, Arizona, New Mexico

West North Central: North Dakota, South Dakota, Minnesota, Nebraska, Iowa, Kansas, Missouri

West South Central: Oklahoma, Arkansas, Texas, Louisiana

East North Central: Michigan, Wisconsin, Illinois, Indiana, Ohio

East South Central: Kentucky, Tennessee, Mississippi, Alabama

New England: Maine, New Hampshire, Vermont, Massachusetts, Rhode Island, Connecticut

• **Middle Atlantic:** New York, New Jersey, Pennsylvania

South Atlantic: Delaware, Maryland, District of Columbia, Virginia, West Virginia, North Carolina, South Carolina, Georgia, Florida

Here's an example of their Census Division chart:

Table 1: Monthly Price Change Estimates for U.S. and Census Divisions*
(Purchase-Only Index, Seasonally Adjusted)

	U.S.	Pacific	Mountain	West North Central	West South Central	East North Central	East South Central	New England	Middle Atlantic	South Atlantic
Feb 10 - Mar 10	**0.3%**	**1.1%**	**0.7%**	**0.2%**	**-0.8%**	**0.3%**	**2.5%**	**-0.5%**	**-1.0%**	**0.2%**
Jan 10 - Feb 10	-0.4%	1.2%	-2.1%	-1.3%	0.5%	-0.2%	-2.1%	-1.1%	1.2%	-1.5%
(Previous Estimate)	*-0.2%*	*0.8%*	*-0.9%*	*-1.0%*	*0.6%*	*0.1%*	*-1.3%*	*-1.0%*	*1.9%*	*-1.7%*
Dec 09 - Jan 10	-0.6%	-1.0%	0.7%	-0.3%	-0.3%	-1.4%	-0.2%	-0.5%	-0.8%	-0.4%
(Previous Estimate)	*-0.6%*	*-0.8%*	*1.0%*	*-0.3%*	*-0.2%*	*-1.1%*	*-0.4%*	*-0.9%*	*-1.1%*	*-0.5%*
Nov 09 - Dec 09	-1.8%	-3.0%	-2.8%	-0.9%	-0.8%	-1.9%	-2.3%	-0.2%	0.1%	-3.2%
(Previous Estimate)	*-1.9%*	*-3.1%*	*-3.1%*	*-0.8%*	*-0.8%*	*-2.1%*	*-2.2%*	*-0.3%*	*0.1%*	*-3.2%*
Oct 09 - Nov 09	0.3%	1.6%	-0.9%	-0.3%	0.2%	-0.2%	-0.5%	-0.6%	-0.3%	1.7%
(Previous Estimate)	*0.3%*	*1.5%*	*-0.7%*	*-0.2%*	*0.3%*	*-0.1%*	*-0.5%*	*-0.7%*	*-0.3%*	*1.6%*
Sep 09 - Oct 09	0.3%	2.0%	0.1%	0.3%	0.5%	-0.7%	2.3%	0.8%	1.1%	-1.5%
(Previous Estimate)	*0.3%*	*2.0%*	*0.1%*	*0.2%*	*0.5%*	*-0.6%*	*2.3%*	*0.7%*	*1.2%*	*-1.5%*
12-Month Change: Mar 09 - Mar 10	-2.2%	3.1%	-5.9%	-1.8%	-0.9%	-3.9%	-1.0%	-3.3%	-1.5%	-5.1%

In addition to Census level data there is also home price information at the city and town level for hundreds of areas. This allows you to track home price trends for your local area.

The main differences between this index and the Case-Shiller are:

1. While they both track resales of the same property, this one also tracks refinances and uses government mortgage data.
2. FHFA analyzes the combined mortgage records of Fannie Mae and Freddie Mac, which form the nation's largest database of conventional, conforming mortgage transactions.

When the U.S. markets were in deep trouble from 2006 into 2011, the Case-Shiller Index had more exposure in some of the worst-hit metropolitan areas. The FHFA Index did a better job of showing what was happening at a more local level in areas that didn't react in as volatile a manner to the ups and downs of the markets.

Both indexes have value, and they're easy to track, since you can sign up to receive the monthly reports at their websites.

REGIONAL & LOCAL REAL ESTATE MARKET RESEARCH

We've zoomed down from a global view to a national look at market research. Now it's time to get more regional and local, which is where the bulk of our research will be concentrated. It's an old though accurate axiom that "real estate is local". No matter what's going on internationally or nationally, there is always something unique about a local area that will dictate the real estate market there. Whether it's a new major employer locating in the area or the lure of vacation and resort type amenities, there is something unique about every area.

Local government initiatives, as well as public and private investment, will determine in large part the strength of a local real estate market. Tax incentives to businesses and developers play an important role in the strength of local real estate markets, as well.

Local business organizations and publications are the first resource for real estate news and market information. Real estate investment clubs bring together mortgage brokers, bankers, appraisers, surveyors, real estate brokers, and others who have day-to-day dealings in the market and a current perspective on trends.

When we discussed selecting your first team members, we went into detail about the market information services available from tech-savvy real estate professionals. While some areas have public disclosure of property sales prices, many areas do not. Email alert reports of sales from the MLS are an invaluable resource. Once the agent sets up the alert reports, it's all automated, so the agent shouldn't mind doing it.

Absorption Rate

It's a good time to discuss a market measurement that helps us to get a picture of the current inventory of unsold and listed properties. It's called "absorption rate", and it's a really good measurement for you to develop and use on a regular basis, probably monthly.

The simplest explanation is that absorption rate is the rate at which inventory is being sold off in relation to how fast it's coming on the market. It's really an easy calculation if you have the numbers to do it. Choose a time frame, monthly, six months, or a year, and find out how many homes have sold in that period. Let's say that we are going to track absorption rate based on sales over the last six months. First, get the number of homes sold in that period and divide it by six, which is the number of months being measured.

Then we get the total number of current listings. If 600 homes sold in the last six months, then 100 homes are selling on average each month. If we have 700 homes currently listed, then we have seven months of inventory. Our absorption rate is 100 homes/month and we have seven months of supply.

Tracking the current number of months of inventory can give us a snapshot of how things are going and maybe even allow us to predict market movement. If our inventory has been holding steady between seven and eight months of homes listed, then suddenly having a month or two with only six months of inventory could signal market improvement. More homes are selling or fewer homes are being listed. Either way, supply decreased so the market may see higher prices.

If you're receiving regular sold property reports from a real estate agent, you have half of what you need. Now all you need is to know how many homes are currently listed. Get this information once a month or so, and you'll have a snapshot of how the market is moving.

Government Initiatives and Development

Some of the most valuable information you'll ever get is information about local plans for development or government initiatives that will impact employment, zoning, or property usage.

Let's say there is some land owned by the county that is undeveloped and pretty much just a wooded area. The county meets and decides to convert it to a greenbelt and park area with paths for walking and biking, as well as a small body of water for activities. There will also be tennis courts, soccer fields, and other group sports facilities.

Two trends in housing come into play here. With the cost of vehicle fuel constantly rising, people tend to gravitate to areas close to work and play. So a green area with recreation will normally be a draw for surrounding development and housing.

The second trend is the desire of government to prove their decisions have been good ones. There will likely be favorable zoning and development initiatives in place to encourage building in the areas around our new green park.

Maybe there is already a great deal of housing around this area, but it's older and in need of improvement. This is a great time to look into purchasing rental properties in anticipation of a renewal of interest in the area, rapid improvement of properties there, and an increase in property demand.

THE MORE YOU KNOW, THE MORE YOU PROFIT

Don't be one of those investors who looks back and says, "If only I'd known that". There are very few surprises in real estate development. There are normally signs that indicate change, such as new road construction or fund appropriations for government use of land.

Keep up with local business and government news, join the chamber of commerce, and read news about business and local government. It's easy to jump into deals after the general public is totally aware of what's happening. It's a little harder to be on the front end and takes more awareness, but it's a lot more profitable.

ACTION STEPS

1. Develop your print and major media resources for national to local real estate news and information.
2. Do the same for Internet resources. Begin to build a file or database of notes, information, and statistics that you receive from your research sources and consider important.
3. Learn about any local organizations you can join to keep up with current local real estate-related events.

WHAT'S NEXT?

You'll be able to start getting your feet wet and start locating properties. We're going to give you resources for finding the best deals for rental property purchases and before the competition does.

CHAPTER 10

The Many Sources for
Great Investment Properties

"Michael, there's got to be a better way. We've been driving around for an hour and haven't seen a really good house for our next purchase".

"I've called our real estate agent, but we should try to find other ways to locate bargains, Scott. Looking for signs is the least efficient way, I think".

In our early investment days we just looked for signs and relied on a real estate agent to feed us information. Both of those are ways to locate homes to buy for rental, but there are others. And some of the other ways will land you a bargain without built-in commissions. It's never been our goal to cut real estate agents out of deals, but they don't have everything that is available listed in the Multiple Listing Service.

"Love the numbers, not the house".

Loving the numbers requires knowing all of your costs, including acquisition costs for closing. How you locate a home and purchase it can make a big difference in these costs. Then there is the price to buy, as well. Finding bargains in places other than MLS listings can cut your costs and increase your ROI.

In this chapter, we're going to jumpstart your buying knowledge with experience we gained the hard way through trial and error over a number of years. Some of the resources we mention here may not fit your market, and some may require more research and time on your part than you want to spend. However, knowing about them will give you other opportunities to locate great rental homes to buy.

MLS LISTED PROPERTIES

Of course, the vast majority of local properties available for sale will be listed in the Multiple Listing Service. As we've mentioned several times, you should get automated listing reports from a real estate agent so you'll get daily updates of new listings as well as homes that have been reduced in price.

You can specify the criteria for your automated searches based on a number of MLS database information fields, including price range, size, area, etc. If the agent is willing to provide it, a report on expired and withdrawn listings may be of value to you as well. You may be able to call on these owners later to see if they've given up and would be willing to talk with you about a purchase. Look at cumulative "days on market" to see how long they have been trying to sell.

You will no doubt end up buying homes that are listed through real estate agents, so you'll want to get regularly updated information to get out in front of bargains.

OTHER WEBSITES FOR LISTINGS

Sites like Trulia.com and Zillow.com are large sites where homes and properties are listed for sale. These sites also allow homeowners to list their homes as "For Sale by Owner", giving you a resource outside of the MLS to locate properties not listed by real estate agents.

"For Sale by Owner" websites are very common, and a Google search on "for sale by owner" will bring up a great many sites for you to check out. Some may even be specific to your area.

FORECLOSURES

While many banks list their foreclosures in the MLS, they're usually listed at prices below normal market value, so watch the MLS for properties listed as foreclosures. If you are unable to search on "foreclosure" as an MLS field, you can look at owner names to find the ones that are bank-owned.

Here's where you can really get into "loving the numbers". From a real-life example, let's say there is a $200,000 home listed in foreclosure. You know that you can get pretty good rent payments on this home, and you have run the numbers carefully. It would be a decent buy with decent cash flow at $175,000. It would be a super buy with super cash flow at $150,000. Jane, our investor, offers $95,000.

This is where it helps to have a buyer agent who understands your business and wants to be involved for the long run. Many offers like this may get presented, but few will be responded to and even fewer accepted. So they have to do some paperwork, but you're trying to get the very best deal you can. In our example, the bank didn't respond to Jane's offer.

However, Jane is patient and kept watching. The bank reduced the asking price a few months later from $200,000 to $175,000. Jane came right back with that $95,000 offer. Again, there was no response or counteroffer. Then, a second price reduction to $160,000 was published, and Jane brought a third offer at $90,000, a bold move that told the bank she was serious about price. The bank was tired of holding this property so this time they countered. A deal was made at $120,000! Jane is happily taking her rent checks to the bank every month.

Finding Foreclosures in Other Ways

If you watch for mortgage default notices and announcements of properties that are being sold on the courthouse steps, you can sometimes step into a good deal on a foreclosure property before the bank lists it with a real estate agent.

There are foreclosure websites as well. Realtytrac.com is a large site keeping comprehensive records of bank owned properties all around the country. A quick Google search on "foreclosure listing websites" will give you some sites to check out. You may even find some sites that are more localized to your area.

If possible develop relationships with the people at major banks who handle foreclosures. Get to know the asset managers employed to manage and liquidate bank-owned properties. Let them know that you're always in the market for value, and maybe you'll get the chance to pick up a property directly, before listing and agent commissions. The bank doesn't like paying them either.

SHORT SALES

A short sale is the purchase of a property at a price below the balance due on the mortgage. This can happen when a homeowner is having trouble making their payments and can't sell in the current market for at least the amount due on the mortgage. Basically, they're trying to avoid foreclosure.

The key here is that the bank must approve the sale; the homeowner has no real power in the negotiation. As the buyer, you're negotiating with the bank. Short sales are tough to get to closing, and even when successful, it can take months. Generally, you'll be able to better expend your time and resources in other ways that will locate value properties than trying to buy via short sale. However, it's something you may want to investigate.

Advertising for Sellers

This is a good time to discuss advertising for sellers, since that's how many short sale deals are begun. You can run classified ads in newspapers stating that you are looking for property to buy. Craigslist.com is another place to run these ads, with the advantage that it's free. Other investors use those "bandit signs" you see on street corners saying "We buy houses". You can also place notices on bulletin boards and prepare business cards to hand out or tack on boards, as well.

Put out the word to real estate agents that they can steer impossible deals your way. What are those? A homeowner concerned about continuing to make their mortgage payments contacts a real estate brokerage about listing their home. The truth is that there is no way they can sell it for what they owe plus cover the closing costs and commissions. So the agent generally isn't going to take the listing. Even if they do list it a few months later everyone might have to admit that it isn't going to work.

Let the agents know that you are out there actively seeking the right kinds of deals, and that you'd like to know when one like this comes along. Even if they don't notify you about an opportunity, they may be willing to hand the owner your business card and tell them to give you a call.

PROBATE INVESTING

This may sound like a small niche, but there are trillions of dollars of real estate in probate at any given time. Probate investing is actually a highly profitable niche for investors who either flip or hold the properties.

Depending on where you live and do business, you will have different levels of technology for accessing the public probate records. However, they are public and you can locate properties held in probate and destined for sale by the "personal representatives" of the deceased. These normally aren't attorneys, but people designated by the person before their death to handle their estate. They are people who are tasked with selling off assets and paying debts of the deceased, and they usually want to get the job done and get back to their normal lives.

A misconception is that you'll have to deal with bereaved relatives and heirs, which is not the case. You are dealing with the personal representative, not a judge and seldom an attorney. The single largest asset in most estates is real estate, so they naturally want to dispose of it as soon as possible, since the proceeds can pay down debt.

While it's not going to be a process where you can simply look up "real estate for sale" at the courthouse, it can be well worth the effort. Generally you would have to access the court probate records to find real estate listed as one of the assets. Then, using the tax ID number for the property, you can determine where and what it is. Then you can go do a drive-by to see if it's something you'd like to investigate more. Contact the personal representative and ask to see the property.

Once you've seen it, don't appear to be too eager or say too much. Take detailed notes and ask if you can call the personal representative after you've run the numbers. Then do very detailed research and cost estimations, including any rehab or repairs you'll have to make.

Do a spreadsheet of costs, a very conservative, even understated, rent you can expect to get, and then make an appointment to see the personal representative. Go over the numbers as an investing professional, pointing out all of the issues that justify your offer, which will be low, by the way.

Currently you may be the only person who has discussed the value of the real estate with this personal representative, someone not in the real estate business or "in the know" about market values in the area. Right now you are in the driver's seat.

While it's likely that a low offer will be problematic for the personal representative, they may have nothing else to compare it to at this point, and the property may be free and clear of any mortgages. Looking at the debt that the sale would pay off, the personal representative may be inclined to do a little negotiating and let you have the property at a deep discount.

Take a look at probate situations to see if there is opportunity there and decide if it's worth your time and effort. Sometimes it may present a way to own a rental property in an established area where income properties are hard to find or buy.

FIXER-UPPERS

While this is a property category and not a way to locate homes, this is a good place to talk about the opportunities presented by properties needing work. You will be presented with damaged properties in many of the situations discussed in this chapter, including homes listed in the MLS.

In a later chapter we'll go into detail about repairs and After Repair Value, or ARV. However, for this chapter, let's just be general about the opportunities presented by properties needing work. The retail buyer, and even the casual rental property investor, can be easily turned off to a property if they think it needs extensive repairs.

Because you'll be getting an education from us and on your own about what is entailed in repairs and renovation and how to cost it out, you'll have a much more pragmatic view of the situation. It's all about "loving the numbers," and you'll just sit down and do them to see if it's a deal for you.

Knowing how to do a lot of the work yourself, or how to supervise and hire without a general contractor, will reduce your costs and improve your ROI.

INTERNET SEARCHES & ALERTS

Craigslist

We've touched on advertising for sellers on Craigslist. However, Craigslist can be a valuable tool in locating properties and getting to them before the competition. You don't have to entice the seller to call you, as you're going to watch for their advertisements.

Many motivated and distressed sellers will place ads on Craigslist. It's free, and they have used it to sell other items, so why not try it for their home? They may have been trying to sell in other ways, even listing with a real estate agent. However, they're not getting it done and they may be getting closer to problems paying their mortgage or even approaching foreclosure.

You can do searches on Craigslist, and you can save your favorite searches for quick reference. Just build searches for key words and phrases that motivated homeowners might use when they list their homes on the site.

- "need to sell home"
- "must sell home"
- "home for sale, motivated"
- "must sell home fast"

You're getting the idea. People will let you know via these searches that they have a home that may meet your needs. All you have to do is have the searches saved and check on them.

Google Alerts

Another really great free tool is Google Alerts. You can't use it for a specific area like Craigslist, so you'll need to modify your search terms a bit. Google Alerts searches all over the Web though, and it will find "for sale by owner" ads anywhere they are. So using some of the same key phrases just add your local area to them. That could be the city name or even names of neighborhoods.

Google alerts will send you emails when new items turn up, and you'll find for sale by owner ads soon after the owner puts them anywhere on the Internet.

IF IT'S FOR SALE, YOU'LL FIND IT

Using the resources we've provided in this chapter, you can develop a powerhouse property location system. This is something you couldn't have done nearly this well 10 years ago, but the Internet has created a property information resource that can't be equaled.

ACTION STEPS

1. You began the contact with real estate agents in the team building chapter, so get in touch with one or more of them and get those automated reports coming to your email and cell phone.
2. Go through each of the other sections in the chapter and research the resources for finding homes. Check out foreclosure sites and other large property sites.
3. Check out real estate listing websites and "for sale by owner" sites.
4. Develop searches through Craigslist and Google Alerts to deliver properties to you.

WHAT'S NEXT?

You're moving rapidly toward actually locating a home and running the numbers to see if it will meet your investing and cash flow needs. In the next chapter, we'll take you through the other costs involved in purchasing a home--other than the price of the home. It's critical to the process of "loving the numbers".

CHAPTER 11

Cost Is An Iceberg

In this chapter, we're going to talk about the costs involved in the purchase and rental of a property. Many studies have shown that as much as 75% to 85% of the body of an iceberg is hidden below the water's surface. While there won't be a loss of life involved, don't let your rental property purchase become a movie with "Titanic" in the title.

In the next chapter, we'll go into detail about financial calculations and analyzing the numbers in order to select the right property and assure the cash flow you desire. In this chapter, we'll be examining the many costs involved in purchasing and managing a rental property. Some of the calculations in the next chapter will use the information and concepts in this one.

COSTS TO BUY

The Purchase Price, Down Payment & Mortgage

The largest costs are the most obvious and visible part of the cost iceberg. The purchase price of the home is the single largest cost, though financing will mean that you're not out anywhere near that much cash. Remember leverage.

We have discussed mortgages and the factors that will enter into your selection of the best mortgage for each purchase. The interest rate will determine your payments, and you'll be very much on top of that rate and the monthly principal and interest payments for your rental home.

Now that we've identified the portion of the iceberg above water, it's time to look at the many cost items that impact your cash flow but may not be as visible or apparent to you.

OTHER MORTGAGE-RELATED COSTS

We mentioned that these costs differ significantly based on where you're doing the borrowing. While many Canadian brokers get all of their compensation directly from the lender, many U.S. brokers charge various fees to get the loan done. Which of these will apply to your deals will be something you'll need to investigate.

Origination Fee

This is usually based on "points" of the mortgage amount, meaning a percentage of the loan amount. Usually, this is a fee charged at closing of between .5% percent (point) and 1.5%. So for a $100,000 loan amount, this would be between $500 and $1,500.

This is definitely a negotiable fee in most cases. Early in your relationship with a mortgage broker, you may not have the clout early in your relationship with a mortgage broker to ask for cuts in this area, but as your business increases, you should definitely be thinking about negotiating this fee.

Credit Application or Mortgage Application Fee

A flat fee, usually between $100 and $500, is charged to do credit checks and prepare a credit report for the lender. This is one that you may or may not be charged, but do a thorough check of any fees to see if it's there.

Processing Fee

This is an arbitrary fee to process your application, and is not charged by all mortgage brokers, but it's one to look out for.

Appraisal

Passing along the cost of an appraisal of the property's value to the buyer is the normal procedure for most loans in the U.S. The buyer will be liable for a charge usually somewhere between $300 and $500 for this appraisal.

Re-appraisal or Appraisal Review Fee

Although they've existed for a long time, these fees began to show up more frequently after the U.S. mortgage crisis beginning in 2006. Some of the blame for the mortgage mess was laid at the feet of appraisers who were accused of inflating values to satisfy lenders' desires for more deals.

Whether this was a significant factor or not, lenders became much more cautious. Many deals will end up with a request by the lender for a new appraisal or an official review of the appraisal. While this can't be anticipated in every case, if required it will add a cost that can be comparable to the original appraisal fee.

Mortgage Servicing or Escrow Fees

Lenders usually want control of the payment of taxes and insurance to protect their interests in the property. They don't want the borrower to get behind on taxes or stop paying insurance. So they require that money be placed in an escrow account for the payment of these items by the lender.

While it's your money, and not really a "cost" of the deal, there is a small cost added in many cases to pay the "servicer" entity to handle this money to collect the payments from you, and to pay the taxes and insurance. Most of this money is just a prepayment by the buyer to cover the first six months to one year of taxes and insurance, so it's a cost you'll already have evaluated over the entire ownership period.

OTHER PROPERTY INSPECTION & VERIFICATION COSTS

In determining whether a deal will make it to closing, there will be a number of inspection and investigative activities, all of which carry costs.

Survey

Unless the property is a condominium with no land ownership, you will normally be required to survey the property to determine the true boundary lines as well as any encroachments across those lines by neighboring properties. The exact location of the home and other improvements will be drawn. The payment for the survey is normally a negotiable item, with local custom dictating whether it's common for the seller or the buyer to pay. However, it can be negotiated in the contract.

Title Insurance & Binder (Commitment)

Insurance to protect your title and ownership is provided by a title insurer. In many areas, the title company also handles the transaction and closing functions, as well. If so, there will be a fee for their basic services separate from the title insurance.

The first thing you'll normally see is a title insurance binder or commitment. This document tells you that the title insurance company promises you a policy at closing if certain conditions are met; they will also note any items or situations that won't be covered in the policy. The cost for this binder reflects the fact that deals don't always make it to closing and the title company wants to get paid for the records search that they do to create the binder.

The premium for the actual title policy is separate and based on the level of coverage, with some options available to the buyer. Who pays for the binder and the policy is negotiable. However, it's common in many areas for the buyer to pay for the binder and the seller to pay the significantly higher amount for the policy premium.

Inspections

There are a number of inspections that may be done to determine the condition of the property. They can include:

- General structure
- Foundation
- Roof
- Equipment, heating, and air conditioning
- Mold
- Destructive insects
- Radon
- Soil
- Wells and septic systems
- Asbestos and/or lead-based paint

Often a general home inspector can combine several of these together in one inspection. Depending on area or type of utilities, some inspections are not necessary.

The buyer generally pays for these inspections and the cost can vary considerably, from $300 to $1,000+ depending on which are selected.

Legal, Documents & Other

Deed preparation and any other services that may require an attorney will result in costs for someone. These are also negotiable, but local custom usually provides some history for who pays.

The normally small costs of recording documents at the courthouse will be borne by the buyer or seller, depending on what's in the contract.

If documents must be priority mailed or shipped, those charges will be on the settlement statement charged to the buyer or seller, depending on the documents and their use.

Wire fees and notary fees, though small, shouldn't be forgotten. Every dollar that goes into your purchase has an impact on your ROI.

COSTS TO HOLD AND RENT OUT YOUR PROPERTY

"Hey, Scott. Harold over in the Smith Street property just called to say that the plumbing is backed up again. What's with those guys?"

"I'm not sure, but this is the third plumbing bill in two months, and it's killing our cash flow. Let's figure out if it's the plumbing or the tenants' lifestyle".

Owning rental property is a business, and businesses have costs. It's a natural part of doing business, and nothing to fear. It's only a problem if you've failed to anticipate a large enough chunk of the cost iceberg. Education, planning, and budgeting will not only get you through, they will get you through very profitably. That's why we're here.

Our goal is to eliminate for you the expensive process of trial and error.

There's our goal again. We have experienced many surprises in the area of rental property management and maintenance costs over the years. Through this book and our courses and mentoring, you won't have to go through these problem situations, because we'll have alerted you to them up front.

TAXES

Property taxes are just part of the deal. Learn how tax assessors work, how they value your property, and the levies that they use to calculate your taxes. While there is usually not anything you can do to reduce property taxes, at least understand how yours are calculated. When a notice of a tax levy increase is in the news, you should be able to quickly do a calculation to see how it's going to impact your cash flow and maybe consider if a rent increase should be in the plan.

INSURANCE

You will have some control of the cost for property insurance. You'll want adequate coverage for replacement of the property or damage repairs, but you'll also want to be covered well for liability with tenants in the home. Liability is very important, since lawsuits are more common than house fires in many areas.

Minimizing costs should always be a concern, but be careful about insurance. Compare policies to verify what makes premiums higher or lower. Notably, full value replacement coverage is usually more expensive, but it will pay out enough to rebuild the property. A less expensive option would offer you a set value that you'd have to check on now and then and upgrade for appreciation. This isn't a bad thing, because you may check this in conjunction with an anticipated rent increase.

MANAGEMENT

You may never hire professional property management services, or your business may grow to the point that requires it. However, you should always consider management as a cost of doing business. In other words, pay yourself. No, you don't have to cut a paycheck, but always consider that there is some cost involved in what you're doing as an owner/manager.

If you are using employees or subcontractors for management functions, don't forget to budget this in when you're running the numbers. In the next chapter, we'll get into cash flow worksheets and "loving the numbers".

LEGAL

You may think that getting an attorney at the beginning and getting things lined up for forms and tenant applications will be a one-time expense, and it might be. However, add a little something into your budget for every property; this will build up some allowance for unexpected legal expenses. Even if it's a one hour consultation before an eviction, there will be times when you'll need to consult an attorney.

VACANCY & CREDIT LOSSES

Within the limitations of the current market's supply and demand, you can control your rental income by setting your rents. However, this only controls "anticipated" gross income, since you will experience periods when the anticipated income doesn't make it in the bank account.

Vacancy

Leases expire and tenants move around. Even if you manage to keep them through the agreed-upon lease periods, you'll experience vacancy between tenants. If you're doing well at lining them up in anticipation, you could still have lost income while units are cleaned and readied for new tenants.

Besides lost income, there is the cost of painting, cleaning, and other maintenance between tenants. Factor this into your budget when setting rents.

Credit Loss

Things happen and people run into financial difficulty. Good interviews, credit checks, and tenant application forms can minimize problems with unpaid rent, but there will be some of this in your future. Rental property owners generally develop numbers for vacancy and credit losses based on experience over time. You can probably find out what the average number is for properties in your area. It's expressed as a percentage of rental income, and you can budget for it and build it into your rents.

MAINTENANCE AND REPAIR

Maintenance and repair covers a lot of ground.

- Structure maintenance and repairs for broken windows, exterior and interior wall repairs, doors, floors, and other structural components.
- Mechanical repairs and replacement would include maintaining heating, air conditioning, and appliances. The budget should also anticipate periodic replacement of equipment.
- Landscaping and yard maintenance.
- Plumbing and electrical maintenance and repairs.

Over time you'll build some really great historical numbers that will help you budget for new properties in the future. Also we can help you with pegging down these estimates to avoid missing too much of the submerged iceberg. We're getting you out of the drain of trial and error.

IMPROVEMENTS

We're working on lifetime cash flow and generational property ownership. As long as a property is generating acceptable cash flow, we will normally want to keep it. Over time, improvements and renovations will keep the property rentable and even allow us to raise rents in many cases.

Keeping long term property improvement projects in mind will allow you to project rents and maintain or increase cash flow over time.

ACTION STEPS

We'll get into some real number-crunching in the next chapter. For now, familiarize yourself with these various cost items.

Try to get a title company or real estate agent to give you a sample closing/settlement statement showing all costs to the buyer and seller. Or get a Truth-in-Lending or Cost Estimate from a mortgage broker to determine many of the costs involved. Get both if you can.

WHAT'S NEXT?

We're finally going to share some of the "love the numbers". You'll get some calculations for cash flow, as well as other evaluation methods and numbers for rental property.

CHAPTER 12
Love the Numbers, Not the House

~~~~~~

We have been throwing around that "love the numbers" quote quite often in this book. Now it's time to get an education about these "numbers", and learn how they will assure you of profitable investing with very low risk. All you have to do is understand the ways in which to numerically evaluate a property for long term rental cash flow, and your investments will pay off.

We just worked with you on determining the costs involved in purchasing, holding, and managing properties. Use those numbers to plug into the evaluations we'll be taking you through in this chapter.

Some You'll Use – Some You Won't

You may not need to know some of the math and number crunching we'll talk about in this chapter right now, and maybe you never will. However, if your future investing moves beyond single family homes, some of the calculations here will be invaluable in determining the feasibility of larger multifamily investments.

Knowing the math and finding useful formulas when you need them are essential, so get acquainted with the various calculations and investment measurements here and apply them when necessary.

The Value of a Spreadsheet

Whether you sit down and do it the old-fashioned way, such as drawing out rows and columns for your data, or you use spreadsheet software, you need to have your property data formatted correctly. It will be SO much faster and easier if you use a computer spreadsheet program; then you can build in your calculations and automatically recalculate the results when you change data or inputs.

Most new computers come with some type of spreadsheet software. Microsoft computers usually come with Works or MS Office, both of which have spreadsheet applications. However, if you don't have or want software on your computer, there are two great and free online spreadsheet solutions:

- http://docs.google.com
- http://sheet.zoho.com

Using these, you can work at a library or coffee shop computer to build and save spreadsheets for your investing. You can even share them securely with others.

"Hey Michael, I can't make our meeting today, but log on to our Google Docs sheets account and get the latest numbers for these homes we're checking out".

"Yeah Scott, and I just got an update on a couple of new sold properties, so I'll add them to the sheet and you can see the results".

You can download a cash flow analysis spreadsheet at our website
http://scottsinvestorsedge.com/book-resources/cash-flow-analysis

DOING A BETTER CMA THAN MANY REAL ESTATE AGENTS

Even if you use a real estate agent to do a Comparative Market Analysis for you, you will want to know what makes up a thorough and reliable CMA. Once you begin to gather your own data on property sales, you can choose to do your own CMAs. With what you'll learn here, yours will be better than those done by many real estate agents.

What do we mean by "better"? There is really only one measurement of how good a CMA is: is it accurate in determining the true market value of a home at the time it's calculated? True market value that isn't biased in favor of the buyer or seller is the primary consideration. If there are underlying reasons why a home that seems identical to another should sell for less or more, you need to know this from the CMA.

When considering a property for purchase, you need a CMA that tells you the market value as compared to recently sold properties in the area.

What You Need

To prepare an accurate and useful CMA, you will need recent sales statistics for properties in the area. These comparables should be as close as possible in proximity to the property you're considering. The more time that has passed since a property's sale, the less valuable the comparable, so you'll want to get the latest sales information.

We told you how to work with real estate agents to get sold information, and it's also a matter of public records in some areas. You try to find recently sold properties that are very similar, or comparable, to the property you're evaluating. There will be differences, and we'll talk about those "adjustments" here as well.

Unlike many real estate agents, we're also going to teach you how to do a CMA based on the current competition--homes currently listed that would be considered competition because of location and features similar to the home you're evaluating. While you'll be following the same process, you'll be doing one set of numbers for SOLD properties and another for Active Listings. We'll show you how this is important for determining final valuation. You'll also need the current listing information for homes similar to your subject property.

Choosing the Comparable Properties

We've already said that the comparable properties should be as similar as possible to your subject property, and that they should be in the same neighborhood or as close as possible. You'll also want to use the latest "comps". A CMA is most accurate on the day it's run. Homes come on the market and sell daily, so a lapse in time in making a purchasing decision could mean having to run another CMA with up-to-the-minute data for both sold and listed homes.

It isn't necessary to choose properties with exactly the same features, such as number of bedrooms or baths nor does the square footage need to be exactly the same. However, the more similar the properties the better, since we'll have to make adjustments for any differences between the comp home and your subject property.

How many comps you use is up to you. Usually, the more comparables the better your results, and getting about six will give you a good data set. However, when markets are slow, it can be impossible to get six or more properties that are nearby and have similar features, simply because there haven't been any sales in the recent past.

Do the best you can; stretch the area a bit and move farther away if needed or adjust as you can for varying features. Aim for at least three properties as your minimum goal, with six or more as your ideal.

Example Subject Property

For our calculations, let's assume that we're trying to determine the current market value for a home listed for sale in a popular neighborhood. We know that we can get tenants for this home, and we believe that rents will be stable in the area. So we've located a home in this large and popular subdivision with these characteristics:

- three bedrooms
- two baths
- 1600 square feet
- standard ¼ acre subdivision lot in the middle of the block
- formal living room with dining off the kitchen
- single car garage
- reasonable but not very special landscaping
- normal home in good condition, not overly fancy, with no major problems or damage
- listed for sale for $192,800
- has been on the market for 110 days when we do our CMA

This is what we have for information about the home we're considering purchasing. While the real estate agent probably did a CMA to come up with this listing price, we don't know which comparables they chose or how thorough they were. We also can probably be certain that they haven't done a follow-up CMA in the 110 days that the property has been listed.

Our Comparables

It's been a little slow in this market, but this is a popular subdivision so we were able to find three homes in the immediate area that have sold within the last few months and are similar to our subject property.

Comparable A
- three bedrooms
- two baths

- 1800 square feet
- two car garage
- standard ¼ acre subdivision lot in the middle of the block
- normal home in good condition
- sold for $189,000 after 92 days on the market

Comparable B
- two bedrooms
- one-and-a-half baths
- 1400 square feet
- half acre cul-de-sac lot
- single car garage
- extremely well-maintained with upgraded appliances and finishes
- sold for $187,500 after 78 days on the market

Comparable C
- three bedrooms
- three baths
- 1600 square feet
- standard ¼ acre subdivision lot in the middle of the block
- two car garage
- condition issues required repairs, painting & other work
- sold for $167,500 after 130 days on market

Now that we have the properties for our comparison, it's time to make adjustments so we can equalize them with our subject property.

Adjustments

Appraisers use this same technique, with a lot more detail, using information they maintain on construction costs and the value of certain improvements. It isn't necessary for you to become an expert on construction and how much a bedroom is worth in order to run a useful CMA, though. We'll need some idea of what the differences between the properties are worth in dollars, however, so we can adjust accordingly.

One way to get to some of these adjustment numbers is to have a real estate agent do some comps for you and then show you the calculations. You can see the numbers they are using for the value of an extra bedroom or garage space, let's say. Even better, if your appraiser team member will give you some numbers to use, you'll be in great shape.

Also go to publications and the Internet to get ballpark figures. You can find building sites and real estate sites to help you work out approximate numbers. Remember these are just approximations, so don't stress out over it. Even getting close to the adjustment figures will give you a much better idea of the real market value of a home. We're going to use these numbers, plus or minus, in our adjustments:

- additional bedroom $15,000
- full bath $5,000
- single garage space $3,000

There are other, more subjective things we'll look at, as well. Also it's easier to compare properties when the lot sizes are all the same, as they are here with the exception of our cul-de-sac lot (that one will require an adjustment for the larger lot size). Let's get right to it with adjustments using the following practices:

1. If the comparable house has more bedrooms, then we would SUBTRACT the value of the bedroom(s) to make the price more comparable to our subject property.
2. The same would apply to more bathrooms or garage spaces.
3. If there are fewer of these features, we'd ADD the value to the price, as our subject property would carry extra value if it had these extra spaces or rooms.

Comparable A
- The only major difference is the two car garage, so we'll subtract $3,000 from the sold price to more closely compare to our subject property.
- $189,000 - $3,000 = $186,000 comparable price

Comparable B

- Add $15,000 to bring it to a three bedroom comparable.
- Add $2,500 to do the same for a half bath.
- Based on land prices found through research, subtract $11,000 for the extra quarter acre and the more desirable cul-de-sac location.
- Somewhat subjectively, subtract $10,000 for the much nicer finishes and appliances.
- $187,500 + $15,000 + $2,500 -$11,000 -$10,000 = $184,000

Comparable C

- Subtract $5,000 for the extra bath.
- Subtract $3,000 for the extra garage space.
- Add $10,000 for the condition issues.
- $167,500 - $5,000 - $3,000 + $10,000 = $169,500

Some real estate people would not do this last repair adjustment, and there are arguments both ways. However, if the home had been in better condition, it most likely would have commanded a better price.

Now we have three sold prices that are adjusted to reflect the same features as our subject property. The most common way to go forward is to take these comparable prices, divide them by the square footages, and use an average of that number to value our property.

- Comp A: $186,000 / 1,800 = $103/square foot
- Comp B: $184,000 / 1,400 = $131/square foot
- Comp C: $169,500 / 1,600 = $106/square foot

We can see that Comp B, the one with the upgraded finishes and appliances, definitely garnered a higher price because of its condition. This is good information if we want to do some improvements to this property later. However, right now we just want to get a value on the table.

1. Average the three square foot prices to come up with $113/square foot.
2. Multiply $113 x 1,600 (our subject property size) to come up with a value of $180,800.

Immediately we see that this home appears to be listed about $12,000 over its true value. This helps us determine what we're willing to pay if the other numbers work and we want to purchase it for rental property.

After doing a few of these, you'll rapidly gain confidence in your ability to quickly decide if it's worth doing more investigation and research. If it's unlikely that this home can be purchased right now for the true value or less, then your time will be better spent finding another home.

You don't have to do your own CMAs, but understanding how they work will help you be able to examine one provided by a real estate agent. You'll know if a home is in the ballpark or not in terms of market value.

The Other Side of the CMA

Generally, a real estate agent puts together a thorough CMA before listing a property. Some of them drop the ball by stopping at this point. We, the buyer, have an accurate picture of the value of our subject property in relation to sold properties, but those sales are in the past.

The market is evolving daily. New properties are coming on the market, while others are expiring, selling, or being withdrawn from the market. Economic situations are changing. This means that we need to do one more CMA, but this time we'll use currently listed properties to compare to our subject property.

Go to the MLS wherever you're used to searching current listings and get the active listings in the neighborhood. Select the best comparables. If there is a lot of comparable inventory (high supply), it could mean that the price you were considering as an offer should be reduced. The seller is in a competitive market and supply is high, giving you more choices.

If there isn't much inventory, and especially if there are very few properties comparable to your subject property, then you may have to pay more for the home. If the only comparables are higher in price than the offer you are considering, your purchase price may rise. If they're lower, you can start with a lower offer.

You have now done more to determine the value of a rental property in the market than most real estate agents do. If you want an agent to do these CMAs for you, at least now you know what you want to see. It's the beginning of "loving the numbers," because you'll want to feel confident that you've come up with the appropriate value before looking at the other numbers to see if it's a deal you want to pursue.

Now we'll look at a number of interesting calculations used by real estate investors at all levels of the business.

GROSS RENT MULTIPLIER OR GRM

This is one calculation that shouldn't be relied upon to make decisions about purchasing; it is more useful as a tool to weed out multiple opportunities and focus your attention on those that should be the most profitable and provide the highest ROI.

First, you're going to need to know the gross rental income of properties. If a home is generating $8,400/year in gross rent, or $700/month, then we can use that number to find the GRM.

$$GRM = \text{Market Value} / \text{Gross Anticipated Income}$$
$$\$110,000 \text{ selling price} / \$9,200 = 12 \text{ GRM}$$

In this case, the price or value of the property is 12 times the rent.

Now if we're evaluating properties for purchase and we have plenty to check out, this could be a way to get the best to rise to the top of our consideration list. While many will not be rented at current market value, you'll need to estimate the rent that could be charged. We'll talk about how to estimate income potential later in this chapter. Let's take four properties listed for sale and the anticipated rent income (or actual, if they're currently rented) to get their GRM:

- $125,000 property generating $10,200 in rent = GRM of 12.3
- $100,000 home generating $8,900 in rents = GRM of 11.2
- $112,000 home generating $9,800 in rents = GRM of 11.4

This gives us an example so we can study the numbers. In reality, you could see GRMs in some areas running as low as 5 and only as high as 10 or 11. However, let's use these to see how GRM works.

If you haven't noticed yet, we want lower GRMs, not higher ones. Huh? Well, look at how those examples worked.

- If the home costs more but the rent stays the same, the number goes up. We have more invested for the same rent, so it's a less desirable situation.

- If the home costs less and the rent stays the same, the GRM goes down. We pay less for the home to get the same rent, which is a good thing.
- If the price stays even and the rent goes up, the GRM goes down. We're paying the same for a house as compared to another but getting a higher rent, which is good.
- Same price with lower rent so the GRM goes up. You're getting the picture.

So we're looking for lower GRMs. It's obvious now that the second two examples are better candidates for immediate research than the first one. However, we may have three homes that shouldn't be considered at all. The only way to know is to have an idea of the average GRMs in the area.

These can be derived by studying advertisements that include rents and looking at the value of the homes, or from actual sold properties that go into rental and advertise the rent. Here's where your ongoing record-keeping comes into play. If the current GRMs for the area are around 9, then none of these are where we want to put a lot of effort right now. If, however, the average GRM in the area is 13, then all of these look like reasonable purchase candidates.

GRM, at best is a quick way to see how a property looks in the overall rental property availability pool. It's used more by multi-family investors than by single family home rentals property buyers.

CASH FLOW

We've been talking about this in every chapter, and it's the goal of *lifetime cash flow* that brings you to this book and to our courses and mentorship. Remember our ratty couch and the "aha moment" when we realized that our landlord was taking in $500 more each month than he was paying out for the house we were renting.

We're after the cash flow, so let's be certain everybody is on the same page with what that is. It's really not too complicated:

Cash flow is the net result of subtracting all cash outflow from all cash coming in.

This has nothing to do with taxes or deductibility; it's straight cash. Subtracting every dollar out-of-pocket from every dollar coming in on a property will give you your cash flow number.

- Rent receipts actually received and deposited are normally the only inflow of cash. However, if there is some other amount received, such as extra payments for cable or satellite, they would be a part of the inflow.
- All expenses that are paid, whether deductible for tax purposes or not, are part of the outflow. So property taxes, insurance premiums, mortgage payments, repairs, remodeling expenses (not the portion financed, but, yes, the payments on the improvement loan), and any other payments for improvements are all cash outflows.

Basically, it's cash in minus cash out. While you will have cash flow goals in dollars, you will balance your cash flow goals with ROI, or Return on Investment. In other words, if you can buy a home for $100,000 with a $20,000 down payment or a $120,000 home with a $24,000 down payment, you need to consider the ROI as well as cash flow.

Taking those two homes as an example, if both would provide the same $500/month in cash flow due to rents and expenses, then you'd want to buy the one that costs less in order to get a better return on your investment.

Calculating Your Profit/Cash Flow

Calculate your income: To cover vacancy, we use 11 months of rent for our income.

Income = Projected Monthly Rent x 11

Calculate your annual expenses: Expenses include mortgage payments, insurance, property taxes, utilities, maintenance, repairs, homeowner/condo fees, and management costs. Every dollar going out should be included here.

Subtract expenses from income: Subtracting the expense total from your rent income, as calculated in the first step above, will give you your profit/cash flow.

$$\text{Income} - \text{Expenses} = \text{Profit}$$

Calculate monthly profit: Dividing by 12 will give you your monthly profit.

$$\text{Profit} / 12 = \text{Monthly Profit}$$

We've created a cash flow worksheet to walk you through this process. You can find it on our website at www.scottsinvestorsedge.com/cashflowworksheet.

NEVER BUY NEGATIVE CASH FLOW!

Would you put your money into a bank savings account that required you to pay them every month to hold it? Buying zero or negative cash flow hoping to cash in on appreciation is just not smart. Appreciation is probable, but it can't be predicted. Using the calculations and techniques we're teaching, you'll be able to peg your cash flow going into the deal, and you want it to be POSITIVE.

Two Brothers – Two Approaches

Two brothers are rental property investors. Both of these brothers are profitable investors, but they have different approaches due to other things going on in their lives.

Andrew – has a job and family and prefers to have others do repairs, maintenance, and management tasks for his rentals. He is willing to realize a lower cash flow due to these extra expenses.

Carl – has more time to devote to his rentals and prefers to do as much of the maintenance and management as possible, saving the costs and realizing higher cash flows.

As time moves on, either of these brothers can change their approach, putting more or less time into their investments. This is one of the best things about rental property ownership. You can tailor your involvement by using the appropriate numbers to assure you of a positive cash flow based on your approach.

The trading off of your time and labor for cash flow is a factor in your calculations of expenses. Know going in what you're willing to do and what you're going to have to pay others to do. If you're not sure, err on the side of caution by adding in anticipated costs for these items. Then if you decide to do some or all of them, your cash flow will be better.

RETURN ON INVESTMENT OR ROI

Let's look at a couple of ways to measure ROI. Each has its own importance and use.

Cash on Cash Return

Many investors do not consider the Cash on Cash Return calculation as a very powerful measurement tool, since it doesn't take into account taxes or other factors. However, it's a great way to look at the first year of a property's ownership and see how this investment would compare to placing the money into something completely different, like a Certificate of Deposit or bond.

$$\text{Cash on Cash Return} = \text{Annual Cash Flow} / \text{Cash Invested}$$

This is cash invested, not the cost of the property that's mortgaged. So if we purchased a $100,000 home with cash invested for down payment and closing costs totaling $25,000, and we are renting it out with a net cash flow of $400/month, here's how it looks:

$$\$4,800 \text{ cash flow for year} / \$25,000 \text{ invested} = .192$$
$$\text{or } 19.2\% \text{ Cash on Cash Return}$$

Go find a bank savings account or even a risky bond that will do anything like this for you! It's easy to see why real estate rental property investors always seem to be doing so much better than investors in any other market or commodity.

Return on Equity or ROE

Return on Equity can be calculated in two ways. One is very much like the Cash on Cash calculation we just did. The difference here is that you're taking the Cash Flow After Taxes, CFAT, and dividing it by the cash invested. So you take out of the Annual Cash Flow the income taxes you'll pay on that money.

While this is a number people want to know, it's highly variable because it's based on your individual tax situation, so it isn't really a helpful way to compare properties; it's more of a comparison based on your financial situation.

However, there's another way to calculate ROE, and this one could influence your investment decisions down the road. Let's say that you purchase a rental home for $200,000 with a $50,000 down payment. You are renting it out for $1,400/month with a net cash flow of $400/month or $4,800/year.

In the first year, your equity is close to the $50,000 that you put down on the property. So here's the ROE calculation:

$$ROE = \text{Cash Flow} / \text{Equity (value less what you owe)}$$
$$9.6\% \text{ ROE for } \$4,800 / \$50,000$$

You will find this calculation useful in later years of ownership. As you're paying down your mortgage and the home is appreciating in value, each year you will find that your equity will be growing (you'll owe less on the property but it will be worth more). Rent will change as well; it will probably grow, though not likely at the same rate as your equity.

Let's take a look at this property in five years. Now, due to appreciation and a decreasing loan amount, your equity in the property is at about $68,000. You have been increasing rents, so your cash flow is at $500/month. Here's the new calculation:

$$\$6,000 / \$68,000 = 8.8\% \text{ ROE}$$

These are made-up numbers, and the equity may not have increased that much. However, it illustrates an important use for this calculation. As you pay down your loan, the amount going toward the principal increases at a faster rate. If appreciation is also going well, it's unlikely that your rent increases will keep pace. So each year your ROE will be lower.

When you begin to see other opportunities that will yield higher ROE, then it may be time to borrow against this equity for other investing or to sell this property and roll into a larger one--or more than one.

RENTAL YIELD

Rental yield is simply defined as the return from rental income as a percentage of the money you have invested. It's an easy calculation and, depending on the method, it can help you make comparisons to other investments.

Rental Yield – Property Value

Here we're calculating the yield based on the cost of the property. If you own a home that cost $200,000, regardless of whether you have a mortgage or not, you would use that number and divide it into your net rental income after expenses. So if you're taking in $9,000 after expenses:

$$\$9,000 \ / \ \$200,000 = 4.5\% \text{ Rental Yield}$$

Rental Yield – Cash on Cash

This is the same as the Cash on Cash ROI calculation we showed you earlier. You take your net rental income after expenses and divide it by the cash you have invested in the home. Using the example here, we paid $50,000 down on the $200,000 home. Now we're dividing by that number to get cash on cash rental yield:

$$\$9,000 \ / \ \$50,000 = 18\%$$

Why do the same calculation as the ROI Cash on Cash we discussed earlier and call it Rental Yield? It's just because you'll bump into these two uses out there, so you want to know what's going on. You'll also see "rental yield" numbers quoted and you'll need to know if they're based on the full price of the home or on the cash invested.

SEE FUTURE POTENTIAL BUT BUY AS-IS

We're doing a whole lot of analysis and number-crunching here, and it's all about ending up with positive cash flow. However, there is another aspect of purchasing property that you should always have in mind: future potential. While it needs to be profitable immediately, a property can have future added value based on its characteristics or the area.

For example, you may be able to subdivide a large house into two units for an increase in rental income. It could be as simple as adding a separate entrance, which isn't a high-cost renovation. Adding bathrooms or another kitchen could be more expensive, but splitting one unit into two can increase cash flow significantly.

There are a number of things you can do to a home to make it more desirable to renters or to increase rental income. Since we're buying with an "as-is" approach that generates cash flow immediately, these projects can be done whenever we want, or never. However, use a checklist to identify potential in properties:

- ❏ Is the house bigger than most area rental units?
- ❏ Does it have more than one entrance?
- ❏ How much parking is available on site?
- ❏ Is there street parking?
- ❏ Will the city allow another unit to be built on the site?
- ❏ How difficult is the permit and building process?
- ❏ Can a bathroom be economically added?
- ❏ Can a kitchen be economically added?
- ❏ Is there space for outdoor amenities like a pool, hot tub, playground, picnic area, etc.
- ❏ Could an unfinished basement with a separate entrance be finished out for a second rental unit?
- ❏ Are infrastructure improvements planned in the area?
- ❏ Can a room be converted to a bedroom in order to raise rents?
- ❏ Can a loft or attic be converted for more rental space?

❑ Could an addition be built to increase the number of bedrooms?

❑ Can a large lot be divided and partially sold off?

❑ Are there adjacent lots that could be purchased in the future for a larger development project?

Fall in love with the numbers, not the property.

You want to have this checklist and keep the potential in mind, but always buy based on numbers that will provide a positive cash flow as the property exists now.

DOWN PAYMENT OR CASH FLOW?

We're back to discussing leverage again here. How much down payment should you put into a property? The more you invest, the lower the mortgage payment and the higher the cash flow. However, tying up cash in one property that could be used for two properties is a consideration, as well. How do we make these decisions?

It's part of the "numbers," so we're looking at leverage again here. Now that you have a firm foundation in the calculations to determine an investment's cash flow potential, you can make better decisions about leverage.

With mortgages available from almost zero down or with down payments of 5%, 10%, or 20%, you have choices as to how much cash to invest in a property. In our earlier leverage examples you saw how buying all cash isn't the best approach, since leverage is one of the greatest advantages of real estate.

Our Two Sisters Example

Finding a better example than Maggie and Sharon for this would be difficult. Their uncle Mike gave them each $20,000 when they graduated from college. His only stipulation was that they invest it in real estate.

Maggie and Sharon had differing views on how best to invest their money. Since this example is all about the cost of financing and leverage, we're going to leave out closing costs and monthly expenses. We'll focus solely on the cost of financing.

Sharon's Approach

Sharon wanted a lower monthly payment to increase her cash flow. She put her entire $20,000 down on one $100,000 home. Her monthly mortgage payment was $515, and she rented it out for $800/month. She generated monthly cash flow of $285, or $3,420/year. That is a 17% return on her investment. Not bad at all!

Maggie's Approach

Maggie put a small 5% down payment on a $100,000 home, which was a $5,000 investment, and put the rest into a bank account. Her monthly payment was $612. With $800/month collected in rent, her cash flow was $188/month. Though this was almost $100 less than Sharon's cash flow, Maggie did point out to Sharon that her return on that $5,000 cash invested was 45%, a nice 28% increase over Sharon's.

Leveraging The Difference in Approaches

Maggie quickly saw an opportunity and went right out and put her $15,000 remaining cash to work, buying three more homes with 5% down each. Now her cash flow is $752/month, a nice $567 extra cash deposit to her account each month.

To help illustrate this, here are a couple of charts. The first compares Maggie's and Sharon's investments and the resulting cash flow.

	Maggie 5% Down	Sharon 20% Down
Money required	$5,000	$20,000
Mortgage payment	$612.09	$515.44
Cash flow	$187.91	$284.56
Marginal increase/$5000	$187.91+$187.91+$187.91	$187.91+$32.22+$32.22
Cash flow/$20,000	**$751.64**	**$284.56**

The other nice thing for Maggie is that she now controls $400,000 in real estate, while Sharon has only the single $100,000 property. Maggie will enjoy four times the appreciation potential.

The next chart shows the decrease in return on each dollar invested as the down payment increases.

	5% Down	10% Down	15% Down	20% Down
Money required	$5,000	$10,000	$15,000	$20,000
Mortgage pmt	$612	$580	$548	$515
Cash flow	$188	$220	$252	$285
Marginal cash flow increase per $5,000	$188	$32.22	$32.22	$32.22

These charts clearly illustrate the value of leverage, since Maggie is definitely in a much better financial position than Sharon because of her prudent use of leverage. There's positive cash flow in every one of her homes, and Maggie will participate in property appreciation on $400,000 instead of Sharon's $100,000.

RENTAL EVALUATIONS

Everything so far has been about evaluating a property for purchase. In many of the examples, we've used rental income numbers. Now it's time to determine how we know what rents we will be able to charge. Overestimating rents will damage your cash flow. Underestimating them could cause you to pass up on a good purchase because the cash flow calculations don't pass your tests.

It's very important for you to have valid rental income estimates based on your market and to keep them updated. We discussed this in the chapter about research and learning your market. Let's look at it a little closer now in regards to the rent number--the pivotal cash flow component.

The good news is that much of the information you need to estimate how much rent you'll be able to charge is out there trying to get your attention. Start keeping records of apartment projects and single family home rental ads. They'll normally tell you a lot about the property, bedrooms, baths, etc. They'll usually tell you the rental amount to go with those features. You have the components of what you might call a Rental CMA.

Get the data on comparable properties in comparable or nearby areas. Build a file and a spreadsheet to keep tabs on average rents for certain size homes. When you're evaluating a home for purchase, pull out your rental records and look at comparable properties to get a pretty close estimate of what you can get for rent for the subject property.

There are some subjective items in your comparison. Proximity to parks or green areas and to major employers can result in higher rental income. You looked at these types of variables when you were doing a purchase CMA. Now you're using these same factors to adjust anticipated rents.

Advertising to Get Rental Demand

Running an inexpensive classified ad and a free ad on Craigslist can provide valuable rental estimate information. You don't have to own the home yet. If you run an ad for rentals in a certain area, when you get a call on it, ask the potential tenant some questions. You can tell them that you don't have anything at the moment but will look for something for them.

Find out what they're looking for and, more importantly, what they're willing to pay for it. Now you have both sides of the equation. You know what properties landlords are advertising for rent and for how much. You also have feedback from actual renters as to what they're willing to pay.

When you're running the numbers to evaluate a property for purchase, use this data to build a solid expectation of the rent you can charge for the homes you're considering for purchase.

Love the Numbers, Not the Property

What you've learned in this chapter will be the basis for your evaluation of properties to produce lifetime cash flow. Never shortcut the numbers.

ACTION STEPS

1. For each of the investment calculations in this chapter, run your own examples. Choose the numbers from actual homes for sale or just make them up.
2. Begin to build your rental database, including the price properties are renting for as well as their characteristics and features.
3. Do a sample "Property Potential" checklist.

WHAT'S NEXT?

We're going to work on expanding your investment team in the next chapter. You'll begin to add team members to help in building your investing business.

CHAPTER 13
Expand Your Success Team Stage 2

At this point in the book and in our courses, some readers may be farther along than others. We've covered the major components of successful rental property acquisition for positive cash flow. You know how to go about locating prospective properties and how to evaluate their rental potential and value. This is a good time to look at Stage 2 of building your Success Team.

We'll be looking at the contributions and attributes of these future team members:

- Accountant/CPA
- Bookkeeper
- Appraiser
- Handyman
- Partner

As in Stage 1 team member selection, you should begin your research and networking to locate these team members now. You may not need one or more of them at this moment, but you don't want to be urgently looking for a team member after a need arises.

ACCOUNTANT/CPA

Making money through real estate rental is our plan, and we plan on creating lifetime cash flow. One lifetime cash flow component that works against us is taxes. We all want to pay our share, but that share can be very different for each investor and frequently is more than it should be.

While an accountant or CPA's services can cost between $300 and

$1,000 a year--and even more for a corporation--it's money well spent. Not using one, or using the wrong one, can cost you much more. Also, consider the future value of every dollar you save this year when it's invested in rental property many years from now. So, without any hesitation, find an excellent accountant.

What to Look For

You want someone who works with other real estate investors and understands real estate taxes. While a corporate accountant dealing with retail businesses may be quite good in that specialty, he may not have the specific expertise you need as a real estate investor.

Where to Start

Ask your other team members for referrals. Real estate agents, mortgage brokers, and attorneys may have experience working with accountants who serve real estate investors. Join a real estate investment club, a place where there may actually be an associate member who is an experienced real estate accountant. You'll definitely be able to ask other investors who they recommend.

What You Get

Primarily, you get services that help you stay out of trouble. Not having the money to pay the taxes you owe when you owe them is a tough situation to be in. Your accountant can keep you on track, meet with you regularly, and give you a plan to be certain that your tax planning is on track.

Another area where business owners get into trouble is with payroll taxes and workers' compensation insurance. The government is serious about these withholding obligations. Shortages in these areas can result in more than fines; court action and business closure are real possibilities. Your accountant will keep you informed about your obligations and help you set up procedures to make these deposits.

Accountants also reduce your audit risk. They can alert you to potential "red flags", such as when your deductions in a certain area are higher than the norm for your type of business. It's possible that you merely categorized some of your business deductions incorrectly, but you'll need someone to monitor this for you.

Your accountant or CPA will help you avoid overpayment and

underpayment of taxes. Overpayment is negative cash flow and takes away resources you could be investing for greater lifetime cash flow later. Underpayment creates penalty fees and interest payments, which are definitely not a wise use of your money.

Set up periodic meetings with your accountant to bring them up to date on changes in your investments and your business. They can't do their job in a vacuum, so you'll need to provide them with timely and accurate data. Subsequent to these meetings, your accountant may adjust some of your withholding or tax payments in response to your business adjustments. It's better to be out in front with accounting and tax issues than scrambling at the end of the tax year.

BOOKKEEPER

You don't want your accountant keeping your books, even if they are willing to do this, because the cost would be too great. You need a bookkeeper for this function, and they'll be very hands-on in your daily business. You can usually find a detail-oriented and efficient bookkeeper for between $20 and $30 per hour. Depending on the size of your business, you may be spending up to $500/month when you're managing a group of properties.

Where to Look

As with all team members, ask others for referrals. If you joined an investing club, you can ask other members. Definitely ask your accountant, since they'll know bookkeepers who are sending in data from their clients. The accountant will know who are the most organized and up-to-date with information.

Doing it Yourself

At this stage, you can be looking around for a potential bookkeeper but shouldn't be hiring one just yet. Early in your investing business, the record-keeping should be manageable for you on your own. That's unless you hate numbers, can't use spreadsheets, don't want to learn, or you're bad with math and numbers. If this is you, or if you're very busy with no extra time, then hiring a bookkeeper is wise. Otherwise, you should be able to do this yourself for a while.

You may have a trusted family member who is good with numbers and spreadsheets and can help you with bookkeeping. We like to do our own. We track all of our receipts and have all of the proper forms, as well as great spreadsheets to keep up with costs and income by property.

There are also many good property management software packages out there. They can be inexpensive or very costly to purchase, so you shouldn't jump in unless you really need specialized software. And then be sure to thoroughly research the features.

When your business grows to the point where you want to incorporate, a bookkeeper is even more valuable. There will be more paperwork and record-keeping involved in running a corporation. If you have one or more employees, a bookkeeper is almost a necessity. However, as a real estate investor, you'll probably be using contractors so you won't have payroll obligations. You will have tax reporting requirements for payments to those contractors, however.

What to Look For

You want someone experienced with keeping books and financial records. They must be proficient in the use of spreadsheets, since they'll be tracking a lot of financial data. Good spreadsheets have alerted many investors to areas of their business that needed attention before they became big problems.

Bookkeepers serve a variety of functions, including helping you to:

- pay bills.
- prepare checks.
- balance bank statements.
- analyze operations, costs, and revenues.
- manage tax records.

A good bookkeeper will significantly lower your end-of-year stress levels. Your records will be in order and up-to-date, and they'll be forwarded to your accountant periodically to keep you on track for financial and tax planning.

APPRAISER

Appraisers assess property values and prepare value reports, mostly for lenders. If you're making a cash purchase, you will want to use your own appraiser. If you're getting a mortgage, the bank or lender will choose an appraiser from their list of those they use regularly. While you may not be able to influence the selection by the lender, knowing something about the local appraisers is helpful. Some are more conservative than others and some select comparables a little differently.

An appraiser normally gets paid by the job--somewhere between $200 and $500, in most cases. If you're getting a mortgage, it will be a cost charged to you in the closing process. The price depends on the size of the property, geographical location, and whether or not a site visit is necessary. These days, computerized appraisals are becoming more accepted, but it's an individual situation in each deal. Most will require the appraiser to physically inspect the property.

Who Pays May be Negotiable

If you're doing a refinance, the bank will choose the appraiser, but you'll pay for the appraisal. In most cases, you'll also pay when a new mortgage is being sought. However, we've built up a track record of purchases with our mortgage broker and certain lenders, and we always ask for the lender to pay for the appraisal. Sometimes it works, sometimes it doesn't, but it's always worth asking the question.

Where to Start

The bank will take care of this for you. However, as you progress in your business, you may want to hire an appraiser for cash deals or to help you evaluate a property for other reasons, so research into finding an appraiser for your team is appropriate. Now and then you may just want to bounce off a question about investment valuation or market trends. You'll appreciate having an appraiser you can call for this.

Ask other team members or investment club members for referrals. Even if you just meet and get to know an appraiser with the goal of asking a question now and then, it's good to have one on your team. Appraisers keep detailed data on market trends, which could help you in decision making.

What an Appraiser Does

Banks want to make loans that are as secure as possible. They want the security of knowing that the money they have loaned on the property is well-covered by its value. If the borrower defaults on the loan, the bank wants to know that they can get the full value of their loan when they foreclose and sell.

When the appraiser provides an opinion of value that's lower than the purchase price, the bank will not approve the loan, or they'll want more down payment from the buyer in order to get the loan value to an acceptable level relative to the appraised value.

When the appraiser provides an opinion of value that is at or above the purchase price, and you have the required down payment, then the deal goes to closing. The appraised value is influenced by a number of factors including:

- Comparable sold properties in the area, as in our CMAs.
- The condition of the property.
- The quality of the finishes, appliances, and materials.
- Amenities and upgrades that enhance value.
- Size, bedrooms, baths, floor plan, and livability.
- The current market conditions in the area.

Appraisal isn't a structured science; it doesn't offer a table of values to apply to a situation as we might plug values into a spreadsheet. Some of the job is done that way, but some of it is subjective, as well--more art than science. This is particularly true when expensive amenities are involved, such as a swimming pool.

The appraiser must add some value for the pool, but how much? It may depend on how many days in the year the pool can be used, or whether every third home on the block has one as well. If many of the homes on the block have granite countertops and the subject home has Formica, how much does this lower the value, if any?

It's in these more subjective areas that differences in appraisals can be found. If there are plenty of potential comparables but the appraiser hasn't been inside them, then even the selection of comparable homes can influence the value opinion. If the appraiser happens to choose the only three homes in the area with Formica, then this home will fare well. If the selection is three homes with granite, then it may not.

Get Involved

The banks select the appraiser, and the bank or one of the real estate agents involved will likely schedule the appraiser's visit to give the appraiser access to the home. They aren't going to call you up and tell you about it. You'll need to call them and tell them you want to be there for the appraisal. Whether you're buying or selling, you should be there, as your actions and information can help you get a better result.

As a Seller

If you're selling, you want as high an appraised amount as possible. There is already a contract, and the appraiser has a copy of it, so they know the minimum number they must hit to not kill the deal: the purchase price.

There's some reality to understand here. The appraiser knows the purchase price and knows that hitting that number will allow the deal to go forward. Coming in below that number will probably kill the deal. As the seller, you want the purchase price to be hit as well, but any amount over it will make the deal look better to the bank and smooth the path to closing.

However, the reality is that even if your home is worth significantly more than the selling price, there is no incentive for the appraiser to say so. They have that purchase price number to hit, and a small cushion is a good thing, but much more just adds risk for them. A default later will have the bank looking to capture that appraised value, so keeping it at a level not too far above the purchase price is less risky.

You want to be there during the appraisal. Bring along some comparables that either you or your real estate agent compiled and that are favorable to your deal, and make sure to give them to the appraiser. They don't mind you saving them a little work, particularly if they see that they are recent and solid comps.

Also, bring along a list of all of the improvements you've made to the home over your ownership period. New heating and cooling equipment, roof work, new appliances, and all major renovation or repair work should be listed. The appraiser is supposed to notice all of this, but you can help them with your list.

As a Buyer

It's no great leap to know that your interests as a buyer are very much the opposite of those of the seller. You want to purchase a property at the lowest price possible for ROI and cash flow. While it's true that you have already signed a purchase contract by the time the appraiser arrives, this doesn't mean that the price must stand as is.

You are getting a mortgage, and the deal may completely fail if the appraisal comes in lower than the contract purchase price. However, there could be another outcome. The seller could reduce the price to the appraised value to keep you as a buyer. You just negotiated a better deal, and the appraiser did all of the work!

Meet the appraiser with a good attitude and a list of problems you see with the home. You have done your due diligence, you know the problems, and your inspector has verified them. Between your team handyman and some contractor estimates, you can give the appraiser a list of all of the home's condition issues and the costs to make repairs.

Your list could result in lowering the valuation by thousands of dollars and, possibly, a price renegotiation. At the very least, presenting your list of home condition problems will serve as a checklist so the appraiser will not forget any of them when preparing the report.

Whether you're buying or selling, there will almost always be an appraiser involved. It's a good idea to learn about the local appraisers and keep some contact and information data on each.

HANDYMAN

A handyman or home repair person is a must-add to your Success Team early on. In the appraisal section, we mentioned that the handyman is a person to help you assess the condition of a home and the cost of repairs. However, over the long haul, their real value is in providing repairs to your rental properties and keeping them in good working order for your tenants.

What to Look For

> *"Hey Michael. The furnace in the Hall Street house is down again. Jack says he's done all he can do with it and replacement should be our next step".*
>
> *"I'll get some estimates, Scott, and maybe Jack can help with the installation to save us some money".*

This exchange points out one of the most important criteria for selection of a home repair person: being trustworthy. You want someone who knows what they're doing but is also willing to tell you when you're spending too much on them and should take other action. Other attributes you should look for include:

- a knowledge of carpentry, electrical, plumbing, and general repairs.
- an accessible person who'll come when you call.
- someone who is mobile and has the right tools.
- a personable approach when interacting with your tenants.
- trustworthiness is very important since you'll be giving them keys to your homes.

The home repair person will be one of your most valuable and relied-upon Success Team members, so choose well.

What's the Cost?

Repair people normally work on a "time and material" basis. They charge a labor rate, and they mark up the cost of the parts they provide in order to make a profit. This type of work generally carries a labor rate of between $40 and $60 per hour. If you give them steady work, many will discount their labor rate, since they want to stabilize their work week and have less down time with no income.

Some repair people will also discount their parts, but it's a nebulous number, since you really don't know what they're paying wholesale. If you have a number of rental properties and you're using a steady stream of parts, you might want to buy some yourself through a wholesaler and keep them in stock. It speeds the repair process, especially on weekends.

Where to Start

As always, ask your other team members. Ask real estate agents, since they are frequently calling on this type of help for their sellers who are getting properties ready to list. If you know a real estate agent who handles a number of foreclosure properties, they definitely have a repair person on call, and they probably are dependable and reasonably priced because the bank is paying the bills.

Your handyman is an independent contractor, so you won't have to pay wages or worry about payroll withholding. However, you will have reporting requirements to show what you paid them in the course of the year. Especially in the beginning when your business is still small, your handyman can help you out when you're too busy by doing small jobs around the properties.

When You Grow

Once you have multiple properties, you'll move past the single handyman phase and need a general contractor or home repair company. At this stage, be sure to verify that they meet their legal payroll and workmen's compensation insurance requirements. You could pick up some liability if they do not and one of their people is hurt on your property. We'll talk more about this in Stage 3 of building your Success Team.

PARTNER

Whoa, you say! I want all of this profit for myself. I don't need a partner. We're living proof that *you'll reap 10 times the rewards by splitting half of the profits with the right partner.* Two people can get much more than double the work done, and the leverage from having two people involved in financing properties will allow you to grow faster and larger.

What to Look For

In a nutshell, YOU. You're reading this and working with us because you're totally committed to building lifetime cash flow. You know it will require hard work, and you know that it won't happen overnight. You want someone with the same attitude, for sure.

Motivation is important, and you want a partner motivated for success and willing to give 150% in effort to make it happen. Two of you doing this creates a 300% output for success. In this case, 1 + 1 = 3.

While you'll probably become friends, that isn't a requirement on the short list. You need someone with motivation and the right attitude and commitment; most of all you need someone you can trust. Tying your financial future to someone else, both legally and personally, is a big step, so the choice of a partner is far more critical than any other of your Success Team members.

Where to Start

It's also "when" to start. While your business is a small sole proprietorship, you may not want to consider a partner. However, you could partner with people on individual deals. This could allow you to complete a deal you couldn't have otherwise handled financially. And, in the course of the partnership, you will be able to evaluate this single deal partner for future deals or a business together.

Later, as your business grows, and when you are considering changing its structure, you can consider whether to partner or not. Synergy is a great business builder. Two people bringing similar attitudes but different skill sets and opinions to the table can bring better decision-making as well.

You and your partner will have double the financial ability, so you can buy properties faster. You'll halve your risk in the venture. Creativity is likely to more than double, since you have someone to bounce ideas off of and you'll get new ideas back.

Your partner is not an investor--someone who loans you money for a stake in a property or your business. They are a part of your business, a co-owner. You must share decision-making and they'll have their say in how things go. However, you'll be surprised how often you agree when the business principles are sound. They make money and lose money when you do, so you're a true team.

ACTION STEPS

1. Go to http://scottsinvestorsedge.com/book-resources/team-stage-two and download your stage 2 team worksheet
2. Start looking for a good handyman right away. You want to be able to take your time and get references, so starting before you have a property is fine. Also, if you own a home, you can use them for your home repairs.
3. Begin to network to find a good accountant. Before you bring in the first dollar from rentals, you need to have the right accountant on board. Guidance before your first purchase could help you get a better start.
4. Add a bookkeeper when you're ready.
5. Begin to think about a future partnership and to size up potential partners as you grow your business.

WHAT'S NEXT?

Some of the best deals you'll make will be homes that the casual retail buyer doesn't want because of repair or renovation issues. The ability to size up the problems and to come up with the cost to repair them is half of the battle. The other half is in the After Repair Value (ARV) calculation. We'll help you with both in the next chapter.

CHAPTER 14

Repairs, Renovation & ARV

Some of the best deals out there for rental homes will be houses with minor problems and repair issues. Some may be in good repair but have "functional obsolescence" issues. That's when the floor plan or certain areas have become out-dated and are not the best for today's living and entertainment preferences. Appraisers adjust property values down for functional obsolescence.

An example might be a small formal dining room. If a wall is removed, it could open that area up to the kitchen or living areas, or even join the two. This fits much more with today's lifestyle. While repairs to correct livability problems will probably require immediate action, renovations may be something you want to do in the future to increase the value of the property.

There are two property condition values used by investors, the "As-Is" value and the After Repair Value, or ARV. Wholesale property investors (fast flippers) are only concerned with the as-is value of the property and whether they can flip it to another investor for a profit without doing any work on the house.

Other flippers like to buy fixer-upper properties, do the work, and then immediately sell them for a profit based on the ARV of the home. Still others, including us, will hold the property as a rental but may still want to purchase a home in need of repairs or renovation. Foreclosure properties can present some of the best values out there, but they will frequently need some amount of work, and this can sometimes be major work.

DIY – Do It Yourself
We are a couple of guys who like to get our hands dirty, especially when it saves us money while increasing our ROI and cash flow. So we do a lot of our own repair and minor renovation work on our properties. In some cases, we act as the general contractor and put some subcontractors on the job.

If you're handy this way and have the time, this is the best way to maximize the value of the property at the lowest cost. "Sweat equity" is the term for doing the work yourself. You're increasing the value of the house with your own work, which increases your equity right away.

Hiring Out the Work

If you don't know the front end of a hammer from the back end of a shovel, then you'll want to hire professionals for repairs and even minor renovation work. Even if you do have the ability, you may not have the time.

Whether you're doing some or all of the work yourself or hiring it out, you will need to determine the cost to complete it and the value of the home after the work is done. Figuring the After Repair Value is actually the easier of the two jobs. The accurate estimation of the costs is every bit as important and is actually a trickier task.

ARV FOR THE RENTAL PROPERTY BUYER

Rental property investment ROI has two components--the cash flow and the equity increase over time. Equity can be increased quickly with repairs and/or renovations, and that's what we're dealing with in this chapter. It's great to be able to buy a house and immediately put in a tenant and create positive cash flow.

However, some really good deals will require at least some repairs before move-in day. If you purchased a home at a significant discount due to the condition and need for repairs, sometimes extensive, then you will have added value once they're completed.

You'll recognize possible future improvements or renovations that will increase the property's value and cash flow through higher rents. You may see great potential at the time of the purchase, but you hold off on doing the work until after you've rented it out for a while.

After Repair Value is simply defined as the value of the property after the work is done. Whatever you see that must be done or could be done to improve the property is considered, and a value is calculated for the house as if the work is completed.

The good news is that you know exactly how to do this from what you learned in the Comparative Market Analysis chapter. All you're doing is a

CMA that considers the property to be already repaired or renovated. You select comparable sold properties and make your adjustments as if the home were in the repaired and renovated state.

Let's go back and refresh your memory about the CMA, because it's the best way to assess the ARV of a home. Why bother to do this if you aren't planning on doing any renovation? It's because today's plan is tomorrow's old plan. You can't anticipate what may be in the future.

We're long term investors for cash flow. While we'll do the necessary repairs to get the home occupied, and they may add to the value immediately, we may also recognize opportunities for renovations or more extensive work that will increase value and equity down the road. Changing market conditions, such as a new high tech employer moving to the area, could be the impetus for a remodel or other simpler renovation. Changes in the demographics of our tenant pool could bring about a desire to change up the property a bit.

Earlier in the book, we mentioned large houses and how there may be an opportunity to make changes, add entryways, or divide a single property into two rentals. This increases cash flow and the value of the house. If our tenant pool is moving from families to young professionals, this type of renovation could be quite profitable for cash flow reasons and it will increase the value of the home, our equity, and our ultimate ROI.

Equity for Future Business Growth

We're in this for the long haul and for lifetime cash flow. Reaching financial independence will happen when we grow our holdings to exceed our cash flow needs and can move to the next level. This requires financial leverage, and there's opportunity in property improvements.

We discussed the appreciation of a property's value over time. However, an immediate infusion of value from renovations can speed the process a lot. At some point, by coupling normal appreciation with renovations over time we can build a nice pile of equity against which we can borrow to fund other purchases.

Converting a basement to a tenant space is an excellent example of multiplying the value of existing square footage for equity and cash flow. Adding the value of the improvements to the value of the extra cash flow will free up leverage to add to our rental property inventory.

ACCURATE COST ESTIMATION IS CRITICAL

Doing a CMA that considers the property in its After Repair Value state is the easy part. However, it's just a plan when you want to buy a property for $150,000, believe you can renovate or repair it for $20,000, and anticipate an ARV of $200,000. It's not a reality unless you can make the cost numbers work.

In Stage 3 of building your Success Team, you'll be selecting contractors for major repair and renovation work. Right now we'll just refer to them, as well as to the help your handyman can provide in estimating the less extensive work.

When couples renovate their own homes, cost overruns are almost a cliché or a bad joke. Divorces over these projects are legend, and movies like "Money Pit" starring Michael Keaton are fun, though painful, to watch. The last thing you want is a money pit. What you do want is a final result that's on or under budget. This requires attention to detail, using your team members properly, and the use of other material, labor, and renovation estimate resources.

Estimation Resources

We'll run through some online and print resources here that can educate you in the costs for repairs and renovation projects. Nothing will be spot-on, since much of the labor and material costs vary depending on locality. However, if these resources do nothing else, they will prompt you to leave nothing out of your estimates.

www.homerenovationestimate.com

Estimate Calculators

Roof Renovation and Roof Repair
Sloped Roofs — Estimate Costs
Flat Roofs — Estimate Costs

Exterior Wall Siding — Estimate Costs
alluminium, stucco & more..

Eavestroughs — Estimate Costs

Deck Construction — Estimate Costs

Patio Construction — Estimate Costs

Fence Construction — Estimate Costs

Driveways and Walkways — Estimate Costs

Landscaping — Estimate Costs

Garage Renovations — Estimate Costs

Windows: — Estimate Costs
Replacements and Window Installation

Exterior Doors — Estimate Costs
Installation and Build

Stairs and Railing Renovations — Estimate Costs

The screen shot shows some of the free cost calculators available on this site. These are simple calculators, so they don't provide enough in-depth information to use for your final estimate. However, they can quickly give you a picture and help you to decide if you and your team should spend putting together more detailed estimates. Here's a screen shot of the data input page for window replacements:

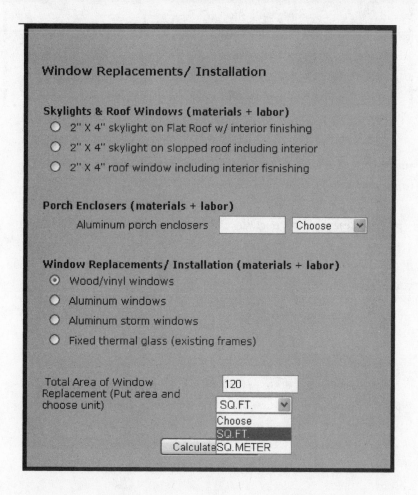

You can see that there isn't a lot of detail here. They just ask for window type and dimension in square feet and meters. Here's the result page:

Estimation: The estimated cost for your project is $6,000.00
Find a Home Contractor

Window Replacements/ Installation

Skylights & Roof Windows (materials + labor)
○ 2" X 4" skylight on Flat Roof w/ interior finishing
○ 2" X 4" skylight on slopped roof including interior
○ 2" X 4" roof window including interior fisnishing

You can see that the estimate for 10 windows of 12 square feet each is simply a number with no extra details. This site probably makes its revenue from contractor recommendation referral fees.

However, this is a really easy number to obtain and it allows us to see if replacing these windows might be a future project. We now have an idea of cost. Working through all of the appropriate items for a renovation can be done very quickly on this site, and you'll at least have a ballpark figure to help you plan your next step.

http://www.scottsinvestorsedge.com/book-resources/cnn

Over at CNNMoney.com, there's a really easy calculator to help you compare the project costs to potential resale value. When you look at these types of comparisons, the first thing to remember is that they're quoted based on the cost of hiring contractors and are usually at the upper end of market prices. Sites and resources would rather their readers be pleasantly surprised by lower costs than be mad at them for under-estimating the real cost of a project.

However, all information is of value, and the next two screen shots show how fast and easy it is to get information about average costs for given projects.

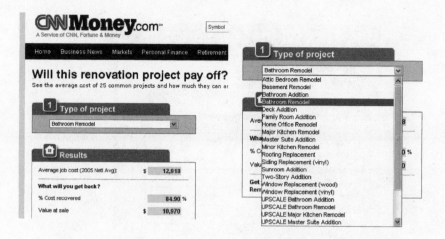

The data for that quick reference chart comes from a site with much more localized and detailed data.

http://www.remodeling.hw.net/facts-and-figures/cost-vs-value-report

This site provides maps for various regions. You are then able to narrow your search down to specific cities. Here you'll find detailed project data based on your local area. Here are some screen shots:

Cost vs. Value Report

2010-11 Cost vs. Value Data is Now Available
View the annual report on the relationship between remodeling costs and resale value. You can compare national and regional averages for 33 popular remodeling projects and you can also download a PDF with project data for any one of 80 U.S. cities.

Find out how...

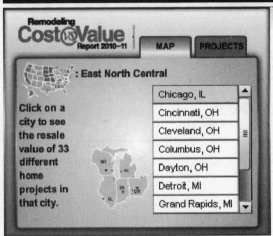

Chicago, IL

Select another year 2010-11 ▾

Select another region East North Central ▾

Select another regional city Chicago, IL ▾

City data for 35 projects, including:
- City Job Costs
- City Resale Value
- City Cost Recouped
- City/Region Comparison
- City/National Comparison

East North Central — Midrange				2010-11 National Averages			
Job Cost	Resale Value	Cost Recouped	Project	Job Cost	Resale Value	Cost Recouped	Change vs. 2009-10
$54,517	$38,934	71.4%	Attic Bedroom	$51,428	$37,142	72.2%	⬇
$15,606	$6,316	40.5%	Backup Power Generator	$14,718	$7,136	48.5%	⬇
$67,533	$37,967	56.2%	Basement Remodel	$64,519	$45,186	70.0%	⬇
$42,919	$19,571	45.6%	Bathroom Addition	$40,710	$21,695	53.3%	⬇
$17,304	$9,516	55.0%	Bathroom Remodel	$16,634	$10,668	64.1%	⬇

It's a great place to get more local information about costs to repair and remodel homes. It also compares the data to previous years.

http://scottsinvestorsedge.com/book-resources/costestimate

Not to leave our Canadian friends out, we found this site advertising the same type of estimating tools for Canada. Even better, this site covers the U.S., as well.

Entering a postal code in the Toronto area, we selected "Kitchens". The

next page gave us different layout shapes for a kitchen remodel.

Clicking on the L-Shaped Kitchen, we get this screen:

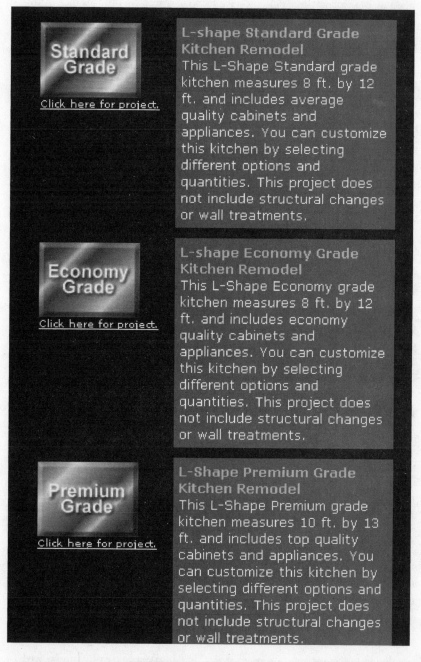

Now we can select grades for our project, from economy to premium. We'll end up with a localized estimate of the project cost adjusted by the quality of materials we would select.

You're getting the idea, and there are a great many more websites with this type of information. All you have to do is search on phrases like "home renovation", "home remodel estimates", or "home renovation cost calculator". You'll have no trouble finding plenty of ready information.

If You Want It In Print

If you want something to carry around in the pickup truck, there are plenty of books to be found. A quick search at Amazon and Barnes and Noble turned up titles like these:

- *F.R. Walker's Remodeling*
- *R.S. Means Construction Books*
- *Affordable Remodel: How to Get Custom Results on Any Budget*
- *Sweet's Repair and Remodel Cost Guide*
- *Dodge Repair and Remodel Cost Book*

There are many more of these remodeling guides. We recommend that you get the latest edition, though, since project costs are always changing.

USING YOUR TEAM

Of course, the busier you are, the more you're going to rely on your Success Team members to pull together this type of data for you. However, it is critical to your success that you understand how it's done and where to find and verify the information.

There should also be consideration for your team members. If you're evaluating a dozen deals every month or so, it helps to be able to do basic estimates to focus in on the ones most likely to be feasible. Calling up your contractor several times every month to do detailed estimates for deals that will likely never happen could cause you to have to find another contractor.

ARV and Costs Go Together

In this chapter you've learned that ARV can't stand alone. The costs needed to get there must be accurately calculated or you could end up with that "money pit", or at least a small "money pothole".

ACTION STEPS

1. Start compiling and bookmarking online renovation cost calculation resources.
2. Run through some sample projects to become familiar with the way they work.
3. Buy a book if you want a print resource.

WHAT'S NEXT?

We're ready! In the next chapter we'll go out and actually look for a rental property.

CHAPTER 15
Let's Go Find a Property

〰〰〰〰〰〰〰〰〰〰〰〰〰〰〰〰〰〰〰〰〰〰〰〰〰〰〰〰〰〰〰〰〰〰〰

This is the transition you've been waiting for and progressing toward throughout this book and with our mentorship and training. You want to go out and actually locate a property, evaluate it for rental opportunity and cash flow, and get to the point of making an offer. Let's work our way through this with a "real city" example pulled out of a hat.

DALLAS, TEXAS RENTAL PROPERTY PURCHASE

Actually, we threw a dart at a map, and we hit low and center. There is no other reason for using Dallas, TX, but it's as good a place for this exercise as anywhere. We're not going to get into neighborhood selection, since we're all from different places in the U.S. and Canada, so we'll just keep this a numbers comparison that assumes similar neighborhoods in and around Dallas, Texas.

Rental Research

What Are Homes Renting For?
There are a number of websites you can use to look for rental homes by area, and we just chose one out of the Google search results for "homes for rent Dallas TX". We entered some criteria to narrow down the results:

- minimum two bedrooms
- single family homes
- rent between $1,000 and $1,500
- yard (size not indicated)
- dishwasher
- air conditioning (it is Texas!)
- washer and dryer

It was a very productive search, with more than 170 homes in the results for this narrow rental price range. Next we went through those to get some similarly sized homes with three bedrooms and two baths. Here are five homes we found that compare well:

3 Bedrooms	$1150	1662sq. ft.	2 Bath(s)	$1150	For questions or availability call: ~~(866) 555-3711~~ Contact the Property

Available Rental Property	Price	Sq. Ft	Bath	Deposit	
3 Bedrooms	$1495	1832sq. ft.	2 Bath(s)	$2000	For questions or availability call: ~~(866) 526-1337~~ Contact the Property

Available Rental Property	Price	Sq. Ft	Bath	Deposit	
3 Bedrooms	$1250	1610sq. ft.	2 Bath(s)	$1250	For questions or availability call: ~~(888) 788-8851~~ Contact the Property

Available Rental Property	Price	Sq. Ft	Bath	Deposit	
3 Bedrooms	$1275	1860sq. ft.	2 Bath(s)	$1275	For questions or availability call: ~~(888) 404-8887~~ Contact the Property

Available Rental Property	Price	Sq. Ft	Bath	Deposit	
3 Bedrooms	$1395	1755sq. ft.	2 Bath(s)	$1000	For questions or availability call: ~~(888) 888-8888~~ Contact the Property

Let's recap these, all of which are three bedroom, two bath homes:

- Home # 1 1662 sq. ft. for $1,150/month
- Home # 2 1832 sq. ft. for $1,495/month
- Home # 3 1610 sq. ft. for $1,250/month
- Home # 4 1860 sq. ft. for $1,275/month
- Home # 5 1755 sq. ft. for $1,395/month

We'll add all of the square footage numbers together and all of the rent figures together and then divide each total by 5:

Rental amounts total / Total square feet = Rental per sq. ft.
$6,565 / 8719 sq. ft. = $0.75/sq. ft.

This is a simple calculation to help us to get a feel for how single family homes are renting in the area. Of course, we're also going to do thorough market research to determine several other things, including:

- demographic trends--who is moving in and out
- employment trends--jobs coming or going
- which neighborhoods have rent competition and which don't
- neighborhoods with fewer available rentals
- how neighborhoods look and feel based on drive-bys

We now know how much we can rent a home for on average, assuming it's in normal condition and isn't too fancy or too plain. We're going to act like a tenant and call or even go see properties to get a very detailed look at what amenities are drawing the higher rents. It could be area, features, or simply proximity to green belts or employment.

If you're talking to landlords, ask questions like, "How is it going with your rental? Is it hard to keep tenants in it? How long has it been vacant? Are you flexible on the rent?" You'll think of others.

If there are several comparable rentals in a neighborhood, check them out to see what makes a difference in the rents they're charging. It could just be what they need to cover their payments, but it could also indicate which features are valued in the area. If corner lots or cul-de-sac lots command higher rents, you want to know. If you are comparing two homes for purchase that are very much alike in features and price, the one in a cul-de-sac may be the best choice.

Finding a Home to Buy

We've discussed using a real estate agent to keep you supplied with automated reports of new listings and sold properties, so you'll be watching those. However, we don't have those right now for Dallas, so we're going to go to the Web to search for Dallas homes that we can purchase for our cash flow goals.

Let's talk about IDX versus sites like Realtor.com and other mega-sites. IDX stands for Internet Data Exchange. It is the agreement between real estate brokers in the Multiple Listing Service to exchange data for display on their websites. The agreement allows all brokers in that MLS to display certain fields of information about other brokers' listings.

IDX searches are the best choice for your purposes because they're the most up-to-date, and the data hasn't been manipulated before you see it, other than limiting some of what you can see. Here are some notes about why we say this:

1.   IDX is a search of all of the participating real estate broker listings in the local MLS.

2.   IDX is usually updated at least once each day.

3.   Realtor.com is fed most of the IDX data for member sites, but Realtor.com manipulates the text to fit their format and ultimately changes some of it. There can also be more of a delay in seeing data there.

4.   Trulia.com, Zillow.com, and other sites are not fed data from local MLSs, in most cases. They must get it in other ways, and you're likely to miss listings simply because they're not there.

5.   Those sites also have old data that doesn't get removed in some cases. Buyers have been upset to see their new home still listed for sale on those sites months after they moved in.

Those are the major reasons for choosing to search on a local MLS IDX site. If you've already started working with real estate agents, it's likely that you're using their site and you're where you need to be. If you want to find one, just do a search as we did on "dallas real estate idx".

The Property Search

We easily found a site with all of the Dallas area listings and began our search. Now, at this point, we must make some basic assumptions that may not fit your situation. The good news is that we found a lot of homes available in the area that were priced between $100,000 and $150,000. Right now the market is great for our purposes.

For our example situation, we're going to assume that you have a 20% down payment. Don't fret if you do not have this much, since there were plenty of home choices and some would have been in your price range. We have to use an example, so here's what we're using for our investor buyer capabilities and desires:

- This investor has up to $40,000 cash to invest in the home.
- Using the rental information we previously obtained, we want to rent out the home for around $0.75/sq. ft. and realize nice cash flow.
- We're assuming certain numbers for taxes and insurance

> that were recommended at the website where we did our search.
- We're also buying a ready-to-rent home that doesn't need substantial work, just minor touchup and make-ready repairs.

There were plenty of homes to choose from, but let's settle on a couple of them to see the potential for us:

MLS #: 11546622	Bedrooms: 3	Full Baths: 2
Type: Residential	Square Ft: 1,574	Half Baths: –
Class: Single Family	Lot Size: 0.217	Year Built: 2004
Price: $140,000	Fireplaces: 1	Stories: 1
	Garage Capacity: 2	

MLS #: 11545877	Bedrooms: 3	Full Baths: 2
Type: Residential	Square Ft: 1,678	Half Baths: –
Class: Single Family	Lot Size: 0.152	Year Built: 1986
Price: $140,000	Fireplaces: 1	Stories: 1
	Garage Capacity: 2	

As you can see, in terms of characteristics, these fall right in line with the rental homes we studied earlier when gathering data. Let's see how these could rent using our calculation:

Square feet x $0.75/sq. ft. = Potential rental price
Home 1: 1574 x $0.75 = $1,181/month
Home 2: 1678 x $0.75 = $1,259/month

Both are listed at $140,000. We're going to assume that these are very similar homes in the same area and that their condition and other amenities are similar, as well. Jumping right to Home 2 due to the higher rent potential, we'll run some numbers before we decide to go look at the home.

First, asking price is just that-- asking. Stats from our real estate agent and a good CMA show that the home isn't overpriced, but we should be able to get it for $132,500. We want to put 20% down and get a 30-year mortgage at the current interest rate of 5.5%.

- Amount of the loan is $106,000
- Down payment is $26,500

- Payments with taxes & insurance will be $825/month
- Gross rent cash flow $1,259 - $825 = $434/month

Let's be conservative and assume other costs of $54/month for repairs and miscellaneous expenses, leaving a monthly cash flow of $380. Now let's run some other numbers:

- $380 x 12 = $4,560 annual cash flow.
- Net cash flow of $4,560 / Cash invested of $26,500 = the ROI of 17.2%.
- Use 11 months instead of 12 and the ROI is now 15.7%.

Let's make it clear that there were several dozen lower-priced homes with the same features and amenities, and there were also many that were higher-priced. However, we didn't want to use an unrealistic example. In fact, it's very probable that a home could have been located and purchased for around $110,000 with 1500 square feet of space, and the numbers would have looked like this:

- $22,000 down with $88,000 mortgaged.
- $700/month payment with same terms as the previous home.
- Using $750 for miscellaneous expenses, rent of $1,125/month, and 11 months of income, our annual cash flow would be $4,125.

Notice that the annual cash flow is almost the same as in the previous example, since the home is smaller and the rent lower. However, here is our ROI:

- ROI =$4,150 cash flow / $22,000 invested = 18.8%

And we have an extra $4,000 or so in cash to use elsewhere.

We haven't even talked about foreclosures or other bargain basement properties. While they may need work, they can be purchased at deep discounts that could make it well worth the effort.

A Foreclosure Example

Listing Information:

Address: ~~11818 Glendale~~ Lane

City: Farmers Branch

State: TX

Zip: 75234

Area: 22

County: Dallas

Price: $94,500

MLS #: ~~11591858~~

Property Type: Single Family

Listing Type: Resale/New

Subdivision: Heritage Park 05

Status: ACTIVE

Property Information:

Style: Traditional

Bedrooms: 4

Total Baths: 2

Full Baths: 2

Year Built: 1971

Sq. Feet: 1881

Lot Size: 0.1856

Basement: Slab

Garage: Attached, Garage Conversion, Outsid

Parking: 2

Construction: Brick

Stories: 1

Exterior: Deck, Patio Open

Interior: Other

Appliances: Cooktop - Electric, Dishwasher, Disposal, Range/Oven-Electric

Utilities: City Water; City Sewer;

This is an actual listing on a bank foreclosure website. The text of the listing indicated that the appliances were there, not stripped, and it appears there would be some repairs but nothing extensive.

First, it's very possible that this home can be purchased for significantly less than the asking price, but let's be conservative again and assume that it will cost you $90,000. It needs about $5,000 in work before we could take on a tenant. Here are the numbers:

- $18,000 down and $72,000 financed.
- $550/month payment (we'll allow $600 for misc.), and should rent for $1,410 based on square footage, but let's use $1,375/month.
- Cash flow = ($1,375 - $600) x 11 months = $8,525/year.
- NOW we're talking!
- With $5,000 for repairs, $23,000 in cash is invested.
- ROI = $8,525 / $23,000 = 37%

The reality in your area could be anywhere inside these example results we've presented. However, these are all positive cash flow properties with very nice ROI numbers.

You're doing this for multiple properties. Fall in love with the numbers, not the house. Be out there working these numbers on a group of possible homes. Narrow down the pack, and look for potential tenants to make your final decision on which property to buy.

DO YOU HAVE TENANTS? YOU SHOULD.

Before you make decisions and offers on properties, you should be looking for tenants. Advertising for the area, as well as the other techniques we mentioned earlier, should give you a list of potential tenants who want to live in the area of the homes you're considering. And they'll want the features and amenities, as well.

When supply meets demand, lifetime cash flow results.

ACTION STEPS

1. Do rental research based on your financial abilities and goals right now. In other words, don't look for $2,000/month rental homes when your ability to buy dictates homes in types and sizes renting for $1,000.
2. Start searching the MLS and foreclosure listing websites for homes that are within the basic price range and feature set you've determined to be rentable.
3. Narrow down the possibilities to three or four homes and run the numbers.

WHAT'S NEXT?

We're going to take you through a home purchase transaction from the initial offer through the closing. It's going to be a thorough explanation of what's going to happen and what to watch out for.

CHAPTER 16

From Offer Through Closing: Your First Property

You did your searches, viewed properties, ran CMAs, and finally "loved one set of numbers". You went back and viewed the property again, taking your handyman with you to help you spot condition issues that could change your numbers or opinion. You found a few small things to fix, but nothing jumped out to tarnish the deal.

This is a listed property and you're working through your real estate agent team member, so you call him up to make an offer. He's been with you to the property and is familiar with your goals and ready to "write it up". In this chapter we're going to take you through the process from the first negotiations with the seller through picking up the keys at the closing.

HOW MUCH TO OFFER

You think it's a great house, but mostly you love the numbers. So the only way you want to end up the owner of this house is if you can negotiate a deal that fits your numbers and produces the ROI and cash flow you want.

The listed asking price for the home is $139,000, and it's been reduced in price one time. You have enough cash to put 20% down for a mortgage. However, you've determined that the only way the numbers will work for you is to buy the home at $135,000 or lower.

When discussing the initial offer with your real estate agent, you have several things in mind.

- It's been on the market longer than the average Days on Market (DOM) for the area.
- The price reduction was over a month ago, but it was well after the property was first listed.

- The current price is lower than comparable properties in the area, and it's the only home in this neighborhood priced such that you your numbers work.
- The home seems to be in great condition, and you shouldn't have to spend much money to make it rentable. (Of course, this is pending inspection results after you're under contract.)
- Your rental research shows there is demand for comparable rentals in the area, and you should obtain a nice cash flow given the normal rents commanded by similar homes.
- The sellers have owned the home for five years, so they should have some equity in it. A check at the courthouse shows that their mortgage five years ago was recorded in the amount of $110,000.
- You want to pay no more than $134,000 for the home, and a quick calculation from recent MLS sold properties shows sold prices coming in about 4% lower than list prices overall, which would be about $133,400 in this case.
- A few other properties met your numbers requirements, so it would not be a terrible thing to walk away from this deal. While it looks like your price number is possible, you need to start with a first offer of $129,000.

As you can see, there are many things to think about when you're going into a negotiation of this size. It can help to find out the motivations of the seller(s). However, the area dictates whether you can get this type of information or not. It may be offered to you, as seen in the statement that they're moving for job relocation, but sometimes you can't determine why they're selling.

Of course, if it's a short sale situation, you know there is a motivated seller trying to get out from under the costs of the home. If it's a foreclosure, we know the bank's motivation. In this case, you'll focus on the homeowners and their reasons for selling.

The Lowball Offer

While this situation indicates that you should keep the offer reasonable, there can be situations where your offer would be well below the asking price. We talked about one when we discussed foreclosure properties. If you are bargain hunting and have other options, making low offers can work for you now and then. Sometimes it will backfire, upsetting a seller and terminating negotiations. Sometimes they'll counter offer and continue to negotiate for a while.

In this case, the seller had reduced the price by $12,000 about a month ago. This seems to indicate that they're motivated to sell, but they're now at the best price in the neighborhood. In fact, that's how they grabbed your interest, through an email alert from your real estate agent's system that showed an excellent price reduction.

Balancing all of the considerations, including the fact that you already have interest from possible tenants, you think that a $129,000 offer is the way to go. While you want to buy it at the best price possible, settling in at around $134,000 would be a roughly equal compromise between you and the sellers.

THE PURCHASE CONTRACT

Whether you call it a contract, an offer, or something else, you'll want to get started on the paperwork. In areas where attorneys handle this type of transaction, they'll prepare the purchase contract documents. It's far more common, however, for the real estate agent to prepare the offer using forms mandated by the state and provided by state real estate associations.

These contract forms are usually developed by a team of attorneys and real estate professionals, and are designed to protect both buyer and seller. In most cases, they are the forms the real estate agent must use. While they can modify them to a certain extent, too much variation could be considered practicing law without a license.

Whether an attorney or real estate agent handles the deal, the steps of a real estate purchase, as well as its contingencies, will be the same. It's important to remember that the group of businesses and people involved in getting this deal through to closing generally want it to close.

While some will get paid even if the deal doesn't close, most will be disappointed and without compensation if it doesn't. You're the one bringing the money to the table, through your down payment and mortgage, so you should never hesitate to ask questions or require explanations for what's going on.

Contingencies

A "contingency" is a condition that, if it happens, will bring about a certain result. There are many contingencies in real estate contracts, some of which are expected to happen and some that you don't want to happen. They can be as small and mundane as the stated contingency that "earnest money will be deposited upon acceptance of the contract by all parties". In other words, we're negotiating, but when we agree and sign the contract, the buyer will put up the earnest money.

There are many areas of a purchase contract that contain contingencies, and they can be part of every step of the path from contract to closing. Here are some examples of contingencies:

- Additional earnest money will be required at certain stages of the process.
- The seller may be required to submit certain disclosures.
- The buyer must approve disclosures as they are provided.
- The buyer must obtain certain property inspections.
- The buyer's requirements for repairs after inspection must be met.
- The buyer must be approved for homeowner insurance.
- The buyer's mortgage must be approved.
- Title insurance must be provided.
- Old liens and claims against the property must be extinguished.
- An approved survey must be provided.
- The property must appraise at or above the purchase price.
- Certain documents must be filed and deeds approved by the lender.
- The buyer and seller must approve various documents or actions before along the way.

Obviously you can expect there to be many places where a certain event can change, or stop, the course of the transaction. These contingencies also carry due dates and deadlines. You should not just rely upon your real estate agent or attorney to meet all deadlines. Since missing just one deadline can create problems, get a schedule of what needs to happen when, and then monitor the progress of the deal, reminding people of deadlines, if necessary.

In our example deal, the contract is being written up with all of the standard contingencies, including property inspections. However, in reading the listing and viewing the property, you notice that there is a really nice outdoor portable storage building that isn't mentioned in the listing as being included in the deal.

You have it placed in the contract as a contingency. Your offer is contingent upon the outdoor storage building remaining with the property and passing from seller to buyer. That's an example of a contingency that pops up often for items like hot tubs, playground equipment, and even yard ornaments.

Disclosures

Normally disclosures are made by the seller as to the condition of the property and other factors that could influence the buyer's decision to buy and at what price. Some of these disclosures are available prior to the contract. For example, many online MLS listings will provide access to certain disclosures about the property.

Generally the contract will specify the disclosures the seller must provide to the buyer, when they are to be made available to the buyer, and the rights of each party if there are disputes over the disclosures. Before making an offer, read and understand any disclosures that are already available. During the process from contract to closing, there may be further disclosures. Be just as careful to go over them and take action if required.

THE OFFER & NEGOTIATIONS

Submission of the Offer

If you are working with real estate agents through the MLS, your next step after signing an offer is to give it to the seller's agent who then presents it to the seller. In some areas, you and/or your agent can be present when the offer is presented, though you must then leave while the seller and their agent discuss it. This isn't done often, since real estate agents usually don't like this procedure. In fact, real estate agents usually don't inform the buyers that this is even possible.

Generally, unless you have reason to be concerned that the offer won't be presented at all, the process will work just fine without you being there, and you'll get a response from the seller within the time specified in the contract.

If you're working directly with the seller, you would then be presenting your own offer, or your real estate agent would present it for you if they're involved. This can happen with For Sale By Owner (FSBO) properties that advertise they will pay a commission to an agent bringing a buyer. You could also be presenting your own offer in a short sale situation.

The Hard Line Deal

There is nothing wrong with a strong negotiation stance that works the seller down to their "rock bottom" price or lower. However, remember that there are still some negotiations to come. If your inspections turn up issues that cause you to ask for repairs or monetary credits, the seller may have no room to give. Deals fall out over repairs and other post-price-negotiation items all of the time. Just be prepared for a "NO" to further concessions if you've really nailed the seller down tightly on price.

The Counter Offer

Of course, the seller could accept your very first offer as written, but that will rarely happen if you're making offers with the strategy of getting the best price you can. So the response from the seller will normally be a counter offer. Counter offers aren't always about price. Almost any contingency in the contract can be negotiated through a counter offer, such as:

1. The price or earnest money amount.
2. Closing dates or other delivery and deadline dates.
3. Buyer financing, such as down payment.
4. That storage building we mentioned earlier.
5. Who pays certain closing costs.

Item 3 is questioned by some buyers. If the contract has the buyer outline the type of mortgage they intend to get and their proposed down payment, as many do, the seller can negotiate those items as well. Let's say that it's a decent market. Sellers are getting showings, and the home you're offering to buy hasn't been on the market very long. You make a price offer and the contract has you spell out that you're going to get a conventional loan with 10% down.

The seller could counter offer that they want you to agree to a 20% down payment if it's needed to get the mortgage. They are simply looking for a stronger buyer and more assurance that this deal can happen and this can happen even when you've submitted a pre-approval letter from your mortgage broker. The seller won't care if you end up using only 10% down, since they just want the strongest possibility of approval from the outset.

Pre-approval for Mortgage

If you need financing to purchase a home, you should always get a pre-approval letter from your mortgage broker or lender for at least the amount of the purchase price. This letter states that preliminary checks have been done, and based on the appraisal of the property and other factors, the lender is pre-approving you for a loan.

It's definitely not a full approval, and things can turn up that may cause you to be turned down for the loan, but it's the best you can do before it's a deal. This letter is required by many sellers before they'll consider an offer, since they don't want to take their property off the market for a contract that could easily fall apart over financing.

Counter offers can go back and forth, with some deals getting done with one or two, and others requiring many more. The good news is that it's not a dead deal as long as you're negotiating.

Using Tenants To Get Into Financing

Since we're on the subject of financing, let's talk about how tenants can help you obtain a mortgage. Having tenants waiting to lease the home you're buying is great from two perspectives. You know you'll have income very quickly after closing (unless the property requires major work). You can also get a letter from the tenants, sometimes called an "Intent to Lease". This is a letter stating that these tenants want to lease the home starting on a certain date.

Most property purchases can close anywhere from 30 to 60 days after the purchase contract is signed, and this happens to be the same time frame in which most tenants are going to move. They usually give 30 days or more notice to their current landlord, so their timing and yours are hopefully in line.

This letter can help you to qualify for the mortgage. Rules change and lenders have differing requirements and limits, but sometimes this letter will make the difference in getting a loan or in receiving favorable terms for the loan.

Your goal for a first property purchase should be to keep it simple. Find a property that doesn't need major work and will be ready to generate rental income almost immediately. Timing your closing close to the end of the month will allow you to put that tenant into the property just days after you own it.

Rent for First Payment Cash Flow

In U.S. mortgages, interest is paid in arrears, meaning that when you make a payment, the interest portion is paying for the previous month's interest or use of the money. Making a payment on March 1 would include the interest for February.

So let's say that you're closing your U.S. loan on April 27th. At closing you would be charged an amount equal to the interest on the loan for the period through the end of the month of April, which is three days' worth of interest. This means you won't have to make your first payment until June 1st. The June payment would pay the interest for May with the remainder applied toward the principal amount of the loan.

Think about how it will improve your initial cash flow to have your tenants ready to move in. If they're moving in on May 1, you get first and last month's rent, which you can use to pay some of your closing costs. You'll get another rent payment when your first payment is due. This is pretty nice cash flow management, since your rent is more than your payment, and you're getting three months rent by the time that first payment is due.

How We Bought Our First Property

> "Hey Michael, I found the perfect second house to start making this a real business. Now it's your turn. Go find some money!"
> "Okay, you go find some tenants, because I'm going to go get us some low-money-down financing, but we'll still need closing costs".

The second property that we bought didn't come as soon as it could have. We didn't have the knowledge and tools that we have now and that we're sharing with you for your business. However, by the time we did figure it out, our second deal was a breeze.

While zero down deals aren't around anymore, this deal is a good example of getting creative in financing your deals. We found a zero down loan and used our tenant's money to get the deal done. We had tenants ready to move in. Here's what we did:

- The new tenants paid first and last month rent for our second home.
- The tenants in our first home paid their rent.
- We closed and used those rent receipts to pay closing costs and move our tenants in.

It's still possible to get 5% to 10% down payment loans nowadays. Once you own a property or two, you may be able to use the equity in your owned properties to finance the next one. Using a HELOC (Home Equity Line of Credit) or refinancing one home can free up enough cash for the down payment on another. Lining up your tenants and having them ready to move in can provide the remaining cash that you need for closing costs to get the home purchased and occupied.

IT'S A DEAL – WHAT'S NEXT

Once you're past all of the counter offers and you agree to all the terms in the contract and counters, you sign the deal and start the process toward closing. While processes overlap and the sequence varies, let's run through the things that are going to happen between that contract agreement and getting the keys at closing.

Title Insurance Search & Binder/ Commitment

While the process can differ in the U.S. and Canada, title insurance is a factor in most deals. Once the policy is issued at closing, it insures the legal owner against threats to their ownership that arise later. These threats could involve anything from mortgage fraud to encroaching fences or outright claims by others that they own all or a portion of the property.

When the deal is presented to a title company, a search of the property's title history is the first order of business. If an attorney is doing the closing, then that attorney or someone of their choosing will do a title search. This search is designed to trace the ownership of the property back in time, as well as to discover any liens or other potential problems with title.

Once the search is complete, assuming there isn't some really bad "cloud" on the title, the title insurer will issue a binder or commitment document that promises that the policy will be issued at closing. This document will specifically state any contingencies that must be satisfied for the issue of the policy, as well as items not covered. These are called "Requirements and Exceptions".

Requirements include things like payment of all taxes up to the date of the closing, satisfaction of all mortgages and liens against the property, and even some documents that may be required due to a divorce and joint ownership. These are normal requirements and usually are handled quickly and easily.

Exceptions are normally not a problem, either. Anything that's recorded in relation to the property, such as easements, will be excepted from coverage. An example would be an easement for the electric company along a property line for five feet of the property to maintain buried electric lines. This is already something that's been agreed to by previous owners, and it's a matter of record, so the title company will not cover you if you build a nice patio on that five foot border and the electric company jack-hammers it to work on their line.

Another more common example would be recorded Homeowner Association documents and Covenants. If the recorded documents say that you can't have your boat parked in your driveway, then you can't later make a title insurance claim that they're restricting your rights as an owner. You knew this going in because it was in your binder.

Inspections

Very quickly after contract signing, you'll want to begin the process of setting up property inspections. There will be deadlines for inspections and for any demands or objections you may have as a result of what the inspections find. You'll want to be present for all inspections. Feel free to ask questions, since you're usually the one paying the inspectors.

In some areas, this is accomplished with an "option" period, during which you have a certain number of days to satisfy yourself as to the condition of the property. If you make no demands or objections during that period, then the inspection contingency is considered removed, and you move on toward closing.

In many other areas, the process is managed by actual due dates in the contract. You will need to have inspections completed by certain dates, and you'll have a certain time frame in which to object to conditions and ask for repairs or other concessions. If you miss deadlines, you can miss your chance to get out of a deal due to inspection results and to have your earnest money returned.

If unexpected problems turn up by inspections, there will be a process for dealing with this outlined in the contract. You will be able to enter another negotiation phase with the seller and ask for repairs or perhaps monetary concessions due to inspection problems. At this point, if an agreement can't be reached, the deal will terminate according to the terms of the contract.

Appraisal

We discussed earlier that you will want to try and be present during the appraisal and gave reasons for you to be there. If the appraisal comes in low, it will either kill the deal or result in a price negotiation. If it comes in at an acceptable number, the lender will proceed to work toward full approval of the loan.

Survey

When the survey is ordered depends on local custom, who's paying for it, and the contingency dates in the contract. As a survey is generally only usable for a certain period of time, the tendency is to order it to be done only after certain other contingencies are met so that the money is less likely to be wasted due to a failed deal.

The surveyor will do his job, and you needn't be there. As the buyer, you'll be given a copy of the completed survey so you'll have the chance to review it to make sure that there aren't any surprises. If there are, such as an easement for a billion volt power line over the top of the house, you can take the action outlined by the contract for survey issues.

Mortgage

The lender will be working through your application and loan documents. They will also receive copies of the title insurance binder and survey. The lender will be sure to protect their own interests and will have an endorsement for coverage under your title insurance.

Deals that don't close on the planned date are frequently those with mortgage document problems. The problem may not even be your loan qualification. It is more likely that certain documents haven't reached the lender in a time frame that allows their underwriters to do their job. Just be aware that you should take an active interest in the movement of documents and the meeting of all deadlines.

The Closing

Let's get some terminology figured out here. "Closing" can be the same as "Settlement", and "Funding" means that money has changed hands. Generally, you won't get the keys until they get their money. Don't time your deal too close to the end of the month in case there's a problem with closing and funding. Sometimes funding may be a day later than settlement.

Depending on local custom and other factors, you may or may not ever meet the sellers, since many closings are only attended by the party or parties on one side of the deal. Your mortgage broker and real estate agent should be there, but it may just be the three of you along with the attorney handling your closing or the title company's closing person.

You'll sign a large stack of documents that are mostly related to the mortgage. You'll receive copies of everything you sign, and there will be other documents sent to you later. Your deed, signed by the sellers, will be recorded at the courthouse after funding as evidence of your ownership, and you will receive an official copy of that recorded deed.

You'll also receive instructions as to how much your first and subsequent payments will be and where to send them. Then you get what you came for--the keys!

Go check out your new rental home and start getting it ready for those tenants you have ready to move in.

ACTION STEPS

If you're not ready to actually write up a deal on a house, no problem. If you are, then just implement what you've learned in this chapter. Otherwise, meet with your real estate agent and ask for blank contracts so you can become familiar with the terms and conditions in them.

WHAT'S NEXT?

We're going to market for tenants, learn about applications, and talk about the tenant interview process.

CHAPTER 17

Marketing, Finding &
Interviewing Tenants

We've discussed marketing for tenants a bit earlier, but let's go into more detail here, as well as discuss the application and interview process.

MARKETING & ADVERTISING FOR TENANTS

Your marketing and advertising plan can grow with your business. It doesn't have to require any real budget at the beginning. The different methods and marketing media can be selected based on how they fit your market area and tenant demographics. You don't have to spend a dime to implement some of them, and others are inexpensive yet effective if done properly.

Newspaper Classifieds

We touched on these earlier. A continuous ad in the classifieds under rental homes can be a good investment. Keeping it short makes it inexpensive, plus you may be able to negotiate a reduced rate for a contract to run regularly.

It can be as short and sweet as:

"Great homes for rent in the best neighborhoods. Call ###-####".

Remember that you don't necessarily need to have a home available. You can learn from your callers the types of homes they want and use information in your purchase plans. You may also be able to purchase a home to fit a tenant. You'll have the time to make that happen if they call you early enough before their planned move.

If you do have a home that will be available soon, then running a longer ad with specifics for that home would be a good use of classifieds. Renters start looking even before they make a decision to move, since they want to see if what's available is worth the hassle of moving. Here are some ads in a small town weekly newspaper:

1 Bdrm./1 ba., 1019 sq. ft., fully furnished. River acess, carport & small fenced yard. No dogs. $685/mo. +
utilities. 1 year lease.
Available now.

2 bdrm./1 ba. 1400 sq. ft. brick/stone flooring, kiva fireplace, office space, hot water
baseboard heat, W/D, large yard, pets ok. $850/mo.
+ utilities.
Available March 29th.

Adobe home recently remodeled. 3 bdrm./ 3 ba. Kiva fireplace, fruit trees; washer/dryer hookups. Natural gas;
community water;
septic. $1,100/mo.
+ utilities.
One year lease.
Available now.

3 bdrm./2 ba. pueblo style home with large fenced yard on 1.25 acres features Saltillo tile and skylights, patio,
radiant heat and garage. Nice mountain views. $1,150/mo.
+ utilities.
One year lease.
Available now.

3 bdrm./2 ba. on 1 acre with 3 car carport, workshop/studio plus a shed for tools,
completely fenced, one pet ok. $1,200/mo.
+ utilities.
Available now.

Craigslist

Craigslist is invaluable as a marketplace for your rental business. It's free, and it allows you to not only place ads but to find out what others are looking for, as well. Because it's free, some renters will actually run "looking for rental" ads that provide information you may want to factor into future purchase decisions.

Looking for A Home to Rent - (Sioux city) apts wanted

$500 Family needs a house - (Sioux City/Leeds) apts wanted

Thu Feb 24

$550 URGENT HOME NEEDED - apts wanted

Wed Feb 23

Looking to rent 3 br house or duplex - (Riverside/Briar Cliff area) apts wanted

$750 Need House or Townhouse 3 to 4 Bed - (Riverside/North Sioux/West of Casselman) apts wanted

Tue Feb 22

$1 3-4 BR WANTED - (Sioux City Area) apts wanted

Just a quick look at one town's Craigslist ads for rentals found two or three renters actually asking for rental properties.

However, you can run your Craigslist ads to get rental applicants, much like you would do in newspaper classified ads. You can be as wordy as you want, describing specific properties or running that general ad to just get prospective tenants to call or email you. In fact, because Craigslist users can search based on words in the listing, you want to have features and other things about the property written there to attract that renter to your ad via a search.

One advantage of Craigslist is the email response mechanism. You can begin to build an email list of renters for when you are buying a new property.

$650 / 3br - Your Dream House - pic

$850 / 5br - 5 BR 3 BA house in Morningside - (308 S. Helen)

$525 AA Completely Refurbished Beautiful 1+ BR - (1037 27th St , Sioux City) pic

	Sun Mar 06

$425 / 1br - Morningside 1BR Lower level - (2514 S Rustin)

$350 / 2br - @ Bdrm Single garage - (Pierson, Iowa)

	Sat Mar 05

$850 / 3br - Acreage - (Close to Sioux City)

	Fri Mar 04

$25 / 1br - Senior Living-Brand New 1 Bedroom Units-Rent Based On Income - (N. Sioux City, SD) img

$520 / 2br - 2 bed room one bath - (morningside, sioux city)

The screen shot above shows some rental ads from Craigslist in Sioux City, S.D.

Bulletin Boards

Whether you're in a college town or you're renting properties near a major employer, there are going to be opportunities to place rental ads on company or school bulletin boards. There may also be coffee houses in the area that are frequented by renters and have bulletin boards you can post on. This is a great resource when you want to advertise a specific property. You can build a small document in a word processor with a photo and your ad text. It's free and effective marketing.

Social Networking

For more free marketing, consider setting up a Facebook page and a Twitter account for your rental homes. The Facebook page can become the permanent home for images and descriptions of your homes, much like having your own website. The Twitter account can be automatically set up to receive new stuff from your Facebook page, or you can work it in the other direction--posting availability notices on Twitter and having them show up automatically on your Facebook page.

You can save searches on Twitter that will notify you based on key phrases like "rental in YourTown", or "need a house to rent in YourTown" to catch discussions going on in your area about home rentals. If you are alerted to Tweets or Facebook postings by people looking for rentals, you can enter the discussion and point them to your Facebook page or a website.

Website

Once you have several properties, you may want to set up your own website to promote them. This can be FREE or very inexpensive. It requires a bit more work, but it can save you a lot of time in the future when you get interest from your other Internet marketing efforts. You can have multiple photos and all the text you want about features and amenities.

Should you receive interest via email, you can just send the potential tenant a link to your website with all of the details. You can even do video to promote your properties, and it's all free advertising on a website. If someone should locate your website doing Web searches for rentals, he will find your phone number as well as a link to your email. These are the primary ways in which you will market for tenants in the future. Of course there are other methods and media, but these are the most cost-effective and they work.

TALKING TO TENANTS ON THE FIRST CONTACT

Sometimes you'll be talking to prospective tenants when you don't have a property ready for occupancy, since your marketing is running continuously. However, once they're on the phone or corresponding via email, you can get valuable information from them, and possibly still end up with them as a tenant based on their timeline and yours.

If they are calling about a specific property and you're ready to lock them up as a tenant, your first contact should be a friendly one, and you should be careful as to which questions you ask. You are subject to certain housing and equal opportunity laws, so you'll want to be very familiar with what you can and cannot ask a renter. You may even want to run your question list past your attorney.

Let's get this out of the way now, as it's also important in your application process. If you can't ask them on the phone, you can't ask them on paper either. It's not something to be fearful of, but you always want to be law-abiding in all aspects of your business operations.

If you advertised the property for a specific rental amount, they should be able to pay that, since they've contacted you. If you haven't advertised a certain amount, you will want to get past any objections to the amount of the rent in this first conversation. Once you have discussed the property a bit and the costs of rent and utilities, if there is still interest, it's time to schedule a showing.

PROPERTY SHOWINGS

"Scott, there are seven groups all waiting to see our only rental! Get over here and give me some help showing it".
"I'll help Michael, but let's rush them through because we need to go out right after and buy another one!"

Remember this box from Chapter 2? We're getting you past our mistakes yet again. We enthusiastically advertised a property with a date and time for showings, and ended up with a bunch of people there all at once. Doing this was a mistake, though; it makes everyone uncomfortable since they perceive pressure and competition for the house. And it makes showing it a hassle because there are too many people there at once.

Showings should not overlap. If you have several people who want to see the property, it's OK to set up the showings close enough together so that you're not sitting there waiting. However, try to keep the two groups from spending too much time together on the property.

Security should also be a concern. You don't know these people, so make sure that someone in your family--a friend or your partner--knows when you'll be at the home for a showing. You might even have a pre-arranged distress signal you can use by calling them on your cell from the house. You must always be aware of safety issues.

Point out features and neighborhood amenities, but allow them to walk through and spend whatever time they want in each room. When they arrive, you might ask them if they want to go through on their own first or if they want you to accompany. Some people want to talk to each other about it without their future landlord being right there. Be quick and complete in answers to their questions.

If they're showing interest, this can be the beginning of your complete "tenant interview" as well. You will have an application ready (we'll discuss in the next chapter), but first you need to determine if you want to move forward with these tenants.

THE INTERVIEW

If you see them in a favorable light based on your contact during the showing, you may sit down right there at the house, at a coffee shop, or at your office if you have one. You can discuss their needs in renting the home, find out where they work, and get a feel for their stability. You can ask how long they have lived in the area.

You can prepare them for the next step, as well. Telling someone with credit problems that you'll be running a credit check and checking rental references will generally cause them to bring up issues right then, since they don't want to go through an application process for nothing.

If appropriate, take notes and ask your questions at this meeting. If they want time to think about it or express any hesitation, set up a phone call to check back with them in a day or two. You may or may not be able to get through your interview questions in this first meeting, but you can finish up on the phone.

It's a great feeling to have several interested tenants for a property. You can feel good about having choices, and you can be selective. Once you have the right tenant selected, you can move on to the actual application and rental/lease agreement.

ACTION STEPS

1. Contact your local newspaper for classified rates and any advertising frequency discounts.
2. Familiarize yourself with Craigslist and check out some ads looking for local rentals.
3. Start working on a list of interview questions and make sure they're legal.

WHAT'S NEXT?

We're going to get into the paperwork and landlord-tenant topics. We'll talk about deposits, rental and lease agreements, inspections, and more.

CHAPTER 18

It's Yours: Rental Property Legal Move-in and Move-out

There's no reason that you can't be a great landlord, both from your perspective and your tenants'. Being a great landlord from your tenants' perspective involves taking care of the property and responding to their issues. From your perspective, it's getting the rent paid on time, keeping vacancy and credit losses to a minimum, and minimizing damage and repair costs.

While very few concerned landlords have trouble taking care of their tenants, they tend to have problems taking care of their landlord and ownership needs. The problems begin with landlords wanting to be nice and trusting, so they don't complete the paperwork and conduct due diligence up front. Accepting a tenant on a handshake with a "gut feeling" that they're OK can work much of the time, but it's not going to work all of the time.

```
Landlord Joke:

   A large family, with seven children, moved to a
new city. They were having a difficult time finding
an apartment to live in. Many apartments were large
enough, but the landlords objected to the large
family. After several days of searching, the father
asked the mother to take the four younger children
to visit the cemetery, while he took the older three
to find an apartment. After they had looked most of
the morning they found a place that was just right.

   Then the landlord asked the usual question, "How
many children do you have?"
   The father answered with a deep sigh, "Seven...but
four are with their dear mother in the cemetery". He
got the apartment!
```

The Tenant Application Form

You should have a thorough tenant application form that allows you to get a great deal of information from them before any decisions are made. Using the information on the form, you should check their credit, call their rental references, and verify previous address and rental history information. Just asking them a few questions verbally can result in a lot of regret on your part. The application at a minimum should have:

- Full name(s).
- If two unrelated people are to be tenants, get a full application from each of them.
- Social Security Number(s) – be sure to safeguard this information according to privacy laws.
- Previous residence history back at least three to five years.
- Contact information for family.
- Rental references.
- Employment and income information.

Research laws on privacy, civil rights, and your area's landlord/ tenant regulations to be sure that you don't include questions that are illegal to ask. These could include family and lifestyle questions and others. Discrimination complaints are not something you want to deal with.

You can start with an application form marketed as legal for your state of residence. A Google search for "state legal tenant application" turned up a number of sites where you can get a form advertised as legal for each state. However, it wouldn't hurt to get it blessed by your attorney, as well. Your attorney may even want to add items to the application.

There are certain disclosures and other requirements for tenant and landlord agreements. One of the legal sites offering forms had these items listed as additional forms to consider:

LEASE PACKAGE DOCUMENTS

These are just some of the 26 documents you can select to include with your lease...
- Lead-Based Paint EPA Pamphlet
- Lead-Based Paint EPA Disclosure
- Pet Agreement
- Zero Tolerance for Criminal Activity
- Co-Signer Agreement
- Welcome Letter
- Emergency Shut-Off Instructions for Electric, Water and Gas
- All Addendums, Disclosures, and Information Documents
- Include a lease cover page and a dynamically created table of contents

RULES AND REGULATIONS

This is an example of some of the selectable rules and regulations in the lease...
- Late fees are strictly enforced and any unpaid fees will not be waived
- The Tenant must notify Landlord of any changes in employment
- The Tenant will be responsible for any fine and/or violation that is imposed on the Landlord due to the Tenant' negligence
- The Tenant agrees to test smoke detectors periodically as well as maintain operational batteries at all times.

This can seem pretty complex, but it's something you need to do right, and you only need to get it together once. Set up your forms and interview process before you find your first prospective tenant, and you'll find that it will become second nature over time. Some people don't enjoy calling employers and references, but it's something you need to do. No matter how uncomfortable you are checking someone out this way, you'll find it a lot more uncomfortable evicting them.

You may be able to use a tenant screening company specializing in this process. You may find their fee acceptable in return for getting all of these reference, employment, and credit check items done for you.

About credit scores: One study in 2010 found that as many as one third of U.S. residents had credit scores that would probably not be high enough to easily qualify for a conventional mortgage. While this sounds great for landlords since it leads to a large supply of renters, how do you decide what score is acceptable?

You can have an absolute bottom line for credit score, and a range that causes you to be more selective if you have multiple applicants. However, some people who have been through rough financial times and have less than stellar credit scores may be great and reliable tenants. Some who have excellent credit scores can turn out to be real problems. You do your best, but sometimes life just gives us challenges.

Calling Rental and Employment References

Call previous landlords and ask more than just if the tenant rented from them. Ask questions about their behavior, rental payment history, attention to the rules, and treatment of the rental property.

- Did they always pay their rent on time?
- Did they ever have pets?
- Did they get along well with other tenants?
- Did you ever have any problems with them?
- Is there anything else I should know?

Most landlords will share this type of information with you, since they would appreciate the same consideration if they were calling you.

As for employers, past and present, you should have a prepared list of questions and a form to record their answers for your files. You want to ask questions that give you insight into the prospective tenant's past, present, and future.

- How long have they worked at the company (or did they work there, if it's a previous employer)?
- Is their current job secure and do they have a reasonable prospect of ongoing employment?
- Are they a good employee?
- Can you describe their character?
- Can you confirm the income indicated on their rental application, and is it a salary, an hourly wage, or compensation based on commissions?

You may not get all of these questions answered by an employer, since some people may be concerned about legal liability, but be sure to ask them.

Qualifying Students as Tenants

The process of qualifying students as good tenants can be a little tricky. When attending school, many tenants will not have steady employment, or they may not work at all. They may be attending school on scholarships or grants, or their parents are giving them financial assistance. Frequently, income can be from a combination of sources.

Always Check with Parents

Checking with a student's parents is critical, since they will likely be candid about their child's ability to make rent. Parents know that they will probably be called upon to bail out their child in a pinch. They want to make sure that their child has a roof over their head, so they will be a good backup if a check bounces or the rent is late. Develop a relationship with the parents.

You should call the parents and try to get them to sign as a guarantor for the rent. This is the best case scenario, since you now have signatures for two people who are promising to pay the rent and honor the lease terms. A call to the parents is usually appreciated, and they can give you insight as to whether their child should be taking on the rent that you'll be charging them.

Roommates

With students, it's frequent to have roommate renters, with four to six being a common number. That's how we were living as college students when we had that "aha moment". That's how we rented out the first home we purchased. It's not a situation to fear, but there are special considerations with a group.

We usually try to contact at least one parent for each of the roommates. Using email, we inform them of the lease terms and try to get some response back. The students sign the lease as a group, but each are individually bound by the lease terms and are responsible for his or her portion of the rent.

If one roommate decides to move out, she will be held responsible for their lease, so you want to make it clear to her that she should be looking for a replacement to relieve her of responsibility. Depending on the law where you rent out the property, you may be able to require as much as 60 to 90 days notice if one tenant is leaving. This gives the tenant and you time to look for someone to take that place.

There is also an incentive for the other roommates to find someone to fill the vacancy. Let them know that you're looking for someone. They have a choice of finding someone they like and can live with, or you're going to have to fill the spot with a stranger. Everybody has an incentive to find the right person.

THE LEASE AGREEMENT

The same legal considerations apply to the lease agreement as to the rental application. Even more care should be taken to adopt a lease agreement that meets all legal requirements and protects your interests and your investment. This is a legal contract so everything should be in writing.

Deposits and Payments

The lease must clearly set out the terms of rent payment--amounts, due dates, and any penalties that you can legally charge the tenant if the rent is late. Make sure that the tenant understands what constitutes "late rent", and that they know what's going to happen if they are late with their payments. It should specify your procedure and the penalties you can assess for bounced checks, as well.

We want first and last months' rents in advance, and record that we have received this money on the lease itself, making it the receipt for the tenant. We also require the full legal amount we can charge as a damage deposit. Check your area's laws on this. We want the tenant to have an incentive to leave the place in good condition. The lease should be very explicit as to how the cost of damage will be determined.

There's no getting around the fact that pets bring damage concerns. However, not allowing pets can significantly reduce your pool of available tenants. You can and should limit the types and sizes of pets, if you allow them at all. Check local law and charge extra rent if allowed. Increase the damage deposit, as well.

Also, follow the law when you determine how long after move-out before you'll send them the damage deposit money owed. Some lease agreements have spaces for initials next to all of these important money-related items. It helps to show that they were pointed out specifically to the tenant.

Other Lease Terms

When we sit down to sign the lease, we set the tone during this half hour or so for our entire future relationship with the tenant. We want to be friendly, but we also want to make sure the tenant understands the terms of the lease and knows that we're serious about enforcing them.

It's usually easy to find standard lease forms that are legal in every state at local office supply stores or online. You may want to run it by your attorney, as well. If it's not clearly specified in the lease, we make sure that we add clauses that state that the landlord is not responsible for loss or damage to tenant property. They are advised to obtain renter's insurance on their personal belongings.

Lease agreements can have any legal terminology you want in them, and we always have rules for how the tenant can use the property, what they can do, and what they can't do. Samples include:

- Tenants cannot use the backyard.
- Tenants are limited to one vehicle parking space on premises.
- There will be no loud music or behavior after 11 PM.
- The tenant agrees to a specified grass cutting schedule.
- The tenant agrees to inform the landlord in advance of any overnight guest staying more than two days.

The lease should specify the allowed occupants of the unit, both in number and possibly even age. Don't worry about requiring specific ages, but if the tenants are a couple with two children, then the lease should state that. You don't want to find that you've suddenly accrued an extra tenant because they invited a friend down on his luck to move in. If you do allow this, it should be your decision and not something they can do because the lease wasn't clear on occupancy.

Signing the Lease

You want to set a professional tone but not an intimidating one. You don't need to sign the lease in your attorney's boardroom. However, you don't want to sign it at the local bar over a beer, either. It's OK to meet at your office or even at a local coffee shop, but be careful that it doesn't seem like just a couple of friends getting together.

Get Organized

A time will come when you have so many tenants that you can't remember all their names and information without recoding it. It is very important that when you grow to this size you stay very organized.

Whether you have 3 tenants or 300, you should have all of their important information recorded in one place. Download our Tenant Tracker chart to help you stay organized and save you time and money!

http://scottsinvestorsedge.com/book-resources/tenant-tracker

MOVE-IN

It's move-in day, and the tenants will be expecting a clean unit in good repair. You will have had repair and cleaning people in the unit, and everything should be in good order. However, things get missed, and your move-in inspection should be very thorough and documented.

At this time you've received the first and last month's rent, but you may want to wait to take the security deposit until this inspection is completed. You will want a very thorough checklist of items, and this inspection can take 45 minutes to an hour. Your tenant will agree to have damage repairs paid for out of their damage deposit, so you want to be certain that all existing damage is recorded to assure that they're treated fairly when they move out.

All furnishings should be out of the unit so that all of the floors and lower wall areas can be seen. You're looking for anything that you would consider being a problem when they move out, from picture hanger holes to a loose handle on the refrigerator. Everything should be recorded.

The checklist should be signed by both you and the tenant, and the same checklist should be used for both move-in and move-out so that conditions are seen right next to each other on the form. A couple of example forms for rental move-in and move-out inspections can be found online here:

http://scottsinvestorsedge.com/book-resources/condition-checklist

You'll be noting any problems, no matter how small, since this will make it clear to the tenant that you're serious about condition issues and damage. They'll feel better knowing that you want to make the unit ideal for them at move-in. You'll want a statement on the checklist or in the lease that says you'll take care of items noted on the move-in checklist within a certain period of time.

Same Move-in Day

Vacancy costs money, so we always try to set up our move-ins immediately when the unit is vacant, bringing in people to clean and repair items while tenants are moving out. We also have moved almost all of our leases to begin on the same day, May 1. While this may seem odd, think about it. We have cleaning and repair people notified and scheduled well in advance, and even rent trucks and dumpsters for this day.

By having all of them come on the same day, we can keep our crews busy, knowing that very little to do at one unit will not be a problem, because they can move on to the next immediately. We enjoy economies of scale this way, since the crews are moving from unit to unit, and they are more efficient this way.

Since we do a lot of student leasing, we like the May 1 date. If we can fill the unit then with a year-long lease, we're in good shape for the school year. If not, we have another shot on September 1. However, if we used September 1 regularly, we could end up with empty units over the winter period.

Utility Service Transfers

The lease should be explicit about the responsibility of tenants to connect and disconnect their utilities and having them in the right name for the period of their lease. Tenants moving out who don't do this could leave you with the liability of having to pay utilities from their move-out until the new tenant puts them in their name.

Give them written instructions and the phone numbers to call to change over utilities. Follow up with them to be sure that it's done.

MOVE-OUT

We'll talk a bit about forced move-out and eviction later. Right now we're addressing the normal end-of-lease move-out. At some point after or very near the removal of all furniture, do the required walk-through inspection of the unit with the tenant. Do it just as thoroughly as the move-in inspection and using the same form that noted problems at move-in.

The tenant needs to be there to see what you see and what you write down, since you'll want them to sign the inspection checklist when it's complete. You want to be fair to your tenants, but you also want to document any items that you consider damaged and for which they're responsible. You'll be paying for the repairs out of their deposit.

Make sure you have a forwarding address from your tenant, since you'll need to mail them a check for any returnable deposit money. It's also just a good idea in case of other issues.

ACTION STEPS

1. Research and adopt checklist and lease forms for your area.
2. Develop clauses and lease agreement additions for any specific properties and for general items like behavior and rules for occupancy and rent payment.
3. Check to make sure you're legal and run things by your attorney if you're not sure.

WHAT'S NEXT?

We'll go through the everyday issues and requirements for management of rental units and tenant relations. There will be information about dealing with problem tenants, as well as general costs and challenges of rental property management.

CHAPTER 19

Property Management

Now that you're past the point of finding tenants and getting them into the unit, let's talk about managing the unit and tenants. It's not just making sure your numbers stay in the black and your property is not damaged; it's also about keeping tenants happy and reducing turnover.

TENANT RELATIONS

Keeping good tenants happy should be one of your main concerns. Turnover costs money because of:

- Lost revenue during vacancy.
- Having to rehab units between tenants.
- The need to market for and move in new tenants.

All of those costs are greatly reduced when turnover is reduced. Keeping tenants happy keeps them in the units, and they really don't like moving, anyway. It usually doesn't take a whole lot of effort to maintain a good relationship with your tenants. When they're happy, they are more likely to overlook minor annoyances and problems, such as your delay in getting to a dripping faucet.

Communication is the foundation for a good landlord/tenant relationship. Since you may want to check out the interior condition of units periodically, approach the question and hopefully get to visit by asking, "How's it going and are there any problems?" Tenants will see this as concern for their well-being and may invite you in. It's not an inspection then; it's a courtesy visit to see if you can help them in any way.

Schedule a visit with your tenant every six months or so. If your lease calls it an inspection, that's fine. The lease and local laws will dictate how often you can inspect and how much notice to give the tenant. You're not there to look for clutter or poor housekeeping. You're there to look for damage or violations of the terms of the lease. We usually drop off a card at Christmas, and visit twice more--once in the spring and once in the fall.

In the spring and fall visits we do a little maintenance, as well. We call them and explain that the fall visit is to check faucets and conditions for the winter and to look for any water leaks. The tenants will appreciate your maintenance, and they'll be happy to let you in to get it done.

After you have three properties or so, you may want to hire a property manager or handyman to make these visits. Scheduling a handyman to do exterior work like clearing downspouts is a call you can make. We ask the tenants to please let the handyman in to look for any other problems that can be corrected. The handyman can then report back to us if there are lease violations or damage issues.

Maintain Goodwill

We drop off Christmas cards and we give gifts as well. A gift certificate to Home Depot will be appreciated and might benefit you, as well. Many tenants will use it to make some improvements to the home, such as new light fixtures or landscaping.

Goodwill is also a function of repair response. When a tenant calls with a problem, it should be handled as quickly and efficiently as possible. We guarantee that necessary repairs will be completed within 24 hours, which is usually not a problem because we have handymen on call. If the washing machine breaks, we want to fix it right away to reduce inconvenience for our tenants. This is greatly appreciated, and we know this because our tenants have told us.

Communication

We have found email to be invaluable as a communication connection with our clients. Just about everyone uses email, and it's free and fast. We remind tenants of their lease expiration dates and keep them informed about maintenance and any other activities that may impact their occupancy.

AVOID PROBLEM TENANTS

Following our instructions should help you minimize or eliminate tenant problems. You've learned how to market for them, interview them, and handle leasing and moving issues. If you do these things properly, you'll almost never have problems with a tenant. However, we all mess up now and then, and you may have made a selection error that will come back to haunt you. This usually happens in two areas:

- Collecting the rent.
- Preventing property damage.

Rent collection can be improved by making it easier for tenants to pay rent. Accepting rent via debit cards, credit cards, or even electronic checks is one way to simplify the process. You don't need a fancy machine or special bank account to do this, either. Setting up a business account with PayPal and connecting it to your bank is an easy way. Yes, there are fees involved, but they are a small percentage of each transaction. You can accept all types of credit cards and electronic checks via PayPal. Tenants may run short of cash at the end of the month, so allowing them to float their own loan by paying rent with a credit card is better than getting an excuse and a late payment.

Debit and credit cards don't bounce, and you don't have to go to the bank to deposit those payments. You simply wait until PayPal notifies you of a payment via email and then transfer it free (with a couple of clicks) into your bank account.

Of course, you can always accept their checks in the mail or dropped off. Some landlords send a stamped envelope to their tenants 10 days before rent is due so they can mail in their check. It's a subtle reminder that works.

When the economy is tough and people are scrimping, you want to make rent payment as easy and flexible as possible. If tenants get paid twice a month, and they tend to run short at the end of the month, allowing them to pay with two payments is one way to be flexible and improve your cash flow, as well.

Late Fees

Learn what the law allows for timing and amount of late fees, and implement a late rent fee policy. It should be spelled out in the lease. A common method is to have the late fee kick in three to five days after the rent is due, and for it to be a set percentage of the rent payment. Depending on the law, charging 5% to 10% of the rent amount may be the way to go.

Rent Subsidies and Tenant Rent Aid

You're encouraging tenants to stay in your unit, developing relationships with them, and making them happy. So it's inevitable that now and then a tenant will run into financial difficulties and have trouble paying their rent in full and on time. It could be due to a job demotion, illness, or a layoff and temporary unemployment. They're in a lease with you, and it can be much better for you if you can find them some help to get through a rough period.

Government rent subsidy programs like CPI in Canada and Section 8 in the U.S. are one resource for tenants having trouble making rent payments. You should become familiar with these programs and have materials on hand to give to tenants in these situations.

We once had a family that had been renting from us for several years, and they fell on hard financial times. They were late on rent several times, and it was becoming a more frequent situation. We looked into available programs and found them rent assistance for a while. However, it became clear that the situation wasn't going to get better, and that they were in over their heads with the rent.

We had a frank talk, and they admitted that they could no longer afford to live in the home. However, we didn't want to evict them, so we got creative and worked out a compromise that allowed them to live there with reduced rent in exchange for maintaining the property and the landscaping. This got them through the summer and gave them time to find somewhere less expensive to live. It didn't cost us that much, since we had been paying someone anyway to do the jobs they took over.

Damage Policy

We talked about stating your policies clearly in the lease agreement, and a damage policy should be one that is clearly explained. The tenants should be made aware of the actions you will take if damage is discovered. They should know if they'll be responsible for the cost, and how you'll collect that amount.

REPAIR & MAINTENANCE BUDGETING

As a landlord, one of your primary responsibilities is to repair things as quickly as possible when they break. If you're not a handyman, it helps to at least learn enough to assess the problem and call the right professional. When they arrive, it's good to have enough knowledge to direct the repair person to the problem and answer questions that will help them to diagnose and repair it.

Remember our recommendation earlier to attend classes at home improvement stores. Buy books and learn about general construction and electrical and plumbing installation and repair. When we discussed After Repair Value, we gave you resources to estimate what repairs and renovation will cost.

Using this knowledge, you need to prepare and put aside a budget for repairs. You don't want to be caught short and surprised by repairs when tenants move out. Repair and maintenance costs are part of your business expenses. Complaining about more cleanup or repair costs than you anticipated isn't the solution. It's much more effective to plan for repairs and maintenance and set aside the money.

We set aside roughly one month's rent for each property to pay for rehab when tenants move out. This is usually more than enough, allowing us to be OK with the infrequent excessive cleanup and rehab for the next tenant's occupancy. The term "preventive maintenance" is the key here. Do ongoing maintenance to keep the property in good shape and help to ward off more expensive emergency breakdowns.

We even schedule two hardcore cleaning visits each year, with our crew doing a thorough cleaning that includes mopping floors and vacuuming the entire home. This impresses the tenants and they see that we're serious about keeping up our properties so they are nice places to live. We schedule one of these cleanings just before their lease is about to expire, putting us out in front of the situation if they move out, since the place is then just a quick light cleaning away from the new tenant's move-in.

FIRE AND SMOKE DETECTOR POLICIES

There isn't much worse that can happen to a home than a fire, even if it's isolated to one room. The smoke and water damage can be very expensive. Then there's your liability as a landlord if the tenant is harmed, or worse, due to a fire. You don't want there to be any doubt that you took every precaution to make the home as safe as possible.

Human lives are irreplaceable and we take fire safety seriously. One thing that we insist upon is that our fire and smoke alarms be interconnected between home levels. If there is a basement, first, and second floor, the detectors on all levels are wired together to go off simultaneously. Sleeping on the second floor, it can be easy to sleep right through a fire or smoke alarm going off in the basement.

While some municipalities have made this interconnection of alarms mandatory, we do it anyway, whether required or not. Immediately upon purchasing a home, we have fire and smoke alarms installed and wired together. We also make sure that they're hard-wired into the home's electrical system to get around dead battery problems. Every visit we or our handymen make to the property, we check the detectors with their test buttons to make sure they are operating.

"Hush" Smoke Alarms

You've probably experienced the "stovetop steak grilling" smoke alarm fiasco. The piercing sound is very annoying, so people's first reaction is to remove the batteries so the alarm will shut up. To counteract this, we install hush alarms. They have a button that will silence them for 15 minutes while the occupants air out the home. This keeps people from removing batteries and forgetting to put them back in.

Not only do we try to inspect detectors and alarms every 60 days or so, we document these inspections in our files. We want to have clear evidence that we've taken every precaution to make our dwelling safe for our tenants.

If you have a number of units, you may want to hire a "fire management company". They'll charge a nominal fee to oversee the operation of all fire and smoke detectors, making regular inspection visits. Should there ever be a fire and the tenant complains that you didn't take adequate precautions, you'll have ample proof that you actively engaged in the right activities to assure their safety and the safety of their personal property.

SMART KEY

The Smart Key system is one of our best tools for both security and cost savings. You can buy this system in most building and hardware stores.

All of our house locks are programmable. With multiple properties, this is a great cost saver because we can rekey and program our locks ourselves. It is a system of rotating keys, with 6 to 8 different keys that can be programmed to different locks.

We don't throw keys out. We rotate them through our properties by rekeying them as tenants move out. We keep records for each house, and make sure that when keys are reused, they are in a home in a different neighborhood. Every 8 or 9 years we will end up rotating through all of the sets of keys.

OTHER EXPENSES

Owning a rental property brings with it many expenses.

- insurance
- taxes
- permits
- utilities
- condo fees

These are necessary components of managing your rental property business, and you'll want to be very aware of how much you'll need to budget for them, as well as ways to minimize them when possible.

Insurance

While anyone who has owned a home with a mortgage will be very aware of the insurance required by the mortgage company, there is another level or two of coverage for rental properties.

- Higher premiums will result due to extra coverage for rental property insurance.
- The landlord is covered for loss of rents if the property is damaged and can't be rented for a period of time.

- Appliances and the structure are covered, but not the personal property of the tenant.
- Liability coverage is extremely important, since your tenant could seek to gain money from you for accidents outside your control, such as slipping and falling on the property.

Develop a good relationship with your insurance agent team member. They can help you to get the coverage you need at better rates as you build experience.

Taxes

Property taxes come with property ownership. Never rely on tenants to pay property taxes, since failure to do so will ultimately result in loss of the property. If you have a mortgage, it's likely that the lender will require escrow payments to have the tax money available, and they'll use a servicer to pay the taxes to protect their investment.

Taxes go up, but rarely go down. They're based on a valuation assessment by your local tax assessor, and they can revisit the property's assessment at any time, especially when property values are increasing.

Your improvements to the property can also result in increased valuation for tax purposes. You should always document your improvement expenses for income tax purposes, since they are normally deductible against rental income.

Utilities

If you have duplex or multiplex properties using common meters, you will normally be paying the utilities for the tenant. However, if each home or unit is separately metered, you'll want to have your tenants pay their own utilities. First, it makes your rent look more appealing, since you do not have to advertise rent at a higher number to account for your utility bills.

However, there's another reason for wanting your tenants to pay their own utilities. They pay attention to their usage when they have to pay that bill every month. Having the utilities as a part of their rent tends to lull them into complacence about how much they're consuming.

Permits

Cities and other municipalities enact building permit legislation for several reasons, but primarily for safety and tax revenue, though not necessarily in that order. While you may be able to replace flooring or paint walls without a permit, you'll definitely need one for electrical or construction projects.

Visit your local building and zoning department and pick up material about their permit process and regulations. Always be in compliance, since fines are always more than permits.

Condominium Fees

By nature, a condominium project has a lot of common area space and the condo board will be tasked with maintaining the property. There is a monthly fee assessed to each condo owner to keep the condo building, maintenance and management functions funded. There will always be a requirement for funds to be in reserve for major projects.

Condo fees do have their benefits though. Usually they include insurance on the structures' exteriors, roofs, grounds and common areas. Water and sewer charges are also typically paid out of the condo fees.

Handyman

We've already talked about having a handyman or two on your team. This is a cost of doing business and a necessary one. You must respond to tenant repair requests, and you also want to do regular maintenance to keep the properties in good condition.

Even if you try to do most minor repairs yourself, you will not always be available. You KNOW you take a trip or vacation now and then! Have a handyman on call to take care of small problems before they become big ones.

MORE ON MOVE-OUTS

The way that you handle move-outs can save you a ton of money. A couple of weeks before a tenant is due to leave, we visit the property to find out what's in store for us. If it's a disaster zone, or if the tenant has a lot of stuff, we know we're in for not only cleanup but possibly disposal of items, as well.

We try to offer incentives to our tenants to get them to do as much as possible toward getting the unit clean. If we can incentivize them to do a chunk of the cleaning while they're still in the unit, it can save us a couple of days of vacancy after they're gone.

Offer a Dumpster

A dumpster costs money, but it can be well worth it. If the home is full of junk, it's likely that the tenant will be leaving a lot of it for us. We offer them a dumpster if they'll agree to leave nothing in the unit when they leave. The cost of the dumpster is a great tradeoff for the labor we avoid in cleaning up, as well as vacancy time.

Letter of Recommendation

We had a family that rented one of our properties for several years. They were good tenants who never caused any problems and always paid their rent. Their family was growing, and when a third child arrived, they needed to find a larger place.

To help them find a new home, we offered to give them a letter of recommendation to show prospective landlords. They were touched, saying, "Wow, we've never been offered a letter from a landlord before!"

When they moved out, we stopped by our property and found that the place was spotless, requiring almost no work on our part to get it ready for the next tenant. That letter, taking just a few minutes of our time, saved us the cost of hiring the cleaning crew and got our next tenant into the unit sooner.

Pay Tenants to Clean

In one instance, we had a home with multiple tenants and our visit prior to the end of their lease turned up the fact that the house was pretty much a cluttered mess. We told them that if the house was empty and clean when they left, we'd give each of the tenants $50. It was, and we did. We got a clean house.

Condition and Deposits

Earlier we discussed damage deposits and the importance of a good policy of move-in and move-out inspections and checklists. This is crucial to minimizing damage and will also help you get compensated for as much damage as possible when it does occur.

The lease should make it crystal clear with a list as to what is considered "wear and tear," and what is considered "damage". Normal wear and tear is not damage, and we consider that part of our normal costs so we take care of it at our own expense. Damage we expect the tenant to pay for out of their damage deposit. Let's look at examples:

Item	Wear & Tear	Damage
Carpet	Dirty and worn	Cigarette burns
Walls	Furniture scrapes	Large holes
Appliances	Loose handles	Broken handles
Tile	Grout cracking	Broken tiles

Deposit Refunds

Be very clear in the lease about what constitutes damage. Specify any situation that could result in you retaining part of their deposit. Check your local laws to see what you can and cannot do in this regard.

We try to arrive when the tenants are almost completed with their moving out process and look the unit over right then using the inspection checklist. One example we've encountered of an on-the-spot negotiation of deposit is a couch left in the home. We informed them that the lease states that all personal belongings must be removed, and that we can charge up to $50 per item for furniture items left in the home that we must remove. This normally gets their attention and they remove the item.

Look behind that poster!

Do a very thorough move-out inspection with your checklist in hand and get it signed by the tenant. We once had a move-out, and we went through the property while the tenant was still there. A couple of posters on the wall went unnoticed. Also the light in the basement was burned out, so the inspection was done with just the light from a couple of small windows, but mostly in the dark.

After the tenants had gone and we had refunded their deposit, the cleaning crew came in and found two large, body-sized holes, behind the posters! When the light bulb was replaced in the basement, it was discovered that the carpet was ruined, black and beyond repair. The cost to repair these problems was $1,200, a number still remembered, and a really good lesson.

EVICTION

One of the benefits of following our systems and our mentorship is the probability that you'll never have an eviction. Doing certain things right will help you avoid ever having to deal with eviction. Remember to:

- Have good tenant interview checklists and procedures.
- Prepare a thorough tenant application.
- Thoroughly check out references, employment information, and credit history.
- Use a strong lease that makes all rules and rent payment procedures and timing very clear.

Even if you do all of this right, you may still have a tenant who becomes chronically late with the rent, getting behind one or more months. Or they may annoy the neighbors to the point that you could lose other tenants. If so, eviction may be your only recourse.

In Canada, the process is not too difficult or time-consuming. If the tenant is two months or more behind in rent, you can just serve them an eviction notice and they must move out. Other problems, like neighbor annoyance, are more tricky, so knowing the law and how to proceed is important.

In the U.S., there are many federal, state, and even local laws that protect tenant rights. We mentioned learning about those earlier in the book, and even running your planned procedures past your attorney. The process of eviction can take months and require a lot of paperwork and hassle. This is all the more reason to work with us to perfect your tenant selection and property management processes to avoid the situation altogether.

PROPERTY MANAGEMENT COMPANIES

As you add to your inventory of properties, you may find that a good property management company is well worth the money you pay them. They'll take over most of your headaches, and they'll present a more professional image to your tenants.

The property management company can take over every phase of the business, including meeting and interviewing tenants. They'll do the reference and employer calls, and they'll get the leases signed. They will collect and forward rents and work with late paying tenants, as well.

Property management companies can present a comfortable image to your tenants, since they are dealing with them in an office. Tenants also believe that property management companies will have more properties to show them, even if they're contracted to only show yours if the prospective tenant is solicited through your marketing.

Property management companies keep up with the landlord/tenant laws and should always have legal forms and contracts. They are trained to deal with problem tenants, and they have experience in the eviction process and doing it legally.

If you have the resources, you may want to consider using a property management company. However, you should only do this if you want nothing to do with the day-to-day management of your properties, since their fee is usually between 5% and 10% of rents collected.

ACTION STEPS

1. Look again at forms, checklists, applications, and leases with an eye toward clarifying what tenants need to understand about the rules.
2. Run through our example situations in this chapter and come up with some of your own. Check your lease documents to make sure it's clear who is responsible for damages and other problems.

WHAT'S NEXT?

You're familiar with the entire process--from marketing through tenant selection, move-in, management, and move-out. Mastering these practices and working with us will assure your success with your first property. This will get you excited and you'll want to grow your business right away. In the next chapter, we'll talk about business sustainability and managed growth.

CHAPTER 20
Growing Sustainably

Diversify, diversify, diversify is the mantra of many financial investment advisors who work with clients in the stock and bond markets. Diversification of your real estate portfolio is also a goal, since it reduces risk and can enhance your ROI.

Now that you have a foundation in how to purchase and manage properties and work with tenants, you'll want to grow your business. When you are taking that rent check to the bank, you'll be thinking about how great it would be to be taking several of them.

For our rental property investment business, diversification can take three forms:

- Property type
- Geographic location
- Cash flow types

There is no rush to build your investment portfolio, but developing a diversification plan is a worthy goal at this point.

PROPERTY TYPES

You will want to purchase different types of properties in order to offer a broader selection to prospective tenants. This selection could be about the property type itself, or every bit as much about different rental costs you can offer due to your costs of ownership.

Condominiums

We've discussed condominiums and the way fees work. Generally, the exterior maintenance and landscaping are included in the condo fees, so your ownership maintenance expense will be reduced. Also, some tenants like to rent where there are common areas, possibly even a clubhouse and pool.

Single Family Homes

Most of our discussion has used examples of single family home purchases and rentals because this is usually the way new investors get their feet wet. Single family homes may end up being the dominant property type in your portfolio, but consider other types of properties, as well.

Duplexes and Triplexes

Economy of scale in purchase and costs enters into these property selection decisions. Having two or three units in one location cuts maintenance and purchase costs per unit. This usually translates into lower rental amounts that attract other strata of tenants.

Geographic Locations

Early in your investing business, you'll be unlikely to want to invest outside of your city, but that could come later. Early on, just make sure to look for opportunities all around the city, diversifying your property holdings by buying in different neighborhoods with different rent points.

People are different, and their needs and desires for housing are different, as well. They could select housing based on proximity to work or play and most of them do consider rent amount as an important factor. By purchasing different types of properties in different areas, you will appeal to a broader base of renters and be less likely to suffer losses if one area trends downward because another may be making up the difference.

CASH FLOW TYPES

While our major focus is on long term, sustainable "lifetime cash flow", there are other opportunities for profit and cash flow in real estate investment. Some of them may present themselves to you in the course of your market-watching.

In our experience, there are three common types of investment opportunities:

1. **Cash flow rental** – The focus of our course, this is the property that generates solid cash flow.

2. **Rental property flip** – You can make such a good deal on a property that you can turn right around and sell it for a profit well over the cash flow you would have received over the first year or two.

3. **Future development potential** – You're purchasing the property with an acceptable, though not necessarily great, cash flow. However, it has the potential for future renovation or development that will significantly increase its value.

In most of this book, we're discussing the cash flow rental property, but let's take a moment and look at the other two opportunities.

Rental Property Flip

There are people who make this the focus of their real estate investing business. They locate properties that aren't renting out to their potential due to condition or just below-market rents. They buy a property, renovate it, and do whatever else they need to do to increase rents. Once the rents are higher, the value of the property is greater—they sell it for a profit.

Underperforming rental properties provide a lot of potential, since the value of rental properties is determined in large part by the income they generate. Locating a property that can be improved or otherwise changed to increase rents will increase its value.

Some landlords, particularly older owners, may have tired of tenant turnover and the management chores associated with that turnover. Frequently they will be charging lower-than-market rents in order to keep tenants and avoid turnover.

Future Development Potential

Many of you reading this book may not be interested in doing any development of a property. However, if you recognize potential, you'll understand that the value of a property can increase with changes in zoning or with population growth in an outlying area of the city. So you may purchase a home in a newly developing area and accept lower cash flow now in exchange for the probability that development is moving that way. You'll be able to sell later at a nice profit.

Or you could actually purchase a large home, as we discussed before, and split it into multiple rental units at some point. It may only be a plan for the future, but you have recognized the potential and that influences your decision to buy.

Resale Due to Surrounding Development

An example would be an older house on two or three acres of property on the outskirts of town. You go to the courthouse and do some research on zoning and population growth and movement, as well as checking out how developers are building more in that direction by creating new subdivisions with tiny lots.

Your research indicates that it shouldn't be too long before development reaches that house, and builders will be willing to pay a pretty penny for the land that could be multiple small lots with houses on them. You're still realizing some positive cash flow, though you could have done better with a home in town. However, the chances are excellent that you'll be able to sell this property in a few years for a really nice profit that will be much more than the cash flow you could have generated in other investments.

ADDICTION TO BUYING REAL ESTATE

> *"Hey Scott, I know we have two already, but it's going so well, let's look for a third house this first year".*
> *"I'm with you all the way, Michael. I love this cash flow thing!"*

We were so happy with our first two home purchases that we jumped right into a third in our first year. It was too much, and we definitely felt the strain because both of us were working, too. Three properties in a four month period for two new investors was not a good decision, and we don't recommend it for most people.

We fell in love with real estate, and you probably will as well. The trick is to not become addicted to the point that you make decisions that grow your business too quickly. Buying properties and seeing the cash flowing in is a strong motivator, but you need to control the urge to multiply your results too quickly. Using leverage, you can also grow your business too quickly, increasing your risk of financial pain due to economic cycles.

When You Know You're Addicted

One of our friends recently became a landlord. I toured the place he's renovating and noticed a mattress in one of the spare rooms. When I asked him about it, he said he had been sleeping at the property many nights because he was finishing late.

You know you're addicted if you're spending a lot of nights sleeping in your properties. A night now and then may be fine, but sleeping there most of the week could signal addiction. And, if you have a family, it could bring about other problems.

We're addicted to real estate and we admit it. The trick is to manage your addiction so that the rest of your life is in some kind of balance.

Don't Quit Your Job Yet

You're watching TV and see an infomercial with a new investor saying, "I bought this real estate investment program a year ago and I already own 27 houses and 13 apartment buildings for a portfolio valued at $6 million!"

While it could be a very inspiring true story, don't quit your day job because of it. It's more likely not true, and you need to understand that few investors go full time quickly, and none do it overnight. Don't buy that first property or two and sing that song to your boss, "Take this job and …"

Reduce Anxiety – by keeping your job. There is still a learning curve involved in the ownership and management of your first few properties. You want to do that learning with as little anxiety as possible. Keeping your job will give you a cushion that will allow you to sleep soundly at night.

"But I HATE my job!" Some people gravitate to real estate investment because they want to get out of a profession or job that they have hated for a while. It's a great goal, and one that can be achieved. However, you may find that generating more and more rental property cash flow can actually make going to work at that job more enjoyable.

Few people will quit a job that's supporting their lifestyle and spending for a job with lower income. Why would you want to quit a $50,000/year job when your properties are generating half that in cash flow? Real estate investing is a process, and before you quit your current job you want to be totally comfortable that your real estate investing business will not only support your current lifestyle and spending but grow and add to your net worth in the future.

Your Job Has Another Role

It's very likely that your job's income will continue to be necessary in order to qualify for mortgages as you grow your rental property inventory. While rental income is considered in mortgage qualification, that steady salary trumps it in value to the lender.

AVOIDING OVEREXTENDING YOURSELF

Overextending yourself can be seen in two ways--financially and in availability of time.

We've seen investors who grow too quickly reach an unsustainable growth rate that runs them out of both time and financial resources. Some will stop, but others will try to hammer through this perceived barrier, and it usually brings disaster.

Here are some quick rules to help you avoid overextending yourself:

1. As long as you have a vacancy, don't buy another property. Fill all vacancies before considering another purchase.
2. If your vacancy rate across all properties is 20% to 30%, consider selling the property or properties with the highest vacancy rates.
3. Re-allocate your resources. Sell high vacancy properties and buy in lower vacancy areas.

Vacancy rates of 20% to 30% usually indicate that you are overextended, or that the market isn't supporting further growth. This usually requires you to cover some of the mortgage payments out of the income from your job. Warning bells are going off, and you need to heed them. You might want to consider selling off one or more properties to get on a more secure financial footing.

Build Cash Reserves

Just because it's coming in doesn't mean you should be letting it all go out. Have some fun and reward yourself but be sure to build up cash reserves. When you have an unexpected uptick in vacancies, those reserves can carry you until you take action to fill the units or sell the properties.

One Property at a Time

We would advise you to only buy one property at a time for most of your first few years in this business. This is especially true if there are going to be renovations required before a property is generating cash flow. You'll have a negative cash flow during the renovation period, and you don't want to multiply that across multiple properties at the same time.

The safest rule to apply is to never buy another property until the previous one is rented and generating a positive cash flow. A red flag to alert you to possible trouble is when you're making decisions based on "estimated" or "projected" income and rental cash flow, instead of actual occupied properties and real numbers.

Discipline in Financial and Management Practices

Rule #1 is to not buy just because you qualify. Real estate agents and mortgage brokers only make money when you buy something, so their goal is to make that happen. Their goal isn't yours, so resist any temptation or pressure to buy just because you can.

Manage what you have before you add to your inventory. It's easy to get caught up in moving forward and growing your business but beware of dropping balls in the management of what you already own. Don't ignore the needs of your current properties from a management and maintenance perspective.

Manage your credit lines. As you grow, you'll use leverage and have various loans and credit lines outstanding. Always seek to minimize and pay down debt with higher interest rates. It can be a much better decision to take the proceeds of a property sale and pay down higher interest debt than to take on more debt to buy a new property.

Just Apply Our Top 10 Rental Practices

1. **Do not overextend yourself** – Don't over leverage to buy properties and always manage your expenses. Ask yourself if you could cover your costs if the property is empty for a couple of months.
2. **Use good agreements, forms and leases** – Do your research and adopt forms that are legal and clear and that protect your interests. Resist temptation to grab one off the shelf at the office supply store.

3. **ALWAYS properly screen tenants** – All of those credit checks, interviews reference, and employment calls are absolutely necessary to avoid problems and evictions.

4. **Late rent requires prompt action** – Whatever your laws and lease terms, follow them to the letter and promptly.

5. **Keep your property 100% safe at all times** – This is a liability issue, but you also never want to experience an injured tenant if it can be avoided.

6. **Handle security deposits properly** – There are laws to follow here, and you want to carefully follow the lease agreement terms, as well.

7. **Provide notice before entering** – Learn the laws in your area for how often you can access the property and the notifications that must be made to the tenant.

8. **Disclose environmental hazards** – You don't want to experience the huge fines and possible legal actions involved due to failure to disclose hazards like lead base paint and mold.

9. **Plan contingencies and budget for damages** – Set aside security deposits and rent amounts to fund anticipated damage and cleaning requirements.

10. **Resolve disputes** – Issues with a tenant should always be resolved without attorneys or lawsuits, if at all possible. It's cheaper to give a little in a disagreement than to go to court.

Just paying attention to what's in this chapter will help you avoid overextending yourself and the financial or life problems that result from an addiction to real estate or from growing your business too quickly.

ACTION STEPS

1. Look back at the goals you developed early in this book. Put more thought into sustainable growth plans and how you can avoid overextending yourself.
2. Start a diversity plan for property purchases by studying your market area. Look for opportunities to diversify your property inventory.

WHAT'S NEXT?

We'll deal with the formation of your business and the protections and tax tradeoffs of incorporation versus other business formations.

CHAPTER 21

Business & Legal Formation

This isn't a long chapter, but it's an important one. You're serious about building your real estate investing business as evidenced by the fact that you're reading this book and consulting with us. Be just as serious about how you structure your business entity.

Our natural tendency is to want to keep things simple. A simple business structure is a sole proprietorship, with everything under our personal umbrella. It's okay to start this way, but you'll want to adapt as your business grows. Moving to some type of corporate structure is usually the goal for:

- dealing with taxation issues
- reducing liability
- protecting personal assets
- creating retirement plans

Depending on your location, your personal desires, and your financial structure, you could consider an LLC (Limited Liability Corporation), an S Corporation, or even a standard full C-corporate structure.

The decision should be based on discussions with both your attorney and your tax professional. Putting off the decision for too long could result in higher costs when you pass your properties to the new business entity. You can't just wake up one day and wave a wand to convert all of the properties you purchased as a sole proprietor to assets owned by your corporation. There would have to be sale transactions, which would involve significant costs.

So be thinking about this corporate structure decision from the time of your first property purchase. It's OK to make the decision very early; that's better than waiting too long. Yes, there is more paperwork and reporting involved in a corporate entity, so you may want to wait until you have a couple of positive purchases and know you're going all the way with this business.

Let's look individually at the reasons for incorporation.

Taxes

Corporations are taxed differently than individuals and usually at much lower rates. You can control somewhat how much you pay yourself and how you take profits out of the company to minimize taxes.

Liability

If you remain a sole proprietor and an accident at one of your properties results in a lawsuit by a tenant, your personal assets are at risk, including your personal residence, your personal bank and retirement accounts--everything.

Incorporating changes that. The tenant can sue the corporation, but can only attack the assets of the corporation, not the stockholder, which is you. Your personal assets will not be involved or at risk.

Retirement Plans

As an individual, there are certain retirement account types available to you, and they're not bad. However, with a corporation, some of the corporate income can be put into matching funds for a retirement account for employees, namely you.

CREATE A COMPANY AND BUY IN THE COMPANY NAME

Get the facts about available corporate structures that you may want to adopt. Go over all of the characteristics of each with your accountant and attorney. Do a comparison chart or T-chart to make comparison easy, especially in the area of taxation.

Compare the management and reporting requirements for each, as well. Look at how money can pass from the corporation to you from a tax perspective, as some can be dividends and some can be salary. Look at the ways in which the corporate structure can create and contribute to leveraged retirement plans.

Keep in mind that corporate protection from liability for debt is slow to evolve. A brand new corporation will not be able to get mortgages without your personal guarantee. So, while you can protect your assets from lawsuits, you will still be standing behind the early debt of the company financially.

One thing to always remember about corporate status is to not "pierce the corporate veil". The protection afforded you in the corporate business structure is at risk if you mix assets or don't purchase everything in the corporate name.

In other words, if you're signing any document or opening accounts to purchase building materials, open them in the corporate name. Do this even if you have to personally guarantee the debt because the corporation must do the purchasing. Also all income in the form of rent checks MUST be made out to the corporation.

If you take rent checks in your personal name, or in other ways mix personal identity in corporate transactions, you risk piercing the veil and losing the protections of the corporation. The law considers it an entity, like a person. Getting the corporation confused with you personally can be considered as misleading as those whom you do business. Keep that in mind.

INSURANCE

While not necessarily different for a corporation or a sole proprietor, you'll want to always purchase good insurance coverage for your company.

Consult your attorney to determine the types and amounts of liability insurance you need. This is very important. Property insurance is easy, since you want to cover your company for the value of the property. Liability is trickier; you need to determine your risk exposure and try to buy enough coverage to protect you without going broke on the premiums.

CREATE A GROUP OF COMPANIES

Take what you've learned so far in this chapter and take it to the next level: multiple companies for your business. This type of structure works very well for real estate. Visualize three companies:

- **Holding Company** – handles the money and financing and owns the other two.
- **Property Acquisition Company** – acquires the properties.
- **Property Management Company** – provides all of the management functions.

At first glance, having three companies would seem like overkill for your needs. However, as you grow, and you will, this is a strategy with great advantages.

Taxation

Your accountant can help here. Using this structure allows you to allocate functions, income, and expenses to take advantage of the corporate structure to lower taxes. The property management company can bill the holding company for management services in an amount that creates the best tax result for each.

The acquisition company gets financing from the holding company but picks up closing costs and other acquisition costs. How much might be passed upward to the holding company can be structured for tax advantages.

Lawsuit Protection

Visualize the lawyer that your tenant hires to sue you because he sprained his ankle while running up and down the stairs chasing his Chihuahua. He'll have to hire help to sort through your corporate structure to see which entity has the assets. Consider that it might not be the same entity that has the liability.

When Do You Do This Structure?

You may never go this far, but we suggest that you consider it when you surpass 15 properties. It's expensive to start and manage corporations, so you'll want to have enough in the way of properties and income to justify it.

ACTION STEPS

Learn about the corporate structures and the advantages and negative issues of each. Make an appointment to discuss them with your accountant and also with your attorney. Take action when the timing is right.

WHAT'S NEXT?

You're on a roll now, getting to the point where you're thinking about all of those properties you'll own and manage. It's time to look at systems and methods to keep your business humming along without stressing you out.

CHAPTER 22
Your Office-Business & Automation

◇◇

There is a personal finance guru person out there who is quite popular and teaches people how to think "richer" so that they'll become richer. She tells a story about "organizing" money for success. By organizing, she means the money in your wallet, pocket, or purse.

Basically, her premise is that you must respect money in order to make more of it. Shoving a wrinkled wad of bills into your pocket shows a lack of respect for its power and value. She was taught to organize bills neatly, flattened, and by dollar value. The 20s would be together, then the 10s, and so on. All bills would face the same way. By doing this, she says that you're respecting money, giving it a valued position, and that this one small organizational practice will help you to make more money.

Whether you agree and decide to make your money neater or not, it's a good entry into our discussion about your real estate investing business. You need to get to at least a minimum level of organization and record-keeping in order to reduce confusion and errors.

Organizing and automating your business practices and activities will make them move more smoothly. You'll spend less time "officing", and more time doing the business of real estate that generates cash flow. You'll also think more like a business if you are in an organized and businesslike environment.

We're talking about more than just being organized in order to save time and reduce management hassles; we're also talking about taking on the early attitude that your business is going to grow quickly. You've set goals and you intend to meet or exceed them on a schedule. Knowing this, you realize that you will need automation and organized business practices before you know it. So why not just start right in the first place?

Of course, with one rental property, some of these methods and tools will not yet be necessary. However, one property isn't your goal, and you'll soon need to address these organizational and automation tools and procedures.

◇◇

THE HOME OFFICE

Most new real estate investors do not need a commercial office space nor the expense that goes with it. A home office space can work for a long time if it's well-organized and allows you to concentrate on your job without too much distraction. You must be able to access key information without a lot of wasted time searching for it.

"Hey Scott, where's the box with all of the receipts?"
"Well Michael, look over in the corner at our new two-drawer
filing cabinet. After that rent check went missing for a couple of days
last month, I thought a little more organization would help".

You'll be spending a lot of time in the field anyway, but you do need an organized space for the business functions. While you can work on the kitchen table, you'll still need a place for files, blank forms and applications, general business and financial records.

If you have a separate room, no matter how small, to dedicate as office space, organize it for efficiency. We like a neutral color to aid concentration and get us into a working mood. That's more difficult at the kitchen table in a brightly painted and busy family space.

Office Equipment

Spend a little money and invest in reliable office equipment. As the world becomes more automated and online, you'll find that computers and online access are major and valuable tools in your marketing and management functions and worth a small expense.

Computer

Computers have come a long way. The biggest ones with the most capability are very affordable these days. Desktop computers are less expensive and offer more memory than notebooks, since the technology to compress into the smaller size factor is more expensive.

We suggest getting a nice desktop computer with at least 3 GB (gigabytes) of hard drive space, since these are very affordable. In this screenshot from an online store, you can see that refurbished models are as inexpensive as a few hundred dollars, while new ones are easily located for $500 or so.

HP XZ776UT Desktop PC
Take full advantage of your business resources with the HP 500B XZ776UT Desktop PC.
Only $499.99
ADD TO CART MORE INFO

eMachines EL1352-07E Refurbished Desktop PC
The eMachines EL1352-07E Refurbished Desktop PC is affordable with reliable AMD processing, rich graphics and plenty of storage space for your media.
Only $299.99
ADD TO CART MORE INFO

Gateway FX6803-35 PT.GBD02.004 Desktop PC
Gaming and graphics glee is the DNA of the Gateway FX6803-35 PT.GBD02.004 Desktop PC.
Only $1,299.99
ADD TO CART MORE INFO

Acer Veriton VM275-UD5700W Desktop PC
The Acer Veriton VM275-UD5700W Desktop PC delivers key technologies and efficient utilities to meet your business and multitasking needs.
Only $399.99
ADD TO CART MORE INFO

Gateway DX4320-19 PT.GAY02.007 Desktop PC
Live your life in HD with the Gateway DX4320-19 PT.GAY02.007 Desktop PC, a powerful entertainment and gaming PC.
Only $799.97
ADD TO CART MORE INFO

HP Compaq DC5750 Desktop PC
This tiny HP Compaq DC5750 Desktop PC is designed to provide you with the performance you need to keep you up and running securely.
Only $199.99
ADD TO CART MORE INFO

Acer Veriton VM275-UD6700W Desktop PC
The Acer Veriton VM275-UD6700W Desktop PC delivers key technologies and efficient utilities to meet your business and multitasking needs.
Only $449.99
ADD TO CART MORE INFO

Sony VAIO VPCL137FX/R All-In-One Desktop PC
The Sony VAIO VPCL137FX/R All-In-One Desktop PC is the ultimate multimedia machine for any room in the house.
Only $1,349.99
ADD TO CART MORE INFO

Printer/Scanner/Fax Machine

These days, "all-in-one" printer/scanner/fax machines are common and inexpensive. They do it all in one box and take up little space in the home office. The most inexpensive are color inkjet printers, but the tradeoff for the low purchase price is the cost of ink. It's like the old business adage of selling the razor cheap so you can keep selling the razor blades in the future.

Moving up in cost by a couple of hundred dollars, you can get faster printing in black and white only with a laser machine, and it will still do all of the other things. Toner for lasers is less expensive, since you get more copies per dollar than with ink for inkjets. They also generally print, scan, and copy a lot faster than inkjet machines.

With the number of hard landline phones shrinking and cell phones increasing, you may not want to pay for a dedicated phone line in your home for your business. Your cell phone will work just fine. If you use a cell phone exclusively, you'll need to take another approach for faxing, however. Actually, it's more efficient anyway.

Online faxing using email is efficient and you get a cleaner copy than most fax machines can print.

► **Free Online Faxing**
World's #1 Internet **Fax** Service Start **Faxing Free** In Two Minutes
www.efax.com

Online Fax Service
Go Paperless - Send & Receive Faxes With **Fax**.com - 30-Day **Free** Trial!
www.**fax**.com

30 Days of **Free Faxing** - Send & Receive faxes through email.
Fax more. Spend less. **Free** trial.
www.send2fax.com

Free Fax · Free Internet **Faxing** ☆ Q
Free Internet **Faxing** - Send faxes to anywhere in the U.S. and Canada for **free**.
Send an International Fax - Faq - Terms of Use - iGoogle Gadget or MacOS X ...
faxzero.com/ - Cached - Similar

Free Fax · Online Fax Service ☆ Q
Send **Free Fax Online** to the U.S. and Canada. International **Fax** and Pay-Per-**Fax** service available.
www.got**freefax**.com/ - Cached - Similar

Five Ways to Send a **Free Fax Online** ☆ Q
Don't have a **fax** machine handy? No problem. You can use the Web to send a **free fax** - and no, you don't have to have a **fax** machine or even find some spare ...
websearch.about.com/od/usefulsite1/tp/**free-fax-online**.htm - Cached - Similar

10 Best **Free Online Fax** Services ☆ Q
Mar 2, 2010 ... There is no need to purchase an expensive **fax** machine or tie up your phone line when you can **fax online** for no charge..
savedelete.com/10-best-**free-online-fax**-services.html - Cached

Send a **Fax** for **Free** – Try **Online Faxing** with MyFax.com ☆ Q
Send **free** faxes with the new MyFax **Free Faxing** Service.
www.my**fax**.com/**free**/ - Cached - Similar

The screenshot shows the first of many Google search results on the term "free online faxing". While some are just free trials, others provide a certain number of pages for free, with a cost to upgrade for more.

The benefits of this method are that you receive faxes in your email as PDF attachments. And if the service you select also allows faxing out, you email in your fax with a PDF attachment and the service takes care of the rest. Usually it's the outgoing that costs, but you can find it for as little as $4.95/month. Faxing is becoming less common due to email, but it's not dead yet.

Tablet Computer or Smartphone

If you find that you're in the field an awful lot and you want to do more than just take calls, a smart phone with email access can do a lot. You can send and receive email, and using one of the services above, you can even do faxing if the document is in your phone.

Tablet computers are another approach, though probably not an early expense you should consider. At around $499, an iPad or one of the Android system tablets will give you much of the functionality of a desktop computer, but you'll have it with you.

Filing & Furniture

Your desk needn't be overly expensive, but it should be functional and not make your work more difficult. A comfortable chair and a desk with everything you need within reach are two important office items.

A filing cabinet is a must, and think ahead. While a two-drawer cabinet is enough at the beginning, and it's less expensive, a four-drawer is planning ahead for growth. You'll spend a little more at the beginning, but you won't be getting rid of one and buying another later.

YOUR FILING SYSTEM

Experts are paid fat consulting fees to come into corporate offices to do "time and motion" studies. They watch employees and record their every movement during the day. They develop time records for every task, particularly for retrieving information and filing. Their reports recommend changes to the system that save time and millions of dollars for the companies.

You want to save time, as well, but you also want to reduce stress and the hassles of running a business. Having your documents and everyday materials filed properly is important. As you'll be doing a lot of communicating by email, there will also be documents all over your computer hard drive. It will help you to think of your computer as a file cabinet and have roughly the same filing system in each.

In other words, you'll have this box with file drawers in the corner of the office. Dedicate one master folder on your hard drive as your business file cabinet. You can even name it that.

As you build your folders and subfolders in your real file cabinet, you can have duplicate folders on your hard drive, since you'll be receiving many documents there. While you will print them out for your physical file, you'll also be able to access them the same way on your computer. If someone needs a copy of something and it's on the computer, it's much easier to just attach it to an email and send it to them than it is to pull out the file and make a copy or manually fax it.

A Place for Every Scrap of Paper

> *"Michael, I've been looking for that plumber's receipt for an hour now. I thought I threw it into the Contractor shoebox, but it's not there".*
> *"That's not as long as I spent last week looking for the hardware store receipt to return some floor tile".*

Building out your filing system as a high first priority will save you a huge amount of time in the future. We ramped up our property purchases and rentals a whole lot faster than we did our organization and filing systems-- and it was a mess.

If you don't take the time to organize your filing system from the beginning, you'll be kicking yourself at tax time. We're here to teach you this and help you learn from our mistakes. We've developed a filing system that is extremely simple yet gets the job done.

You don't need any special equipment or computer expertise. All you need are manila folders, and you can use your scanner if you want duplicates on your computer, as well. You'll have your normal file folders for the general business documents--those not related to specific properties. For each property we own, here's our structure with a master file and subfolders:

- MASTER FILE – Property Address
  - Tenants
  - Utilities
  - Taxes
  - Mortgages

- o Insurance
- o Repairs & Maintenance
- o Capital Expenditures
- o City and Legal

You can see that we create a master file for each property. The Subfolders in that file break out the various components of property ownership and management for easy access later. Doing it this way, you have a place for each piece of paper. Build the file and subfolders when you buy the property, and you'll always have a place to put documents and receipts.

Tenants

Every new tenant gets their own sub-folder created in the filing system. These folders reside in the Tenant section of the Master Property File. Tenant subfolders should include, at the minimum:

- Rental application
- Lease agreement
- Reference & guarantor information
- Lease-to-own contracts or other tenant agreements
- Notes about anything you know in reference to this tenant, including their pet's name, relatives, friends, etc.
- Enforcement actions you take against the tenant or late rent records
- Complaints

For legal reasons, and you may have state landlord/tenant requirements, you'll want to keep these individual tenant files for three to five years or more. You can remove the folders as they move out and put them into another area of your filing system, but keep the tenant files oriented to the property.

Utilities, Taxes, Mortgages, and Insurance

You can subgroup utilities into electrical, gas, etc. folders if you like. You need this information for your taxes. If the tenants are paying their own utilities (recommended when possible), then you'll want to get a copy of one of their bills or in some other way file a record of their account information for each utility.

Mortgage information would include annual interest-paid statements and any notices or other communications you receive from your lender. If you refinance, maintain a separate folder for the new mortgage.

Taxes and insurance files are important and you want to have all tax ID numbers and insurance policy numbers handy. You'll receive periodic tax assessor notices to place in the tax file. File insurance policy premium notices and proof of payment.

Repairs and Maintenance

This is one folder that can get quite large and will need to be broken into subfolders over time. It's also the one that you'll use a lot; it will save you a huge amount of time when taxes are being calculated. All of those small receipts from hardware stores need to go into this folder. It's those small pieces of paper that are often misplaced, and they add up to a whole lot of money each year.

You'll want to break out this folder into whether an item is fully deductible as an expense that year or if it is a "capital expenditure" that must be depreciated. If it's a property improvement expense, it generally goes into capital expenditures. If it's a repair, it goes into repairs and maintenance.

Capital expenditures special – While repairs and maintenance files can be separated by year, and previous years filed away elsewhere after taxes, capital expenditure files and documents stay with the property forever. When you sell it, these expenditures are part of valuation and tax calculations.

City and Legal Documents

This is another document category that doesn't change or become less useful at the end of a tax year. These are documents that have value and may be needed again for as long as you own the property.

- Building permits
- Financing
- City letters and notices
- Fire reports
- Inspection reports

These permanent files should be available for the life of property ownership, and will stay in the cabinet until we sell the property. The others, the ones that are useful for each tax year, can be moved to banker's boxes at the end of the year and stored away.

YOUR TENANT RECORDS

"The customer is always right … unless they aren't". Our tenants are our customers, and as long as they pay their rent on time and occupy by the rules, they're right, and we want to make every effort to keep them happy.

If they break rules, annoy other tenants, don't pay rent, or don't pay on time, then we want to take the appropriate actions. In order to really know how we want to interact with a certain tenant at any time, we need to have good records that will provide the information we need when we need it.

If our records show that a tenant has been excellent in every way for many months, and they come to us with a request or complaint, we'll be more likely to work with them to make them happy than we would be if they've been a source of problems. This approach only works well if our records are complete and easily referenced when we need them.

The Tenant Spreadsheet

The spreadsheet format is great for this type of record-keeping. While it's a bit tedious to enter the items each month, when you need to access the information, it's right there at your fingertips on one page. Using a program like Microsoft Excel, or Google spreadsheets if you want a free online resource, you can create tenant spreadsheets with the following information:

- Tenant name(s)
- Rent amount
- Amount collected
- Amount they owe you
- Lease start date
- Lease end date
- Notes

Go into the sheet each month and update it. A quick sort by lease ending date will give you an immediate warning of leases coming up for renewal. Checking the notes will let you know if you want to keep the tenant or not.

Using the Tenant Spreadsheet

Rent – When we get the first and last month rent up front, we type in the amount in the appropriate month on the spreadsheet, and we highlight those cells in green to indicate that the money has been received. We fill in the anticipated rent amount for the following months, but we highlight them in red until we receive payment.

Lease expirations – Sorting by lease end date, we note leases ending within the next 60 days for action. First, we decide if we want to keep the tenant or not. If they want to renew the lease and we don't want them, we simply decline. Second, in anticipation of losing the tenant or if we're not sure yet, we begin our marketing and looking for a new tenant.

Late penalties – This isn't an income sheet for tax or budgeting purposes, so we don't need a column to record late penalties. However, they should be in the Notes column. We'll want to be able to readily see if a tenant has been late more than once when their lease is coming up for renewal.

AUTOMATE YOUR BUSINESS

Sitting down every month and trying to write checks for utilities and other monthly property bills will quickly become an enormous headache and a time sinkhole. You don't want to do this. The computerized world and the Internet come to our rescue again in this area of our business.

Automatic Debits

Most of your regular utility and other billing accounts will offer to automatically debit your bank account for your monthly payments. This is a time saver, but giving access to your bank account for charges that you will not see until they're taken out may be a bit scary for you. What if there's an error in your bill? Instead of being able to argue the problem before you pay, you'll be trying to get money back from a utility, which is not a fun prospect. You may have to do this in some instances, but check out the next two methods for other approaches.

Debit or Credit Card Payments

Many utilities and large businesses that collect monthly payments, like phone and cell phone companies, will accept payments with debit or credit cards. Having your bill automatically charged to a credit card adds a layer of protection, as you can dispute credit card charges if there is a problem

Another benefit is "cash back" or rewards programs with credit card purchases. If you can use a 1% cash back card for these bills, it's adding 1% to your bottom line. If it's rewards points, then you'll get a nice trip out of paying your bills on time.

Earlier in the book we mentioned PayPal as a method to receive rent payments from your tenants. As a business account holder, they offer you a debit card as well. If you indicate that it's a credit card (not debit) when you make a purchase, you receive a 1% cash back credit to your account.

Online Banking

Most banks now offer online banking and bill payment. You can simply go into the account and set up automated billing to electronically pay large vendors and utilities or mail checks to smaller ones.

Some of the systems will allow you to designate a monthly utility bill as having a "varying" amount. If you do, it sets up all of the steps of the payment process except the amount each month. You simply go into the banking section and enter the amounts and the bills get paid.

Automatic Tenant Notifications and Email Communications

There are a number of systems and email software options that will allow you to schedule emails in advance. The emails will be released at the scheduled date and time without you having to remember or be involved after you've set them up.

We use lockboxes to allow new tenants to move in right behind old tenants moving out. While we put the lockboxes on a week in advance, we let the tenants know that they will receive an automated email the night before at 12:01 AM that gives them the code to the lockbox. If they want to start moving in at midnight, they can.

You can also set up automated emails prior to lease expiration to let them know it's coming up and ask them to notify you if they know whether they want to remain in the unit or if they plan on leaving.

Rent Receipts

Most tenants want a receipt for their paid rent, even though their cancelled check should suffice. If you're accepting other payment methods, such as credit cards or eChecks, they'll receive email confirmation, but many would still like to have a receipt.

We use PDF files as email attachments to send a paid receipt with our signatures. We don't want to send word processor files, since the tenant could then easily manipulate the file to show they've paid rent when they haven't. PDF files are much more difficult to manipulate.

We just pull up a previous receipt in our word processor and change the date, print it and save as a PDF file, then attach it to an email. This works great and the tenants have proof of payment.

FRESHBOOKS AS AN ALTERNATIVE

An online accounting and invoicing service at FreshBooks.com has been getting good reviews from small business. It allows the user to invoice clients, and even create recurring invoices that go out automatically. It works with PayPal and other credit card payment systems, as well.

The service costs $19.95/month for up to 25 clients/tenants, and $29.95/month for no limits. If tenants choose to pay online, they'll get a PDF receipt for payment and it will automatically post as paid in your online account. If they mail you a check (and you can word your invoice to let them know how they can pay) you enter their payment when the check clears and they get a PDF receipt.

You can see when these invoices are viewed in FreshBooks as well. So, you know they got it and opened the PDF invoice. You'll know when it's paid, and the system works for cash or accrual accounting. You can even elect to have invoices sent via Snail Mail for an extra postage charge.

The best news is that it also does your expensing. You can set up recurring payments to post for accounting (not pay them, just the accounting function). This becomes your primary accounting system. Your frequent vendors are in there, so posting a new expense is fast, usually taking less than 30 seconds, and expenses can be categorized.

Also, because the tenants are related to a rental property, you're recording your expenses and revenues by property, as well. It's worth a look as a user-friendly online system you can use from any computer.

Duplicate Yourself

As you grow, you'll reach a point where you'll want to hire an assistant. You want to set up your office systems--filing, billing, and tenant notifications--so that it's easy to train someone else to use them.

Should you get really busy and need to hire a temporary office worker, you'll want a system you can explain quickly so that they can jump right in and manage it.

ACTION STEPS

1. Begin to plan your office setup and buy whatever equipment you think you need right now.
   Research the rest to get an idea of budget.
2. Do an outline of your filing system, or better yet go buy the folders and set one up for your first property. Just leave the front part of the master file empty for the property address.
3. Research how you want to handle a bank account, billing, accounting, and tenant notifications.

WHAT'S NEXT

We're going to do the final and third stage of building our Success Team.

CHAPTER 23

Stage 3 of Expanding Your Success Team

We never delegate major decisions, especially in regards to property purchases. We're at the site gathering information and getting a firsthand view of the house. However, as our business grew, we found that more and more of the paper-shuffling and less critical activities could be delegated to our Success Team members and others.

Where you need to spend the bulk of your time is *focusing on deals.* Following the market trends, seeking out investment opportunities, and evaluating properties is where your value to the business is best realized. So those are the activities you should spend the most time on.

Let's go through the selection criteria and reasons for adding these members to your team:

- Administrative assistant
- Handyman crew or general contractor
- Property manager or management company
- Associations
- Private Investors

These are our top level Success Team members, and they come into the picture as our business grows.

ADMINISTRATIVE ASSISTANT

The role of an administrative assistant is to take over most of the day-to-day office and administrative tasks. Their value is in freeing up your time to develop new business and to buy properties. The cost for an office assistant is usually somewhere between $15 and $30 per hour. If you keep a record of your business income in relation to the hours you spend generating it, at some point you'll see that investing in an administrative assistant is a wise move.

What to Look For

Real estate or property management experience isn't required in an admin assistant and would probably increase the cost, anyway. You can teach them what they need to know. The primary characteristic of a good assistant is organization. They need to be organized in thought and action and be able to handle multiple tasks every day.

Where to Look

Place a classified ad, a Craigslist ad, and search on the Web for people posting that they desire a job like this. Ask for a resume and references and check them.

An assistant who can start by working from home may be a good choice early on, since it could keep you from having to take on office expense at the same time. This may be a positive thing for the assistant, as well, because some people are willing to work for a lower salary for the convenience of working at home.

Your admin assistant should be personable, since they'll be talking to tenants in the course of handling management tasks and repair scheduling. They should be proficient with word processing, spreadsheets, and online services. A little knowledge about accounting would be a plus, as well.

Starting them part time is OK too. You can usually find very competent people who will jump at the chance to be able to work part time on their own schedule from home.

When to Take the Leap

We didn't hire an assistant until we had $200,000 in cash flow. However, you may need to act earlier, especially if you're going it alone without help from a partner.

You have to learn to let go.

Don't bother to hire someone unless you're going to get your money's worth, which means letting go of tasks and letting them run with the ball. If they don't work out, fine. However, if they're getting the job done well with few errors, don't micromanage.

Let your administrative assistant learn and grow with your business. The more they do and learn, the greater their value and the more work they'll take off your back. This frees you up to grow your business and cash flow.

HANDYMAN CREW OR GENERAL CONTRACTOR

Early in your business, when you have few properties, having a single handyman on call is usually enough. However, as your holdings grow in number, you'll need to have a more robust repair and remodel resource. Putting a general contractor and/or a larger handyman company or both on your team will give you more assets in more than one area.

Evaluating Properties

A more established general contractor will usually have bidding expertise and even computer software to help them quickly generate estimates for repair and remodel. Many have these systems in mobile phones and small computers onsite.

Having a company like this on call will give you the ability to get faster responses to requests for help in estimating rehab and renovation costs to help you to evaluate properties for purchase. Once you locate a reliable company, they'll be the ones who'll do the work, so they'll be happy to respond to your estimate and bid requests promptly.

What to Look For

Stability is a major factor in this regard. You want an established company with a track record and references you can check. If they're new to the area, it may be wise to look elsewhere until they've been around for a while and there are more references to check.

Expertise is very important, of course. The wider their experience, the better. A general contractor will have specialized subcontractors they call on for different phases of a project, but the general will need to have the experience to evaluate and supervise the entire job.

Licensed, insured, and bonded are three words to remember. Check out their contracting license, and check for complaints against it if there is a way to do that in your area. They need to be bonded and insured, and you need to verify that they always have workers' compensation insurance in place for them and their subcontractors on every job.

Responsive, yet economical. It's easy sometimes to find a general contractor or handyman service that will jump when you call. However, if their bids are always 20% over the norm, then you're paying too much for response. You want them to be flexible in their estimation and bidding, in that they are willing to do jobs with more economical materials, rather than top-of-the-line.

Check their references and look at jobs they've done. A good contractor will have happy customers eager to show off that great new room addition they purchased. The contractor should be happy to take you to past and present projects and point out their best work.

Where to Look

Of course, all of the old standby resources like yellow pages and advertising are useful. Check with local building code authorities and associations for recommendations. The inspectors working for the town will usually want to recommend the contractors who cause them the least hassle-- meaning contractors who delivered good work.

Better yet, drive around and look for jobs in progress. Many contractors place a job sign in front of their projects with their contact information. If not, you can pull it off a permit posted somewhere on the job. If you catch them there, you can sometimes get an impromptu introduction to their work on the jobsite.

PROPERTY MANAGEMENT

We don't think that hiring property management out is a good decision until you have a minimum of three properties. Even then, it's a big decision, since it adds to your costs and you want to be sure that you can't manage it in a less expensive way, perhaps even hiring an assistant. However, let's assume that you've reached a point where you really want to let go of management, and you're trying to decide how to make that happen. We'll look at two options:

- Hiring an outside property management company
- Forming your own property management company or hiring a property manager as an employee

We'll look at these two options. Remember that we mentioned the formation of a company earlier when we talked about forming a group of companies. Either of these could be just right for you, or you could begin with the employed manager and end up with a company spin-off.

Outside Property Management Company

Hiring an outside property management company is very effective for many investors. They turn over the day-to-day management of their properties, as well as the tenant acquisition activities. For some, this is ideal because they either don't have the time for these tasks, or they realize that they are not well-suited for them and will not do the best job of management.

However, the major tradeoff is cost. With fees running between 4% and 15% of rents, this is a significant expense and impact on your ROI. Making this decision after you already have multiple properties with rents you can't automatically escalate to make up for the expense will result in a period of reduced ROI and cash flow.

We discussed in various places "loving the numbers," and part of that was paying yourself or allowing some expense for management in case you moved in this direction later. Remember that, and allow for management expense when you're sizing up a property for purchase. Then, if you do move to outside management later, the expense impact has been planned.

What to Look For

A major part of the value of hiring outside management is your ability to let go of tasks. You no longer have to worry about finding and interviewing tenants, checking references, calling employers, collecting rents, or dealing with maintenance and tenant problems.

However, in order to truly turn over those responsibilities, you really need to be able to trust that they are being handled legally, efficiently and in your best interests. Due diligence into the qualifications of the company and checking of references is a must so that you can enter the relationship with trust in their performance.

Thoroughly check out the property management company's time in business; ask for references and call them. They should have been in business in the area for a while, as a lot of property management and its costs are the results of relationships with businesses, repair people and municipal governments.

You've learned what good tenant applications and lease agreements look like, so ask to see theirs. Look for the things you want in your leases, and get them to include them if they're not there already. Ask about their tenant notification procedures, and how they handle late rent and evictions.

Questions you might ask include:

- What services do you provide?
- How will you market my properties?
- Do you manage other properties in the area? Which ones?
- Do you offer eCommerce through your website?
- Do you screen tenants and, if so, what's the process?
- How much do you charge and how is it calculated?
- Will you charge less if a property remains vacant?
- When do you send the rental income to the landlord?
- Can you provide references?

Go into this selection process as if you're a large corporation hiring a senior level manager. Interview the property management company with a prepared list of questions. Some of the questions should be prompted by unique features of some of your properties. An example might be one of your homes with a swimming pool. You would want to ask how they handle swimming pools from both maintenance and liability perspectives.

YOUR OWN PROPERTY MANAGER OR PROPERTY MANAGEMENT COMPANY

We discussed having a group of companies when you've grown to a point where it would make sense for tax and liability reasons. One way to move toward that goal would be to hire your own in-house property management person. As your business and inventory grow, you can expand by hiring assistants for that person, and eventually spin off that portion of your operation as a different company entirely.

What's the Cost?

The cost would vary, but you should do some research into local salaries for lower management or high level clerical people. You're going to need someone who can handle a lot of different tasks and situations.

What to Look For

You will need a skilled and very organized individual. They'll need people skills to work with and interview tenants. They will need to be able to deal with problem tenants as well.

Some accounting, or at least bookkeeping, skills would be a definite plus here. This is especially true from a cost perspective, as you may be able to move your bookkeeping in-house, freeing up what you've been spending there for salary for this management person.

Of course, this property management person can, and will, be YOU for a while. However, once you've decided that your time will be much more valuable spent in other activities to grow your business, you'll want to hire an outside firm or fill this in-house management position.

Where to Start & What to Do

So you're handling your property management in-house, and you have a person on the payroll to do this. Even if it's you, everything we're discussing here applies. These are the things that must be considered and the skills that must be employed in order to do an effective job of managing multiple properties.

Marketing & Filling Units

We've been over all of this as an activity you'll be tasked with until you hire someone else to do it. In this case where you've decided to keep management in-house, you'll make marketing media and other decisions, and your hired property management person will implement your marketing plan. At some point, you may turn over marketing to them completely, but you set the budget and expectations.

You will provide the proper system, training, and forms to your property manager; she will be expected to interview tenants, call references and employers, and get leases signed and tenants moved in.

They'll also take over all of the move-in and move-out tasks we've discussed previously. If you've set up your systems and filing as we teach it, you should be able to bring a new person up to speed quickly. You should also be able to assess their performance by checking your filing and other system report output.

MAINTENANCE, REPAIRS AND RENOVATION

In this discussion, maintenance includes cleaning when units turn over. If you're going to handle your own property management, you will ultimately function the most efficiently and at the lowest cost if you become a sort of general contractor.

You could end up with one or more handymen on the payroll, or you could have them as subcontractors on call. However, for the more specialized work, such as more extensive electrical, plumbing, and renovation projects, you'll be calling in other trades people. You can be the general contractor if local laws allow, and you'll need to be able to supervise work and control the projects.

As your property management on-staff person builds experience, she can move into this role. You're spearheading a progressive move toward a comprehensive property management operation in-house with someone in your employ eventually handling the entire operation.

Once your business grows to the point where your accountant, attorney, and you agree that it makes sense, you can then consider spinning off this entity as its own business which is then hired by your holding company to manage your properties.

ASSOCIATIONS, GROUPS & GOVERNMENT

As your business grows, you'll want to become more involved in local affairs and businesses that have an impact on landlords and real estate. Joining associations that are made up of other landlords and influential community members should be your plan.

The cost to belong to these groups is usually a membership fee, which may be a few hundred dollars each year. However, the cost of not joining could be much greater in the long run. Keeping up with government and economic trends that will impact your rents, taxes, and other operational costs is important. These organizations can help you do that; they also help influence actions and policies for your benefit.

Go online and search for landlord associations, real estate boards, city council websites, and real estate investment clubs. While a real estate investment club is a great place to learn and to network with other investors, it's also a place where attorneys, mortgage brokers, contractors, and others influential in the local market gather.

If there's a Landlord-Tenant Board or group in your area, government or otherwise, get involved in whatever ways you can. Attend meetings and voice your opinion. At the very least, keep up with what's going on and with changes in laws, rules, and policies that could impact your business.

If there isn't a local landlord association, consider starting one. Contact local landlords via mail and email and encourage them to meet with you to form a group to discuss and protect your common interests as landlords.

One huge advantage of a group like this is the ability to discuss situations others have had that you may encounter in the future. This is especially true of tenant relations, evictions, and legal issues. Learning how one landlord handled a tough situation and came out on top can help you to anticipate the situation and have a policy ready for action in your business.

Neighborhood Groups, Community Committees & Area Politics

Whether through a landlord association or your own membership and participation in multiple groups, getting involved in all areas of the community that may impact your business is important.

Attend municipal and town meetings. Keep in touch with or follow the activities of large homeowner or neighborhood groups. Sit in on as many local community committees as you can. You want to know everything that's going on that can potentially impact your business, either good or bad.

Sitting in on a community meeting about the possibility of expanding a park or green space is an example of being in the right place at the right time. Maybe your input will have an impact. You do know for certain that the proposed expansion will put this park closer to one of your rental homes, increasing its value and the rent you can charge.

You are going to be a busy person, but you can't overlook the importance of being involved in the community. The more properties you own, the more important it is to be involved and informed.

PRIVATE INVESTORS

Leverage is how we grow a rental real estate business, and sometimes the normal and easiest financing solutions just aren't available. It could be due to current lender tightening or just the nature of one specific deal or our situation at the moment.

When we find a really great opportunity and the normal financing resources are elusive, private investment can get a deal done. These are investors who make money available for real estate funding, but they're not banks or large institutions. They're either individuals, small groups, or partnerships that specialize in lending for real estate.

What's the Cost?

Definitely more expensive than conventional lending sources, these investors will charge higher interest rates, higher loan origination fees, and usually want to loan for shorter periods of time. Interest rates can vary between 2% and 5% higher than more conventional sources.

Don't get confused about their role. You want an investor, NOT a partner. You want little or no involvement from this investor in your business and what you do. They should be a money resource, not a business partner. This is one reason the cost of this money will be higher, since they're investing it with little or no control over how you manage the property.

Where to Start

Actually, the path to these alternative funding sources can be through a mainstream source, like a mortgage broker or lending institution. When their normal underwriters and investors will not take on a deal, many of these conventional resources will have backup private investing pools.

Ask your mortgage broker about private investors or investor groups they've dealt with and see if you can get an introduction. Ask the bank's mortgage professional who they send people to when their rules preclude a mortgage.

Team Members or Business Partners

Approaching your Success Team members can be a great resource for funds. This is particularly true once they've seen your business grow and become more successful and profitable. They may want to take on a more active investing role instead of just being a tool for your business.

Successful contractors and property management companies will have accumulated financial resources and cash that they may be happy to pull out of low interest investments and move into financing your properties. They increase their ROI, and they have direct involvement in the projects in their Success Team member status.

Where these private investor strategies come into play the most is in getting together down payments. If you have 20% to 30% for a down payment, it's usually not a problem to get funding through your normal sources.

These private investors are the ones you approach to pull that down payment together. Or private investors can fund the cash purchase of the property, with no bank lending involved. There are a number of ways to approach financing a rental property.

Financial Splits

You may be borrowing from one of these private sources via a straight loan secured by the property, with a fixed term and interest rate. In other words, they're investing as if they were moving their funds from one bank or the stock market and loaning it to you for a better return.

In most cases, these types of financial split deals will involve the investor's money, your expertise, and your systems. In other words, all of the management is yours to do, and their involvement is their financial investment.

The other approach used by many investors to dramatically grow their holdings is a financial partnership split of the returns generated by the rental. This is when the private investor wants an ownership stake in the property. If they're loaning you all of the money for a cash purchase, many investors want to take this approach.

Instead of you repaying a loan with interest, you take on partners in the property. Splits can be calculated in any way that works for you and your investor. Let's look at an example:

We find a great opportunity to purchase a home, and we "love the numbers". However, we don't have the cash for the down payment right now. We approach a private investor, and the split/partnership could go one of two ways:

1. They fund the down payment, and we get normal bank mortgage funding for the rest. We split the cash flow profits from the rental until the home is sold, and then we split any equity profits realized from appreciation.

2. This is really the same agreement to split cash flow profits and equity growth, but the investor funds the entire deal and the house is purchased for cash. In this case, there could be a special low interest rate mortgage, or no interest at all if the cash flow is excellent.

Think creatively when it comes to growing your business with leverage. Once you have a track record of positive profit performance, you'll be surprised at how many people will want to get involved, since they'll get a better return working with you than they're getting from their other investments.

ACTION STEPS

1. Go to http://scottsinvestorsedge.com/book-resources/team-stage-three and download your stage 3 team worksheet
2. If you're ready for some or all of these team members, go out and start shaking the bushes to get them.
3. If you're not ready for some of them, sit down and write out your plan for when you want them, what qualities you want, and how you'll go about finding them.
4. Start locating and joining associations, going to local meetings, and getting involved in local political and real estate activities.

WHAT'S NEXT

We've discussed marketing a bit in prior chapters, but it's time now to take a deeper look at the ways in which you will market your business as it grows.

CHAPTER 24

Create a Marketing Presence

Marketing is an ongoing function of putting yourself and your business out there for the world to find, learn about, and do business with. Advertising, which is one facet of marketing, involves the placement of ads in media. We're going to talk about your overall Marketing Plan, and the ways in which you will use it to grow your business.

It's not just about growth but also about presenting a professional image and a "big business" image, even if you're working out of your spare room. **Very important:** We're all about not spending a lot of money to present a professional image to the world. And we're about doing it as efficiently as possible. The good news is that the movement of so much marketing to the Web works right into your marketing plan.

Another thing you'll find as you go through this chapter is that there is a great deal of interaction between the different places on the Web where you'll be marketing. When you read the Website section, get ready to hear about it again in Blogging and Social Networks. These come together in a way that makes it more efficient for you with:

"Write it once – Use it multiple times".

First, though, let's look at print and other offline marketing, since much of it is the good old standby stuff that still works, even in the age of the Internet.

Business Cards

Business cards are a portable billboard that shows you're really in business. When you meet contractors, property managers, mortgage brokers, insurance agents, and others, having a professional-looking business card with your business name on it is often the first exposure they get to your business. Make it a good one.

Classified Ads

We discussed classified ads in newspapers earlier, but should talk about it again now that you have much more business information under your belt. With a frequency discount, classified ads are not expensive, and they can help you contact sellers, renters, and buyers.

The key to classified advertising that's focused on building business instead of renting a specific property is consistency. If you decide to place an ad that "you buy houses", make sure that it runs in the same classifieds section on a regular basis, at least weekly. People get used to it being there, and you'll get business because they knew where to find you when the need arose.

Craigslist

We talked about the advantages of Craigslist advertising earlier, as well. We also mentioned using the search function to look for sellers and renters who have posted their ads or needs on Craigslist.

You will want to run regular listings on Craigslist, but be careful to abide by their rules or you will risk getting negative reactions from the other users or, worse, banned. However, because it's online and has an excellent search utility, you must place your property-specific rental ads there. People will find them, you will get tenants, and it is free.

WEBSITE

Now we're getting to one of your major marketing venue--a website. The first myth to get past is that "if you build it, they will come". Many people have an inflated idea of how a website will bring traffic from search engines. It can take months to years for that to happen, if it ever does. However, there are a number of excellent reasons why you need a website for your business, as well as ways in which traffic is built in other ways:

- Image marketing for the business
- Specific property marketing, photos descriptions, etc.
- Lead generation

- Tenant communication and interaction
- Networking and community involvement
- Saving you lots of time in the future

A website will allow you to present your overall business and present each rental property with multiple images and unlimited descriptions. You can even post videos of your properties.

This is where the time saving factor comes into play. It is almost impossible these days to find someone who doesn't have Internet access and an email account. By placing descriptions, photos, and even videos of your properties on your website, you can easily send a link to a prospective tenant that will present your property in its best light. You can show the details without trying to explain it verbally or typing a long email.

There are more reasons for having a website, but just be assured that you should have a website if your business is to be taken seriously.

What's the Cost?

Websites, particularly template-type sites that are simple to use, can cost as little as $10/month or less, which includes hosting the site (space on a web server where it resides).

However, before you think about cost, and before you think about the format of your website, you'll want to go through the next two sections here, Blogs and Combining the Two. You'll see why.

BLOGS AND BLOGGING

Blogs, short for Weblogs, came into being as online journals for people to share personal things with the world. However, once businesses found out about the benefits of blogs, blogs catapulted into the mainstream and became very big players on the Web. What benefits do they offer? Here are a few:

- Content (text & images) is easily created and managed in blog software.
- Unlike websites, blogs don't require the user to know

HTML or learn how to properly position content on a page. The blogging software takes care of that for them.

- All the user needs to do is use an entry page that looks very much like their word processor input area, and they can drop in text and images without special formatting knowledge.
- The ease of use of blogs encourages more frequent addition of content. Search engines like blogs for this reason, so blogs have become a good way to get better search engine position.
- Blogging platforms have now evolved to the point that the average Web visitor can't tell the difference between a blog site and any other website.
- Blogging allows you to easily post up regular commentary about your business, the local market, improvements to your properties, and more.
- The "comments" function of the blog platform encourages interaction with site visitors and with your tenants if you're posting information for them, as well.
- Explained later, the Really Simple Syndication (RSS) feature of blogs makes every new post you write a "mini press release".

From this point on, we're talking about WordPress features. WordPress is now the most-used blogging platform. It is used by millions of companies whose sites you've visited and never realized they were built on a blogging platform.

So for your purposes, there is no need to differentiate between a blog and a website, since you can get the benefits of both if you build your site on WordPress.

Without going into technical detail, there are two ways to get a WordPress site.

WordPress.com

This one is absolutely free--hosting, site platform, themes for design, the whole thing. You go to http://scottsinvestorsedge.com/book-resources/wporg and set up a site in minutes, and then just learn how to use it from their help menu and from the many books and websites on the topic.

The drawback of the free site is that you're limited to the features and themes that their hosting provides. For most who want a real estate website this will not be a problem. However, as you develop knowledge of the power of the platform and use it more, you may want to switch to a more full-featured platform.

WordPress.org

WordPress.org is the site that supports the "self-hosted" WordPress users. This means that you aren't hosted by WordPress.com, but instead pay to host your site elsewhere. You gain control this way, as well as the ability to customize and enhance your site in almost any way you want.

The tradeoff is small, since there are numerous hosts who offer a quick and easy installation of the free WordPress software on their sites for as little as $4.95/month. So for an investment of as little as $60/year, you can have a fully-featured website with huge storage space under your control.

THE WEBSITE THAT'S A BLOG

Remember, the visitor can't tell the difference, and you can do everything with a website hosted on a blog platform that you can do on a regular website plus more. So let's assume that you're going this route and setting up your website on WordPress. The remainder of this section gives you ways in which to use the site for your business.

We've already mentioned that you can upload great rental property ads , with multiple photos, lots of descriptive text, and even a video of the property and neighborhood. This much in a newspaper ad would cost hundreds of dollars, especially in color.

Documents & Forms

You can "host" your documents on your site. Let's think about a prospective tenant who sees one of your ads somewhere, or arrives at your site. If they sent you an email for more information or an application, you can send them back a link to download the application as a PDF from your site. Then they just print it and fill it out.

If they found your site and they're looking at a specific property, you can keep it up to date as to when it is due to come vacant. If this fits their timeline, they can go to links right there with that property and download an application that's already set up for that specific unit.

Requests for maintenance forms or any other form you would like for tenants to use to communicate with you can be "embedded" in your site and filled out online. It shows up in your email immediately, and you can take action.

You can place links to pay rent via PayPal or any system you use to collect rent via credit cards, debit cards, or eChecks. You can make announcements about property improvements as blog posts on the site. This is both an advertisement for the unit and a marketing tool to show the world how well you maintain your properties.

Using RSS for Networking

We mentioned RSS, Really Simple Syndication, earlier. Let's see how it can increase your Internet exposure exponentially through sites like Facebook and Twitter. We also previously mentioned networking on these sites as a way to participate in the community, as well as communicate with tenants and those who you want to be tenants.

The thing is all of this writing takes time. You're probably already shaking your head and wondering how you can write for a website/blog, post on Twitter, and put content on Facebook as well. Or you're thinking you'll have to hire an assistant just for this part of your marketing plan. Nope.

Write it once – use it multiple times.

This is where your RSS feed comes into play. The blogging software produces a broadcast of each of your posts as you publish them. This is sent out over the Web so anyone who subscribes to your feed can read your latest content. An example would be your tenants subscribing to get notices or news from you.

However, that's not the greatest use of RSS. This feed is usable to send your written content to other sites like Twitter and Facebook. Once you have your accounts set up at those sites, you can set it up so for your feed will display on them. So you write your material for your website, and it automatically goes out to your Twitter and Facebook sites as well.

Feel better? You don't even have to write regular content, though it does help with the search engines. You can set up your site and just let it sit, only changing or adding information when properties or business information changes. Or you can dedicate a few minutes each week to write a post about the latest new appliance you've installed or other improvements to your properties. Leverage the power of the Web. Doing it this way will get you the most bang for your buck and your time.

ACTION STEPS

1. Sit down and jot down a tentative marketing plan. Not too much detail yet, just what you want to do and how quickly.
2. Research website and blog platforms and learn more about RSS, Facebook, and Twitter.
3. Do some tentative wording for classified ads. Look through the newspaper for ideas.
4. Do some research on Craigslist to see what others are doing.

WHAT'S NEXT?

You've been introduced and trained so far on effective and profitable techniques for your rental property investment business. It's time now to take a look at some more advanced property purchase techniques.

CHAPTER 25
Advanced Buying &
Financing Techniques

ⵛⵛⵛ

*"Hey Michael, this is fun, and we're making money on every
house. But, we've exhausted our leverage capability for now, so we
have to figure out how to keep growing".*

*"Scott, that's great timing, since I just bought this book on
advanced buying strategies, and there's a seminar too".*

The use of partnerships and private investors is one way to use creative
financing to move forward and grow your business. However, you need to
have multiple methods in your toolbox if you want to grow using methods
outside the "box" of conventional financing.

We aren't experts at some of these techniques, even though we may use
them. However, we want you to know about them and feel that you can
explore them for your area and your needs. You should always consult the
appropriate legal and accounting professionals about strategies like these,
though. Some of these strategies work best in "up" markets, while others
are better used in "down" markets; a few work best in areas that have a
predominance of one type of property.

LEASE OPTIONS

The phrase "lease options" is short for leasing
a property with the option to buy it at some
point. There are two main factors in this type of
purchase method:

1. The length of time of the lease and when the tenant can
   exercise their option to buy the property.
2. The price at which they can buy it.

If you're maxing out your ability to borrow, lease options can be a way to purchase properties with little or no cash out-of-pocket.

Example for buying a home in order to lease it out to a tenant:

You find a home with a seller who is having trouble selling it in the current market. You explore the possibility of leasing it with an option to buy in the future. If the seller is amenable, you go out and try to find a tenant for the property. Here are the components and benefits for you:

- You find a tenant willing to pay a rental amount that is enough over your lease agreement with the seller that it generates some positive cash flow for you.
- The seller gets to move on with their life but is still responsible for the taxes and insurance on the home. This reduces your cash going out, making it a bit easier to install a tenant for positive cash flow.
- Your written agreement gives you the right, though not the obligation, to purchase the property for an agreed-upon price at a set point in the future--usually at the expiration of the first lease period.
- You pay an up-front price for this option, but you can get all or most of that back from your tenant by collecting first and last month lease payments in advance.
- Now you have a positive cash flow coming in every month, and you have little or none of your own money invested.

This strategy works very well when market conditions make it difficult for sellers to sell properties due to a lack of buyers. Benefits to the seller include:

- They collect some rent to offset part or all of their payment.
- They can move ahead with their lives.
- They can usually agree to take a price that's better than they would have gotten by having to reduce for a quick sale.
- They get the lease option premium payment up front.
- The seller keeps some of the tax benefits until the sale.

It's easy to see how you can convince a seller to work with you if they need to sell but haven't been able to find a buyer willing to pay what they need to get for the property.

Example for selling a rental property immediately:

As an exit strategy for you, if you're ready to sell a rental property and the market isn't supporting your desired asking price, you may be successful selling your home this way.

You continue to collect rental income from your tenant, and you agree upon a price for which you sell them the property at a specified time. You also get a lease-option premium in cash from them—now your "tenant-buyer". You continue to reap the tax benefits, as well. Benefits to the buyer include:

- If they have damaged credit, they have time to repair it before exercising the purchase option.
- They have time to put together the down payment they need.
- They know their money is going toward the purchase of a home, so they appreciate it more.

The added benefits to you include the fact that tenant-buyers take better care of the property, since they expect to own it soon. You can usually negotiate for them to take care of minor repairs as well, so your costs of maintenance are lower than they would be with a normal rental.

More Details on How It Works

Now that you know the benefits of a lease option agreement, let's discuss the mechanics of it a bit more:

- The tenant will become the buyer of the property if, and only if, they exercise their option to buy it.
- The seller continues to be the owner of the property and will continue to pay taxes and most other costs of ownership, as well as keep any legal tax advantages of ownership.
- The seller and tenant-buyer agree to an upfront payment called the option premium that is somewhat like a "down

payment". This provides the right to buy under the terms and at the time specified.

- These are generally longer lease agreements, up to three or more years.
- In a three year lease, the option contract would allow the tenant-buyer to give the seller notice that they want to exercise their option and buy the home. This notice must be given during a specified period of time.
- During the lease period, the tenant is working to secure financing, clear up credit issues, and make sure it will be possible to purchase the property when the time arrives.
- The tenant and seller agree on amount of the lease payment.
- The seller and tenant also agree in advance as to how much, if any, of the lease payments will apply toward the purchase.
- The purchase price is determined at the time of the agreement and can be a set dollar amount.
- The price can also be set in other ways, including being designated as "the appraised value as appraised by XXX Appraisal Company".
- If the buyer doesn't use the option to purchase, they lose it at the expiration date and seldom is any of the up-front option premium returned.

There are at least two instances when a tenant buyer might not exercise their option. First, if the home declines in value over the lease period and isn't worth the amount they agreed to pay, the tenant-buyer may just decide to just move and lose the option deposit. Another situation might be if the buyer has been unable to repair their credit or gather a down payment so they may be unable to buy.

THE SANDWICH LEASE OPTION

The previous discussion about using a lease-purchase to lock up a home and lease it to someone else is a straight-forward technique that is used effectively by many investors. However, there's another piece you can add … the "sandwich lease option".

As the name implies, you execute a lease option purchase agreement with the current owner. However, instead of just leasing the home out to a tenant for cash flow until you decide if you want to buy it, you do another lease purchase option with your tenant. You find someone who wants to own but needs time and you do a lease option with them. Why?

- You see the possibility that the home will be worth more when your option to buy is exercised.
- You negotiate a purchase price with your tenant-buyer that's higher than the price you'll be paying for the house.
- You get positive cash flow throughout the deal, and you get a chunk of profit if both sales happen.
- You also offset your up-front option payment to the owner with the one you collect from your tenant-buyer.

Example Deal: You find a home with a motivated seller who needs to move on. You negotiate a lease purchase with a $2,000 option payment and a purchase price of $195,000 at the end of three years. The home is worth more than that now, but you expect it to be worth $220,000 at the end of the lease period when you will buy it. You are leasing the home for $750/month.

You find a tenant-buyer and do a lease option with them. You get $3,000 up front for the option payment. This is in addition to first and last month rents. You are going to get $900/month from your tenant-buyer. They agree to pay $220,000 for the property if they buy at the end of their lease.

Now let's look at how the numbers work for you:

- $1,000 profit from the difference in option payments.
- $150/month positive cash flow for the entire three year period, for a total of $5400.
- If they buy, you will make approximately $5,400 + $25,000, or $30,400.
- If they don't buy, you still have the $5,400, plus you keep the $1,000 excess option payment.

FORECLOSURES

Foreclosures are not a good thing for either the homeowner losing the home or for the bank having to take it back. The homeowner hasn't been able to make their payments and has fallen behind. When the mortgage time frames kick in, default notices are sent out and the foreclosure process begins.

In tough economic times, foreclosures rise. Banks end up with what are called REO (Real Estate Owned) homes. The banks have significant legal costs, as well as maintenance and security costs, for holding on to foreclosed homes. Banks want to sell these properties to get them off the books.

In some states, the law requires the lender to go to court to complete a foreclosure, though in others states this is not required. Either way, at some point the bank ends up owning the home but they want to sell it.

There is a period prior to the bank owning the property when you can bid on it at the foreclosure auction, or courthouse sale. Here's the chain of events in a foreclosure:

1. Pre-foreclosure – This is usually when the homeowner becomes 90 or more days past due.
2. Default notice – The bank sends the homeowner the required legal notice of default.
3. Courthouse/trustee sale – The home is auctioned off to attempt to recover the balance due on the mortgage.
4. Redemption period – This is a period during which the homeowner can buy back the home if they can pay off the mortgage and cover the costs of the foreclosure action.
5. REO – The bank owns the property unless you it is bought at auction.

If you're going to go to the courthouse to try and buy the property, do your homework first. You should have been to the home and assessed the condition, determined necessary repairs or renovation and their costs, and decided what you're willing to pay. Auctions move fast and you want a plan so you don't end up paying more than you should.

More often, the situation is that the bank buys the home at the auction, and it becomes an REO property. You can now buy the property from the bank; actually, this is the least risky way to purchase it, since you will not find unexpected liens or tax issues on the property. The bank will have cleaned those up.

Great deals can be made on foreclosures, but they require that you take a business-like attitude and "love the numbers". Determine what you want to pay, and even if it's far below the mortgage balance or what the bank is asking, stick to that number. Some of the most successful foreclosure investors we know make very low offers and just wait.

Banks will often list the properties with a real estate broker to try and make a profit over the mortgage balance. As the home sits on the market, the bank's costs for security, utilities, and maintenance continue to grow. As the bank begins to reduce the price, these investors will be watching the process, periodically sending in their same low offer. At some point, either someone else buys the home for more than the investor wanted to pay, or the bank caves in and the rental property investor gets an amazing deal.

Foreclosure Rentals

There is a balance between trying to buy at rock-bottom prices and your ability to get the rents you want along with some appreciation in the home's value. The neighborhood should be studied carefully. Too many foreclosures in the immediate area will reduce property values, as well as rents. It will become more difficult to keep tenants in the property.

If you're buying a foreclosure with tenants already in the property, you will need to be very careful. Check out the property's condition thoroughly and try to find out the tenants' payment history. It can be a long and costly process if you must remove a tenant right after purchasing the property.

TAX LIENS

Though tax liens are not legal in Canada, they're a popular investment technique in the U.S. Tax liens can provide investors with 10% to 20% income yields, as well as a way to acquire properties for pennies on the dollar. When a property owner falls behind on their taxes, the county or municipality that handles property taxation will file notice and, at some point, can legally place a lien against the property. This is called a tax lien. Counties need money to provide services, and property taxes are the primary generator of this income.

Depending on the area and the law, once the county files a lien, the county will either sell the lien via a tax lien certificate or sell the property via a tax deed. The enticing thing is that these lien certificates can be purchased for the amount of the outstanding tax owed plus any penalties. This is often pennies on the dollar and can be from 2% to 6% of the property's value.

As an example, you could end up holding the tax lien certificates for a $100,000 property for only $2,000 that you paid for them. The owner does have a "redemption period" during which they can pay all back taxes, penalties, and interest, but guess who gets that money if they do reclaim the property? You do! This is where the hefty returns come in. Because you hold the certificates, the money paid to redeem the property all comes to you.

If the owner doesn't come forward and redeem the property during the statutory period, then you own it free and clear. Of course, during the interim, you will be responsible for keeping up with the taxes, but you can see that tax liens can be an excellent path to property ownership at insanely low prices.

Even if you don't end up owning the property, the yield you receive from holding the tax lien certificates is a nice one. The owner will have to pay a legally mandated interest rate for the entire time you hold the certificates, as well as interest on any penalties.

Learn the rules in your area and how tax liens are handled. Pay particular attention to the redemption period and the yield to make sure that you want to tie up your money in this way. Tax liens are usually a very nice return if the owner redeems the property at the end of the redemption period, as well as a great rock-bottom ownership position if they don't. There are various ways in which tax liens are handled:

- Investor bidding the highest premium wins. This may be an amount higher than the lien amount and may not earn interest.
- The investor willing to accept the lowest rate of return would win the bid. Random or rotating methods break ties.
- Some areas randomly select the winning bidder, sometimes by computer.

- Bidders come up in order, with the first bidder getting the right to purchase or refuse, then the second bidder and on through the list.

Check with local tax authorities to see how they advertise these tax lien auctions and watch for them. As soon as you find a scheduled one, begin your due diligence. Check out the amount of tax deficiencies and use the Internet to research the properties.

Narrow down your choices, if possible, and then go visit the properties. You shouldn't buy sight-unseen based just on the numbers and property valuation. It could be falling down and a hazard. You want properties worth much more than the back taxes owed and ones you can sell at a profit or hold for rental with excellent cash flow.

The fact is that most tax liens do end up with the owner redeeming the property. However, you can see that the excellent return you can realize in interest just for holding them makes it a far better investment than any savings account, stock, or bond.

BUYING AND SELLING NOTES

Real estate notes are created when money is borrowed against a property, and you may see them referred to as:

- land contracts
- trust deeds
- owner-financed mortgages
- seller-financed promissory notes
- contracts for sale
- owner carry-backs

How might one of these come into being? Let's say that a seller has a buyer willing to pay $200,000 for their home. The bank wants 20% down, or $40,000. The buyer only has 5% down; this leaves a balance of $30,000 that has to come from somewhere. The seller offers a real estate note to the buyer to finance that 15% or $30,000.

It's a second mortgage note, and the buyer will be paying the seller a mortgage payment on that $30,000 in addition to the payment on the first mortgage with the bank. How much that payment is and how it's structured can vary quite a bit; it can be interest only, or it might be paid in annual installments or on some other payment schedule.

All of these notes have an agreed-upon term, a stated interest rate, and a payment schedule. Sellers want to keep the term of the note as short as possible, usually 15 years or less. However; 10 years is a common term length also.

Default Risk

Notes carry a risk. They aren't first mortgages, so your claim is behind that of the primary mortgage issuer, the bank. Buyers can default and there may be no money left to pay you after the bank's first lien is satisfied. The borrower can also file bankruptcy, leaving you as one of many creditors trying to get a slice of a pie that can be very small.

Benefits to Offset Risk

Notes bring some benefits with them that can make them very attractive despite the risk. Buying and selling real estate notes is a huge business for these reasons:

- If the borrower pays on time and also improves the property, the value of the note will increase.
- Notes created when interest rates are high are worth more when interest rates drop, meaning you may be able to sell the note for a nice ROI.
- Notes are normally purchased at a discount to the current amount owed in order to offset risk. The amount of the discount is based on the borrower's creditworthiness, equity, and current interest rates.

Selling Notes for Fast Cash

Accepting a cash offer for a note you hold will normally get cash into your pocket in two to four weeks. You don't even have to sell the entire note, depending on your cash needs or desires. If you're holding a note worth $120,000 to be paid in 240 equal monthly payments of $500 in the future, you could sell all or a part of it:

- Sell the first 60 payments and receive the final 180. You would collect $30,000 and begin to receive payments again in five years.
- Sell the final 180 payments now. Collect $90,000 today and still continue to receive payments from the borrower for 60 months.
- Sell 50% of each payment so you and the buyer of your note portion would split payments for the 240 months, yet you receive $60,000 today.

Notes can be purchased at some pretty steep discounts if the holder needs cash. This doesn't mean there is anything wrong with the note or the creditworthiness of the borrower, just that the note holder wants to cash some or all of it out.

WORK WITH DEVELOPERS & LAND OWNERS

To keep it short and sweet: you will find opportunities to tie in with developers and pick up a piece of their planned development projects. Let's say that you find out about a developer buying 500 acres and splitting it into lots for spec houses. It's early in the process, and the developer is looking for cash to get started on all of the costly development things like surveys, permits, zoning applications, street layout, etc.

You buy in for a spot that is planned for 10 homes out of the 1000 or more they're planning to build. You also buy in with the right to modify the homes in your section to your specifications to make them easier to sell or rent.

Another approach would be to anticipate the growth of a major university. Universities don't move around like corporations, and they frequently develop long range expansion plans for both campus and housing development.

If you learn of such a planned expansion, even if it's to be implemented in phases over a 20 year period, you can go out and contact large tract landowners or people who want to own land in the area and partner with them to buy close by. Developing apartments as the expansion is implemented is an excellent long term strategy that will return great cash flows, but even more important, will have huge equity gains.

SELLER FINANCING

Seller financing can be an excellent tool for financing purchases, particularly in down markets when sellers are having difficulty moving their homes. You'll find it a very valuable way to purchase houses when you don't have cash for down payments or can't get conventional loans through the normal lender channels for other reasons.

With seller financing, the seller is your bank and lender. In its simplest form, the seller owns the property free and clear. It's then just a matter of drawing up a mortgage for 15 to 30 years and you pay the seller as you would any other bank or lender.

If the seller has a current mortgage, a **wrap-around** mortgage can be used. In this situation, the seller continues to pay on their existing mortgage and your loan from the seller carries a payment that covers that mortgage.

Of course, just as in the lease option discussion, you can then put a tenant into the property with a rent amount that yields a positive cash flow.

GENERATE CASH AT CLOSING

First you need to consider and investigate the current laws and lender rules. This strategy is best used with seller or private financing, since few lenders these days want to see any cash moving from the seller to the buyer, even after closing. Not telling the lender could be considered fraud, so get legal advice for this strategy.

However, if you're able to use it, you can generate cash for yourself as a buyer by paying more for the home than the negotiated price and having the seller give you that money back at closing.

Why would a seller do this? Sellers who have owned houses for a long time and have a lot of equity, or maybe own them free and clear, may have tax reasons for wanting to sell with owner financing. They may be able to forego capital gains taxes by collecting interest payments or have other reasons for wanting you to pay them over time rather than in a large, one-time cash payment.

Whatever the seller's reason, they would structure such a deal in this way: if you have agreed to pay $200,000 for the home and the seller is financing it, they would actually do the paperwork and collect $220,000. They would then pay you back the excess $20,000 in cash after closing. You have cash to go make another deal, and they are receiving payments and interest on the higher amount.

EQUITY PULLOUT

As you pay down your property mortgages, your net worth increases because you owe less on each mortgage. If property values are going up, as well, you could have a very large amount of potential cash tied up in equity.

The goal now is to keep growing, and this trapped cash is how you can fund your growth. We're going to look at how to use HELOCs to finance other investments. As mentioned previously, HELOC stands for Home Equity Line of Credit.

Banks will loan you money against the equity in your properties. However, HELOC loans are amazingly flexible because they're not for a certain amount of money with structured payments. A HELOC is a set line of credit that the bank will let you use. It is based on the equity in your properties. The greatest features are that you can use it like a checking account and that you can even pay interest-only payments.

Example: You have $1 million worth of properties out there with $400,000 in equity. You go to the bank and pledge those properties as collateral for a $200,000 line of credit. You still have a 20% equity, so the banks are covered, but you now have the ability to draw against a $200,000 line of credit.

You go out and write checks for down payments on other properties, using your HELOC to buy houses, install tenants, and increase cash flow. Of course, you'll want to figure in the interest payments for your "love the numbers" calculation to make sure that the cash flow is going to make you happy. Figure in a little toward paying down the HELOC principal, as well.

As investors pay down their mortgages, many will refinance the properties with regular mortgages to free up cash. However, in most cases they would be better off to refinance with a HELOC. With a regular mortgage, you pull all of the money out immediately, and you're paying interest on the full amount from day one.

With HELOCs, you don't pay interest until you use the money, and then only on the amount you used. Repayment terms are more flexible, allowing interest only payments. The portion of the line of credit that you're not using doesn't cost you anything, but it's there when you need it.

If you run into vacancy issues, you can use interest only payments on your HELOC to cushion the negative cash flow until the property is occupied again. You can also finance improvements or repairs this way, and even do renovations to raise rents and use the increase to pay down the HELOC. Your property has increased in value.

Tapping a property for $68,000

At one point we noticed that our first property had appreciated and we'd paid down the mortgage quickly. It appraised at $285,000, and we only owed $160,000, leaving an equity of $125,000.

Instead of refinancing, we took out a HELOC for 80% of the value, or $228,000, and we used $160,000 to pay off the existing mortgage, since the rate on the HELOC was lower. This left us $68,000 to use elsewhere when and how we needed it.

Even better, the lower rate on the HELOC lowered our payment by $100/month, which was in addition to our previous $800/month cash flow!

Financing Renovations with a HELOC

Remember our discussion a few chapters back about ARV, After Repair Value. Let's say you have a property that would increase significantly in value with a bedroom/kitchen addition, and you could increase rents significantly, as well.

Using a HELOC to fund the construction loan, you could just write checks to do the renovation. Once completed, you would receive more in rents and better cash flow. You would actually increase your HELOC available funds because the property would be worth more after the additions.

IT'S A "WAY OF THINKING"

You've been exposed to a number of new purchase and financing alternative methods in this chapter. Don't jump right into any of them. Take some time to do thorough research and to learn them inside and out. Then apply our "way of thinking" to their use.

> **"Real estate is a way of thinking much more than it is a body of knowledge".**

Always think that your next purchase, sale, or rental MUST increase cash flow and/or ROI. While there are a great many ways to be creative in purchasing and financing, not all of them will be for you and your situation. Always keep the goal in mind, and only undertake a method if it contributes to the achievement of that goal.

ACTION STEPS

1. Take as much time as you need to review these advanced methods, then do Internet and book research to learn more about them.
2. See which might work in your area and for your circumstances.

WHAT'S NEXT?

In the next chapter we're going to move beyond single family homes to other types of properties and larger multi-family investing. It's a step you may want to take, since the economy of scale in multiple single location units can increase your cash flow dramatically.

CHAPTER 26
Moving Beyond Single Family Homes

∾∾

Your business is growing. You have single family homes and perhaps some condos, duplexes, and triplexes around the area. Each is rented to one to three families. It's hard to get any economy of scale, since they're spread out and you're spread thin managing them.

It may be time to step back and look at your goals and do some more planning. While you probably didn't think about anything larger when you first set up your plan, you also probably didn't anticipate this level of growth either. It's all good.

However, with properties spread all around town, each home has a yard and needs exterior maintenance, interior maintenance, repairs, and management. Those needs are spread all over town, as well. How much less effort and cash would you be spending if many of your units were all in the same place? A lot less!

One small example: Let's say that you have a triplex with three tenants. You can't offer one of them free rent for management activities because that would constitute 33% of your income for the property, which is far too much to spend for management.

However, if you have 50 units in an apartment project, you could offer one tenant free rent in exchange for handling many property management tasks, and this would only be 2% of your income.

You're beginning to see where we're going with this. "Economy of scale" is your savings due to the concentration of units in one small area and can include savings in:

- property management costs
- repairs and maintenance
- discounted appliance purchase and installation
- standardization of finishes to save money

∾∾

There's more, but you're getting the point. By having a great many units in one location, you can save a lot in costs, which all translates to the bottom line.

MULTI-RESIDENTIAL PROPERTY

The widely accepted definition of multi-residential is a property with four or more separate dwelling units in one location. They can be all under one roof, or they can be multiple apartment buildings in one location.

Sometimes four-plexes get a mortgage break, with lenders considering them residential instead of multi-unit commercial. If so, you can get a residential mortgage. However, it isn't necessarily a bad thing if you are required to get commercial financing.

Cash Flow Equals Value

Let's just say that our discussion here is about any multi-family property with five or more units. This will be considered a commercial property for financing purposes. When buying single family up to tri-plexes, the residential mortgage is based on comparable sold properties and the financial ability of the borrower to pay the note. While rental income may be considered, it is not the most important factor for the lender.

Commercial multi-family loans use a different set of qualification criteria and right at the top is the amount of income generated, or the cash flow. The comparison of properties is frequently done with a quick ratio called the "cap rate", or "capitalization rate".

Cap rate disregards closing costs and other purchase fees, only looking at two numbers for a commercial multi-family property:

- the net profit after expenses for the year
- the price of the property

Example: You purchase a five unit complex for $300,000. Your gross rent collections are $40,000 per year. It costs you $10,000/year in expenses, leaving a net rental profit of $30,000.

$$\text{Net rental profit} / \text{Price} = \text{Cap Rate}$$
$$\$30,000 / \$300,000 = .1 \text{ or } 10\% \text{ Cap Rate}$$

Depending on location, rental demographics, and other factors, cap rates for commercial multi-family properties usually run between 5% and 10%. In stable areas with excellent rental histories, investors may opt to purchase properties with cap rates closer to the lower end of 5%. In growing areas with less stability history, cap rates may have to approach 10% to get a buyer to commit.

When you're comparing properties with the idea of a purchase, you'll want to get the going cap rate for similar properties in the area. If recently sold apartment complexes have cap rates around 8%, you would look carefully at one with an asking price and income that produces a cap rate of 6%. This would mean that you're paying too much in relation to the area's other properties. There would have to be some reason to pay a higher price for lower income--perhaps some potential to increase rents or cut costs.

While a higher than area average cap rate could indicate a bargain purchase, that isn't always the case. Investigate cap rates that are out of the norm to be sure that there are valid reasons. If the local rate is 8% and you're considering a property with a cap rate of 10%, it could be a great deal because the income in relation to the cost is higher than other properties. However, you need to know if perhaps a major employer has moved away so a high percentage of the leases are about to go vacant. Reduced rents may be required to fill those units. Reduced rents will mean a lower cap rate.

Underperforming Properties

Low cap rate properties can be a great buying strategy if there are certain characteristics that would allow you to raise rents, such as:

- Rents haven't been raised in years.
- There's a high vacancy rate that could be easily improved upon.
- Empty space could be converted to income-producing.
- Repairs and maintenance costs are too high and could be improved.
- Property management fees are too high, but you can easily drop those costs.

As you can see, buying a property and immediately cutting the costs of operation or increasing rental income will immediately change the cap rate. Getting the cap rate up increases value, which increases equity; this in turn frees up cash for more investing.

Loan Valuation for Financing

Your experience to this point has probably been in securing residential mortgages. The lender wants comps, and they want to be sure you have an income separate from the rent to pay the mortgage. The decision-making process is as much about you as it is about the property, and less about the rent you'll be charging. And you need to put up significant down payments to make the deal work.

The game changes significantly when you move over to commercial project lending. Cap rate becomes a dominant factor. The lender is loaning on an income-producing property, not a residential home. So the income is the major factor in a lending decision. Sure, you'll still need to have some skin in the game via a down payment, but it's secondary to the property's financial performance.

Commercial lenders and banks have a number of mathematical qualifiers they use to value a property for a loan, but cap rate is right up there. They will know the local cap rates and want your property to fall within an acceptable range.

Private Investors

Jumping into large commercial multi-family projects, even with great cap rates and nominal down payment requirements, will be beyond the cash capabilities of many investors. Even 10% down is a lot of money on a $5 million project.

This is when you may need to team up with private investors to pull together the necessary down payment to get the deal done. They will also look at the cap rate, and their interest rates will be higher than a commercial bank. Factor that into the financial performance before you apply for the mortgage, because the bank will.

You can even pull together a group of investors. They have the money, and you have the property and management knowledge to do the legwork to pull it all together.

Legal Structure

Each project or single address set of buildings becomes a single unique corporation. In other words, if these are your commercial holdings, each would be a corporation, perhaps named as the address:

- 822 North Main Apartments
- The Garden Arms Apartments

By keeping them separated as corporations, assets are better protected. Should a fire happen in one project and people are hurt or die, you can be sued for the assets of that corporation or that address.

Our First Multi-residential Purchase

When we were at around five residential homes, we found that we were maxed out for financing and couldn't get mortgages, yet we wanted to keep growing. Clearly we already had a lot of debt but the cash flow was great. The lenders wouldn't lend us more, though, because of the way residential loans are qualified and set up.

We talked to our real estate agent and started looking for commercial properties, since we knew that loan qualification criteria for these properties was different, based more on income and cap rate than on our personal financial status.

We found an eight-plea. With a decent cap rate of 8% and an eager owner, it was a good buy in our opinion. We had a few concerns, however:

- There were repairs that needed to be done.
- The main floor, unfinished and basically vacant, would require renovation before it would produce income.
- There was an old boiler room with plenty of space now that the large old boilers had been replaced with much smaller and more efficient models.
- A locker and laundry room was ridiculously large.

The owner didn't really want to deal with these issues, but we knew that we could do most of this work, and it would immediately increase the value of the property and the rental income.

Here are the "numbers we loved":

- Purchased the building for $600,000.
- Refinanced it for $850,000.
- Pulled out of the refinance $150,000, using $100,000 to make repairs and do renovation.
- Ended up with the same 8% cap rate.
- Newly renovated building was generating $20,000 year in net income.
- Sold it a couple of years later for $920,000. This was a net profit of more than $300,000 in less than two years.

Never forget to "love the numbers, not the property", and you'll always love the result.

COMMERCIAL BUILDINGS

We have just discussed five or more living units being considered a "commercial property". However, residential use is just one small component of commercial property, which includes:

- Retail
- Industrial
- Hotels
- Restaurants
- Shopping centers
- Hospitals
- Medical centers
- Warehouses
- Self-storage units
- Factories
- Garages

Breaking away from residential is a natural growth plan for some investors. Whether it's for you or not will be something you can decide as you learn more about it.

Five Steps to Buying a Commercial Building

1. Define your criteria (property size, type, and location).
2. Determine loan availability.
3. Check zoning and land use restrictions.
4. Investigate the property's environmental history.
5. Hire a building inspector to check out the property.

Really it's just an extension of the things you would do to evaluate a residential property. With commercial properties, though, you must be more concerned with zoning and environmental factors.

How Rents are Calculated

Commercial building rents are priced by the square foot on an annual basis. Depending on where you are, commercial rents may be as low as $1/sq ft in remote areas to as high as $1000/sq. ft. on 5th Avenue in New York. Most are in the $2 to $50/sq. ft. range.

Cash Flow

The goal is the same as with a residential property, positive cash flow. Commercial property leasing requires more analysis on the cost side, however, and more accounting, too. Also you'll have a larger mortgage to consider.

In our discussion of cap rates, we talked about comparing current cap rates of other comparable multi-residential properties in order to evaluate a property for purchase. It's much the same with commercial buildings, and lenders do look hard at cap rates in the loan application process.

You can actually shop for a lower-than-average cap rate in order to capitalize on opportunity. Let's say that you find a building with a cap rate lower than that of similar properties. You see that the current owner is charging below-average rents. The potential is in the ability to make a few cosmetic improvements and then increase rents to the average price for the area. You pay the low cap rate price for the property, take the necessary actions, and end up with better cash flow and a property with a higher cap rate and value.

Management

It is a lot more complicated to manage commercial buildings than residential properties. This is one area in which it's best to start out prepared to hire a professional management company, so you should plan for that in your evaluation and calculations before purchase.

If you have a large office plaza or shopping center, you can use "net leases". In these, the tenants pay all or part of the taxes, maintenance, and insurance costs based on the size of their spaces. You manage and coordinate these payments and pass along the pro-rata share of expenses to each tenant monthly.

On-site management, rotating maintenance crews, and tenant assistance will be required for a commercial property. All of these services and management functions add up to hefty expenses, so accurate estimation and budgeting is essential in order to assure good cash flow.

Tenants

The type of tenants in the building will be important to the banks when they consider your loan request. Lenders want stability of cash flow. Restaurants are an example of a lower value tenant simply because they turn over more. This turnover results in periods of vacancy, as well as costs to find a new tenant and refit the space.

Established businesses that are not expected to move around or go out of business are the tenants you and your lender want. It's also possible to attract better tenants, particularly when you have a good "**anchor tenant**". An anchor tenant is an established brand name store or a high-end chain. A strong anchor tenant attracts other businesses that also want that tenant's stability and some of the traffic the anchor will bring into the building or mall.

Banks make good anchor tenants, called "cornerstone tenants" in Canada. Banks seldom go out of business, and they don't move around much. Their presence draws other tenants, as well. If you have a bank with a long lease and options to renew, your lender will be far more likely to look favorably on your loan request.

Leases

Residential leases are for a home. The tenant lives there, and they have a lot of autonomy over their interior space, shorter leases, and many legal protections. In the commercial world, the landlord has more power, much longer leases, and the agreements between landlord and tenant are exclusive to them, with few tenant protective laws to govern the terms.

Many commercial leases are for five to 15 years or even longer. In many cases, the tenant will pay for and complete space modifications to adapt the space to their business. Many spaces are rented as one large open space, and the tenant installs walls, displays, and fixtures to suit their business. The landlord can compensate the tenant for all or part of this cost through rent adjustments or other agreements. Fixtures that are attached will usually remain when the tenant leaves.

While long term leases are the goal, they aren't less risky just because of the term. Business revenues are dependent on the economy and consumer spending. A tough economic climate can result in reduced income and tenant negotiations for lower rents. Or they may simply go out of business.

COMMERCIAL BUYING CONSIDERATIONS

Buying a residential rental property and finding a suitable tenant is easier than doing the same thing in the commercial world. However, the opportunities to increase the value of a property almost immediately are everywhere in commercial rental investing.

Your strategy should be to locate underperforming properties. These would be commercial buildings or malls where the rents being charged are below current market comparables, and they can be raised to market levels. This could be due to building characteristics that can be corrected at reasonable expense, or just because the current owner has been slow to bring rents up to market levels.

Another strategy we use a lot is to locate an underperforming property with one or more vacancies. At the same time that we're researching the property for purchase, we're out trying to find a tenant to move in right after purchase.

We're constantly networking in the area with the many businesses and people we've met in building and growing our business. When we meet, we're always asking how well their business is doing, if they're growing, and about their current space and rental plans. We offer to locate space for those who are growing and need a larger space, or those who want to relocate for other business reasons.

The very best approach is to find the tenants first and then locate the property. If you have the tenant lined up and find an underperforming commercial space that meets their needs, you can buy it cheap, install the tenant, and reap the rewards of an immediately higher cap rate and cash flow stream.

Adding Value By Changing Use

As our business grew, we added people, split out management functions, and were in need of a much larger space. We also maintained a stock of materials used in maintenance and property management, so some warehouse space was needed.

We located a warehouse space which was pretty much just a large open building, but one that could be converted to our uses with the addition of office spaces. Renting out at $10/sq foot as vacant warehouse space, the cap rate was low so we bought the building cheap.

By converting the warehouse to primarily office space, we improved the space so we could rent it for $16/sq. ft. instead of $10/sq. ft. This is an immediate increase in cap rate and value. When we're ready to sell, we'll enjoy a nice profit on this structure due to the change in use.

Use Your Network

The strategy of finding good buys to suit the tenants you have on tap will require that you always be engaged in networking. Many businesses begin to talk about moving or expansion many months or even years before they actually do it. They may be locked in a lease where they are, or they may want to meet certain performance goals before moving.

Whatever the reasons, you need to be networking to learn about these plans. Circulating and being active in the business community will bring you into contact with business decision-makers and growing companies. Then it's your job to get to know them and their needs.

When you learn of a plan for expansion and new space, offer to go out and find it. We did that for our real estate agent. Everyone we come into contact with is part of our network and a potential tenant.

Avoid Risk and Win Twice

What's winning twice? Some investors might be happy to find an inexpensive and underutilized commercial property. Others might be thrilled to have a tenant in hand who has tasked them to find them a space. We require both before we buy.

We consider it too risky to buy without both of these criteria being met. We must first have a tenant, and then we find a building we can buy at a bargain. The cap rate bargain purchase piece is nice, but our risk is dramatically reduced if we're ready to move in a tenant after closing on the deal. Vacancy is a cash flow killer, and we want to know that it will not be our first challenge after the purchase.

GETTING A COMMERCIAL LOAN

What the Lender Wants

Of course, commercial real estate lenders want the same thing as a residential lender--low risk and a profit on their loans. However, commercial lenders are looking at different factors. The residential lender looks at your personal ability to satisfy the terms of the loan. The commercial lender looks at the property and its financial performance.

The commercial lender will look at the whole picture: the condition of the property, any environmental or other issues, the surrounding area and current market conditions, even an appraisal of value. Tenant quality and vacancy will be carefully examined. The lender wants that cash flow to continue in order for you to pay your mortgage and make a profit.

When it comes to the profit portion, the lender wants to see performance numbers that meet or exceed their 60/40 rule. At least 40% of gross income should be profit, leaving up to 60% for operating expenses. If yours is better or worse than this ratio, be prepared to explain why.

A major factor in the lending decision will be cap rate. If you are purchasing an underperforming property with a low cap rate, but you have a tenant lined up and plan to bring up the cap rate quickly, you'll need to give this information to the lender. It will be considered in the decision process. The lender will expect a lot of documentation, including:

- A well-structured business plan
- Completed commercial mortgage loan application.
- Financial statements for two to three years.
- Tax returns for you and the business for two to three years.
- Description of the property.

- A plan for how you will use the loan proceeds.
- Current selling price of the property.
- Cost of improvements you will make to the property.
- Estimate of the property's value after the improvements.
- Proof of funds to complete the transaction.

In the commercial loan process, you'll clearly see the value of those organizational and record-keeping systems we helped you to build in previous chapters. You'll be bringing a lot of documentation to the table to demonstrate why you're a good risk for this loan. Some of this should be your past performance, and the numbers for your owned properties.

Bringing a spreadsheet of all of your properties showing equity, expenses, cash flow, and the length of time you've owned them can make the difference. You are showing the lender a history of past successful rental property ownership and management. However, there can be a much more tangible benefit.

Let's say you have owned 10 properties for a while and they all have good cash flow. The lender looks at their performance and your equity and offers you a loan much like the residential HELOC on the equity in those properties.

You can use that loan as the down payment for a larger commercial property. If you're attempting to buy a $2,000,000 commercial property and need 25% down, the lender may provide that money as an equity loan against your inventory.

Commercial Loan Team Members

Keep your attorney involved when you're buying and financing commercial properties. There will be zoning and land use issues, as well as environmental laws and special costs for environmental impact surveys. A really good real estate attorney can go over all documents and keep you from missing something important.

An accountant is also a required team member in the commercial real estate arena. The tax laws treat commercial and residential real estate income and profits differently. All of that knowledge you've gained in residential investment won't save you from a surprise tax bill on the sale of a large commercial property.

Partners & Private Lending

We have discussed taking on partnerships to fund larger residential deals. The same strategy can work well in commercial property investing, as well. Also, dealing with private money lenders for project or bridge loan financing can get a deal done.

Bridge loans can be used when a short term need for cash will make a deal happen, but you should have an exit strategy to pay off the higher interest bridge loan with funds from other sources at lower rates.

Commercial is Different – Do Your Homework

Consider the information we've provided here as an introduction to commercial property investing. It's a very different playing field than residential investing, but it's just what many investors find to be the logical expansion strategy for their business. Learn more, keep growing your residential business, and start networking and checking out commercial opportunities in your area.

ACTION STEPS

1. Do some research in your area into multi-residential properties of four or more units. Check out some smaller apartment projects for sale.
2. Do some exercises in valuation of multi-family properties for sale to get the feel for a purchase.
3. Learn more about commercial properties, and begin to check out commercial property for sale in your area.

WHAT'S NEXT?

Just from reading this book, you've come a long way in your knowledge. You may have started out not owning a single property, and now you're thinking about a future with multiple residential and even large commercial properties all generating lifetime cash flow. Let's sum it up in the next chapter and look at your future.

CHAPTER 27
Create Lifetime Wealth

After reading this book and getting to this last chapter, how do you feel? Have we realized our goal as authors and mentors to save you time, money, and hassle by helping you avoid our mistakes?

We didn't intend for this book to be the end-all and be-all of training and mentoring. We do hope that it's given you enough information and shared enough of our experiences that you are now firmly of the belief that you can create lifetime cash flow through rental real estate investment.

You should be feeling ready to move forward and excited about your financial future as an investor. Nothing has been left out as to strategies and sound investment practices. It's now time to increase your knowledge and hone the techniques we've introduced in this book.

In doing so, there is some advice and guidance that we know will help you build your business faster and with less risk. In this chapter, let's set the tone for your forward movement and your next business-building steps.

COLLABORATE – NOT ALIENATE

You can compete, as in an all-out race…

or you can collaborate as a team and pass the baton.

The tendency of many new real estate investors is to believe that the best way is the solitary way. Why share your knowledge and abilities with others when you can create lifetime wealth alone? While any single property purchase can lead to more money in your pocket if you go it alone, your career and lifetime business will experience stunted growth and you'll end up with less if you don't learn to collaborate with others.

We've covered the idea of taking in partners to increase your financial abilities, but really there's more to it than that. Multiple rental properties will drag you down personally, financially, and energetically if you continue to grow without some help, delegation, and partnership.

Even if you are doing well handling the load and the multitude of details and management tasks, how much can you grow if you remain a sole investor who only collaborates with others when necessary? Sure, we've given you instruction in building a Success Team, but it's not just about hiring the best and monitoring their activities.

Ask yourself a question: "Would I rather own 10 properties generating $75,000/year in cash flow or partially own 50 to 75 properties generating $500,000+ in cash flow as my share?" If you're still not sure, ask yourself: "If I could spend less time and work less hard to get that $500,000 because I've involved others, which choice is best for me?"

Build and operate your business any way you want. However, be fully aware that the greatest rewards almost always come to those who understand the value of collaboration.

LEAD YOUR TEAM

Let's take this collaboration discussion to the next level and talk about building and leading your Success Team. There is flexibility in how quickly you build your team and which members you choose before others. However, there is a method in our stages.

Stage 1

Stage 1 team members require little or no investment on your part. They are mostly service providers who get paid when you receive the service or benefit. Actually, you could consider the real estate agent and mortgage broker as free, except you know that the property price has the real estate commission built in it, even if the seller technically pays it. And, the mortgage broker's services come with fees, but they're not charged unless a deal is closed.

Your insurance agent is free for advice and help, only becoming a paid team member when you purchase a policy. Even then, the insurance agent's cost is a part of the premium. So there's low risk in involving your Stage 1 team members, and you should be quick to get that part of your team in place.

Stage 2

With home inspectors and real estate attorneys, you're running into fees that may be charged even though a transaction doesn't happen. However, they're protective fees, protecting your interests and helping to keep you out of trouble. Accountants, bookkeepers, and appraisers are also pretty much arms-length team members, only charging you fees for services performed.

Your handyman selected in Stage 2 is really the first time you have someone working for you, either as an employee or more likely as a subcontractor. In this stage you must begin to learn how to not only manage your properties but your team members, as well.

Stage 3

It's in this stage of team-building that you really bump into limitations if you restrict the involvement of the team members in your business. Property management companies, partners, associates, and private investors can only be as involved as you let them be. The more you limit their involvement and intimacy with your business, the more you limit your growth. This is when you really need to learn how to be a leader.

Involve these people by providing leadership, but also by allowing them to become a part of your business. Building these relationships will give them a sense of being a part of the business which will cause them to put more into helping you to grow.

Think of your business as a company that requires one-on-one sales at kitchen tables to consumers. If it's just you at the table, how much can you grow? You need these team members, and they need to be involved enough to foster your growth. This is crucial to building a large and sustainable real estate investment business.

Whether with employees, subcontractors, or hired professionals, you must learn to build these business relationships and nurture them for growth. The good will and active support of these team members, coupled with effective leadership from you, will result in the creation of lifetime wealth.

FIND AND USE MENTORS

Of course, we're here to act as your mentors in implementing everything we introduce to you in this book and our courses. As you grow your business, you'll meet many people who have already been where you are. They can be an invaluable resource for advice and help in reaching another level in your business. You can find mentors in many places including:

- Real estate workshops
- Real estate TV shows
- Real estate industry associations
- Local real estate investment clubs
- Professional associations

You should always be on the lookout for mentors. Whether you're attending real estate seminars or reading about investing, there are mentors out there with invaluable help and advice. We're not talking about the guru who knows it all, though you may find one. We're talking about mentors who may have mastered one type of property investment.

Mentors can be experts in one area or specialists in one type of financing. Others may have formed their own holding and management companies and be an excellent resource for you in those areas. Mentors can show up anywhere and provide inspiration, solid advice, and training in one or many facets of real estate investing.

KEEP YOUR VALUES

It's inevitable in building a large and profitable business to bump into people who are ethics and values challenged. You don't want to go there. Encountering people who have compromised their values can make us defensive; these interactions can even create the desire to change our behavior and values as a protective strategy. Even if you get dinged a few times, you'll make more money in this business if you keep your value system intact.

Transparency

We should always be transparent in our intentions. Hiding our motivations or true intentions can only make it harder for the right people to become involved in our success plan. Defensive mechanisms can sabotage our plans when we hide information or our true intentions from our team members. As an example, not being transparent with our mortgage broker can lead to the wrong mortgage product for our purchase.

Honesty

We may bump into dishonest people in our business dealings, but we always want to be considered honest. Those who do business with us and those on our Success Team will do more for us and contribute more to our success if they always are firmly convinced of our honesty and good intentions.

People who are defensive or less than honest will always seem to encounter roadblocks in their path to success. They'll struggle to overcome these roadblocks and some of these impediments will halt their growth. When you're honest with everyone, roadblocks become speed bumps, merely a short slowdown in your business growth and path to success.

Fairness

Real estate investing isn't a contact sport, nor is it an activity that requires someone to give up everything in a transaction so that the other side gets it all. All participants in your transactions should feel like winners, with each one getting something of value out of the transaction.

Whether it's our real estate agent, mortgage broker, or even the seller, each participant needs to derive satisfaction and compensation from their participation in the deal. We never try to go around our real estate agent to save what they would have been paid in commission. If they're involved, they should get paid.

As landlords, we always examine the fairness of our activities and tenant relationships. Landlords who try to eke every dime out of a property and their tenants without giving something back are the landlords you'll hear complaining about their declining cash flows and deteriorating properties. We're always reinvesting in our properties, making them a nicer place to live for our tenants, and they appreciate it.

Invest in Your Values

We're really big on energy efficiency and the environment. If we restricted our property improvements and appliance investments to those that contributed the most to this year's bottom line, we would never be installing eco-friendly items. However, we believe that it's good to be earth-friendly.

We spend more for energy efficient appliances, adding insulation and making improvements that save our tenants money on utilities. It isn't always a trade-off with profits, either. We have researched and found rebates and government grants for efficiency renovations, and we're constantly filing for a rebate or grant to offset most or all of the extra cost to do the job right.

You also need to look at the less direct rewards of this type of reinvestment in your properties. Because we've increased the efficiency of the properties, the tenants have lower utility bills. Even if they consider moving, they find that a lower rent elsewhere can be more than offset with higher utility bills, so we keep tenants longer.

Take Action and Keep Doing It

Reading this book and learning everything you can about rental property investing is going to assure your success, but only if you take action. Do something to get started in the field, even if the first step is just getting a real estate agent and looking at houses. It could be just what you need to get moving. While one of our goals has been to help you avoid our mistakes, we realize that you'll still learn by doing. Get out there and do something to break the inertia.

Once you're doing something, keep at it. In 1901, Wilbur Wright told his brother Orville that man would not fly for at least 50 years. Even though they believed that, they kept building planes and trying to fly. And they flew in 1903, just two years later. You can't succeed if you don't get out there and try. Keep trying until you create your success pattern.

PAY YOURSELF FIRST

Building a real estate portfolio requires leverage and reinvestment on an ever-growing scale. Your first years you will be plowing as much profit as you can back into the business to add properties and cash flow.

Once you reach Stages 2 and 3, you will have created a steady income from cash flow, but you're still growing the business. You are diversifying into different property types and possibly even into commercial buildings.

However, through it all, you should be paying yourself. In the first few years, it may just be the rewards we set out in our goals. The rest is all plowed into growth. As you build your cash flow, you'll want to do more in the way of retirement planning. Look into the various retirement savings plans, whether 401(k), IRAs, RSPs, or savings.

Begin to build these other accounts as a diversification strategy, but also to build assets that are more liquid than your real estate holdings and as tax-advantaged investments. You're no longer worried about a job because you're the job! It's your business and your future.

It's also your family's future, since you're building generational wealth, as well. Passing along a large portfolio of cash-generating real estate is the ultimate family provider strategy. You continue to provide long after you're gone.

SHARE AND GIVE BACK

The more you grow your business and the greater your cash flow and wealth, the more you should look at how you can help others and give back to the system that affords you a secure and enjoyable lifestyle.

Help New Investors

Remember how it was when you were out there searching for mentors and how lucky you felt when someone shared their real estate investment knowledge and experience with you. Become a mentor for others, sharing what you know and helping them to succeed as you did.

You can be an enormous resource to improve the lives of your family and friends. You've become a successful real estate investor, and your financial future is secure. Why wouldn't you want to help your family and friends to improve their lives and futures, as well? Give them guidance, and you'll find that helping others will come back to you many times over.

Give to Charities

Whether this is donating money, time, or some old windows you removed from a rental home, give back to the community. Help others, and you'll begin to see that it's still all about networking. Those you help will appreciate it and talk about it, and you'll benefit from it in many ways.

We didn't really think that we had the time to volunteer or participate, since we were really busy building our business, working on houses, and dealing with tenants. What we found was that taking a little time away from those activities to give to others was time well spent.

Showing up to help build a house or helping with a charity event, we always meet new people and come away with business cards. The people we meet want to return the favor and help us, or they want to invest in something we're doing.

While mailing in a check to a charity is giving, it isn't the same as showing up at a Habitat for Humanity event with your tools and some materials to help build a home for someone who really needs it. Giving of your time will go many times farther as "image advertising" than running ads in the local homes magazine.

YOU'RE HERE – WHAT'S NEXT?

We don't know if you were dabbling in rental property investment before you picked up this book or what stage of learning you're in right now. If you are new to the business, we do know that having reached this point in the book, you're better informed than the vast majority of those who already own rental properties.

You've read a lot of pages between learning about the Pareto Rule in Chapter 1 and this page. Those pages are upending the Pareto Rule for you. What you've learned in this book coupled with our mentoring will change the odds significantly in your favor.

Right there with the Pareto Rule in that first chapter was our 10/10/80 Rule for success.

- 10% Motivation
- 10% Education
- 80% Implementation

Notice that we've turned the 80/20 rule upside down now. You have the first two, so you're 100% assured of success if you just go out and start doing it! We know you're motivated, and you've amassed a lot of education in these pages. What's next isn't up for debate. You MUST go out and put this knowledge to work.

We're not saying that you have to go it alone or that you don't need some more knowledge, as well as advice and some support along the way. We're here for you.

WHAT'S NEXT?

Do something! Whether it's calling us to get some advice or mentoring, or signing up for one of our more advanced courses, you can't lose your momentum now. Everything you need is here for you. Take the first step today toward your "lifetime cash flow".

NOTES

NOTES

NOTES

NOTES

NOTES